DOING THINGS WITH INFORMATION

BEYOND INDEXING AND ABSTRACTING

BRIAN C. O'CONNOR, JODI KEARNS
AND
RICHARD L. ANDERSON

LIBRARIES UNLIMITED
A Member of the Greenwood Publishing Group
Westport, Connecticut • London

Library of Congress Cataloging-in-Publication Data

O'Connor, Brian Clark.
Doing things with information : beyond indexing and abstracting / Brian C. O'Connor, Jodi Kearns, and Richard L. Anderson.
p. cm.
Updated ed. of: Explorations in indexing and abstracting. 1996.
Includes bibliographical references and index.
ISBN 978–1–59158–577–0 (alk. paper)
1. Information retrieval. 2. Information storage and retrieval systems–Design. 3. Indexing. 4. Abstracting. I. Kearns, Jodi L. II. Anderson, Richard L., 1970– III. O'Connor, Brian Clark. Explorations in indexing and abstracting. IV. Title.
ZA3075.O28 2008
025.04—dc22 2008003774

British Library Cataloguing in Publication Data is available.

Library of Congress Catalog Card Number: 2008003774
ISBN: 978–1–59158–577–0

First published in 2008

Libraries Unlimited, 88 Post Road West, Westport, CT 06881
A Member of the Greenwood Publishing Group, Inc.
www.lu.com

Printed in the United States of America

The paper used in this book complies with the Permanent Paper Standard issued by the National Information Standards Organization (Z39.48–1984).

10 9 8 7 6 5 4 3 2 1

CONTENTS

Preface to *Doing Things with Information: Beyond Indexing and Abstracting* ix
  Freight Trains Have No Steering Wheels: A Metaphor xi
  Templates of Understanding: On Information Interpretation and Meaning xiii
  What Would Wilson Say? Wilsonian Vision of Interpreting and Understanding Information xvi
Acknowledgments xxi

1. Background Concepts and Models 1
  Basic Models 1
  Search Time and Search Space 4
  Context 4
  Definition of Terms 7
  Question: Where Entropy, Function, and Meaning Converge 15

2. Considerations of Representation 21
  Fundamental Concept 21
  Representation History of a Familiar Entity 33
  Sign and Meaning and Function 37
  Where Do We Stand? 43

3. Representation, Function, and Utility 45
  Context for Representation of Documents and Questions 45
  Object/Event Space 45
  Conventions of Observation and Action 48
  Conventions for Representation 52
  Form of Representation in Information Retrieval 58

4. Failures of Representation: Indeterminacy and Depth 63
  Document Structure, Indeterminacy, and Depth 63
  Exercises in Subject Representation 65
  Discussion 69
  Depth of Indexing 82
  A Note on Structure 88

5. Aboutness and User-Generated Descriptors 91
Introductory Comment 91
Difficulties of the Literary Metaphor 91
Aboutness 99
More on Words and Photographs 103
Subsequent Considerations 105

6. Responses to Indeterminacy 107
Learning From Failures 107
"Partners" and "Intermediaries" in the "Search Process" 108
Browsing 110
Discussion 121
Responses to Indeterminacy 122
A Note on Structure 122
Dust Jackets and Their Digital Kin 123
Conversation Representation 130

7. Doing Things with Word-Based Documents 133
Structural Analysis 133
Thoughts on Indexing and Abstracting Systems 134
An Elementary Word Extraction Program 141
Machine Representation Results 151
Appendix A 160
Appendix B 162

8. Functional Applications of Information Measurement 165
Thoughts on Measurement of Information 165
Information Anatomy and Physiology 169
Dancing with Entropy: Form Attributes, Children, and Representation 170
Clownpants in the Classroom: Measurement of Structural Distraction in PowerPoint Documents 174
Expert Verbal Behavior and Document Structure: Modeling a Binary System of Structure and Meaning 185
Functional Analysis of Bellour's "System of a Fragment" 191
Structural Analysis of the Bodega Bay Sequence 194
Method 197
Closing Thoughts 203
A Fruitful Revival 206

9. Functional Ontology Construction 207
A Turn to the Functional 207
Functional Ontology Construction: Components and Ancestors 210
Ontology as Environment 217

10. Creek Pebbles: A Summary Metaphor and Touchstone for Exploration 221
Reflections 222
Documents in the World/Reality 223
Information Environment 224
There Are Still Too Many Documents 225

References 227
Index 235

PREFACE TO DOING THINGS WITH INFORMATION: BEYOND INDEXING AND ABSTRACTING

THIS BOOK EMERGED from a proposal to do a second edition of *Explorations in Indexing and Abstracting*. As we contemplated the reviews of the first edition, particularly those that were most critical, we began to realize the necessity to address some more fundamental questions. We also thought that finding and using information are tasks of interest to many people beyond the field of library and information science. Doing things with information is fundamental to human life and doing things with all the media available today is exciting, empowering, bewildering, and multifaceted. We have kept much of what was in the earlier book; we have updated some of that material; we have added new material; and we have constructed a robust model for doing things with information. We cannot call this a second edition since the content is so different so we have changed the title.

In the preface to *Explorations in Indexing and Abstracting* we wrote the following two paragraphs to explain why issues of access, representation, and use of documents were so critical.

There are too many books, too many records, too many photographs, too many newspapers, too many journals, too many CD-ROMs, and too many World Wide Web sites. No one person can read all the printed works, even those printed just in one language. Millions of people around the world are connected to the Internet and traffic on the net is increasing rapidly. No one person can listen to all the recorded music or watch all the video productions or become familiar with all the sites on the net. One must choose which very tiny portion of all the documents available one will use for education, entertainment, or decision making.

We live in the midst of phenomenal changes in production, dissemination, and use of information. The numbers of information sources are growing at what often seems to be a staggering rate. In 1777 the Dartmouth College Library opened with 305 books. It would take until 1970 to reach one million books, but only another two decades to reach two million books. The collection that

Thomas Jefferson sold to Congress after the destruction of the Capitol in the War of 1812 consisted of about 6,000 books. The collection now numbers in the many millions. The number of people with connections to the Internet is similar to the population of the entire United States in the middle of the nineteenth century. The very nature of information sources is changing. For the cost of one hardcover book one can purchase a CD-ROM that contains the texts of nearly two thousand literary works, along with spoken word selections, music, and a search engine that can find all uses of a word in only a few seconds. Children in over fifty countries routinely chat about war, earthquakes, dating, popular music, and television shows on the KidCafe network. Photographs and movies can now be stored in desktop computers. Telephone numbers for most of the country and street maps for the entire United States are available for home computers on CD-ROMs. Scholarly journals are appearing, which have only an electronic form, giving rise to questions about the very nature of scholarly publication.

On the whole, the Preface to *Explorations in Indexing and Abstracting* remains a robust representation of our thinking, as expressed in this book. Of course a few things have changed. At the time of the writing of *Explorations in Indexing and Abstracting* there had not yet been a dot com explosion and bust; now Web-based enterprises such as Google and amazon.com routinely serve the information needs of millions, though not without controversy. Web 2.0 enables direct and simple interaction with the Web in the form of blogs, image repositories such as Flickr.com and De.lic.ious, podcasts, and RSS feeds. Indeed, we might now add to "too many books," too many blogs. These developments not only expand the universe of documents but they also challenge "the library way of organizing." In the mid-1990s, Wilson commented that an overlooked aspect of Web search engines was the fundamental shift from a small set of organizing schemes that varied from one another in only relatively minor ways to a much larger set of organizing schemes, which had great incentive to experiment and to evolve because of the profit motive behind them. Wilson's point was the burden this variety and evolution put on faculty of schools of library and information studies. The issue is no less pressing now.

The current controversy over the "Googlization" of information retrieval and even some libraries highlights an aspect of representation of information and questions that we have addressed in a more direct manner in this book: "the primacy of the need to bring knowledge to the point of use" (Wilson, 1977, p. 120). It is for this reason that we have adapted Austin's title, *How to Do Things with Words* and changed our title to *Doing Things with Information*. An index, abstract, or any other retrieval tool, no matter how well it follows some set of rules or standards, is "good" if and only if it results in findings of value to seekers of information. That is, the form, the algorithm, the adherence to any set of rules are all meaningless if someone in need of information cannot find useful information.

In the preface to *Explorations in Indexing and Abstracting* we wrote of our central concerns in the following words.

> Grappling with the question *What is it about?* in order to design systems to foster successful searching is at the heart of this book. Its stimulus is the thesis that no matter how facile the retrieval system, substantial failures result because of fundamental differences between the manner in which documents have been represented and the manner in which searchers represent their questions.

The relationship between a person with a question and a source of information is complex. Indexing and abstracting often fail because too much emphasis has been put on the mechanics of description and too little has been given to what ought to be represented. Research literature suggests that inappropriate representation results in failed searches a significant number of times, perhaps even in a majority of cases.

For these reasons this text will emphasize modeling and constructing appropriate representations of each question and each document. Such an approach mirrors the thoughts of wildlife photographer, Paul Rezendes, on searching:

> Many people today think tracking is simply finding a trail and following it to the animal that made it. . . . I think the true meaning of reading tracks and signs in the forest has been pushed into the background by an overemphasis on finding the next track. . . . If you spend half an hour finding the next track, you may have learned a lot about finding the next track but not much about the animal. If you spend time learning about the animal and its ways, you may be able to find the next track without looking. . . . Tracking an animal . . . brings you closer to it in perception.

FREIGHT TRAINS HAVE NO STEERING WHEELS: A METAPHOR

The original working title for *Explorations in Indexing and Abstracting* was *Freight Trains Have No Steering Wheels*. It was an attempt to embody the strengths and weaknesses of traditional tools for information retrieval. We state here just why we thought the metaphor was apt for both general readers interested in doing things with information and for students in library and information science who will be among those designing and implementing models and systems for doing things with information.

Railroad locomotives are not equipped with steering wheels. In a very real sense, the steering has been accomplished beforehand. Those who placed the rails accomplished all the steering. This contributes to the efficiency of moving freight and passengers around the country. Huge loads of items, large and small, can be moved by train to different parts of the country in days. Anyone can board a train and relax, while being transported over large distances.

So long as the passenger has in mind a destination and that destination is on or near the rail line, this is a good system. However, rapid and easy movement along established lines and to established points may not necessarily be efficient for some particular person or task. The passenger whose destination is not on the line may travel the rails as a part of the journey, yet take a bus or car some considerable distance as another part. The traveler seeking the "feel" of an area may wish to travel on foot or bicycle in order to take in the minutiae. The geologist or archaeologist may have to leave all roads entirely. The salesperson or politician may have to stop in places and at times that cannot be accommodated by rail lines and so takes a bus or an airplane.

Efficiency is a measure of the degree to which certain goals or criteria are met. The speed of operation of a system, its fuel economy, its percentage of downtime, and its load capacity may be efficiency measures for some people, but not for others. Each user of a train is faced with questions such as: Does it go where I want to go? Does it do so in a suitable time frame? Is the cost appropriate to the gain? The rail lines are highly efficient for some purposes, moderately so for some, and not at all for others. Indexing and abstracting are components of retrieval systems that hold similarity to train systems. In most instances, the steering has been accomplished beforehand. Indexing terms have been constructed or extracted, classification categories established, and abstracts written before a system user engages the system. So long as the user has a good grasp of what is being sought and can put a question into system terms, most systems are efficient. Yet, for the patron not familiar with system vocabulary, for the patron with a functional requirement that cannot easily be put into topical terms, and for the scholar seeking new connections, most systems are only moderately efficient, at best, and impediments at worst.

Designing indexing and abstracting systems to be efficient requires an understanding of the goals to be served by the system. In most instances this will mean knowing the sort of results any individual user will desire from the system. Some users may be pleased with results achieved within the current mode of dividing and describing the world of knowledge. Other users may require systems of very different sorts.

The traveler in a landscape of documents requires the same elements as a traveler in the geographic landscape. Both require means of navigation, moving about, and evaluating progress.

TEMPLATES OF UNDERSTANDING: ON INFORMATION INTERPRETATION AND MEANING

It is intriguing to be the author of a work that receives numerous reviews, formal and informal. At times one wonders if all the reviewers have all read the same set of squiggles on the page. Of course, they did not. Even though each had the same set of squiggles in front his or her eyes, each brought a different past, a different set of assumptions, a different set of competences. Here we consider those reviews of *Explorations in Indexing and Abstracting* that stimulated some of our thinking while constructing the current book.

For the past decade, reviewers, instructors, students, and readers have been commenting on Brian O'Connor's *Explorations in Indexing and Abstracting: Pointing, Virtue, and Power* (1996), the foundational work for the piece we now present to you with updated considerations and a functional, meaningful model to support an omnidisciplinary information playground. We take the comments and critical comments of original supporters and critics as stimuli to examine more deeply and explain more clearly our explorations of questions, documents, and doing things with information.

We have selected to address three reviews of *Explorations in Indexing and Abstracting*. The first was written by an Amazon.com user who read the text and posted his or her comments anonymously. The second and the third were written for publications in the library and information science fields by those who have library science degrees. To every reviewer and critic, we thank you for your comments. We intend to offer in the current book some clarity, especially for points you wrote that indicate to us that perhaps O'Connor's original intent and purpose were missed.

One might well ask why we take the time to examine reviews of *Explorations in Indexing and Abstracting* here. Some of the critical comments from reviewers and from students in indexing and abstracting courses demonstrated some fundamental misunderstandings of what was being presented in the book. Some of these misunderstandings were likely the fault of the author; however, some seem to bespeak a superficial understanding of representation and the use of documents, substantial misunderstanding of computational analysis of documents, and a lack of a theoretical base for critiquing efforts to enhance methods for doing things with information. Presenting three reviews here augments the preface by presenting a snapshot of the thinking by the three authors during the early period of constructing this book.

Three Reviews

Review 1

Reviewer—A reader for Amazon.com, March 28, 1997:

> While the author tries to make an interesting case for computerized indexing, offering that it allows the user to become involved in the process by choosing depth of indexing, the book completely misinterprets the results that a good indexer can produce.
>
> The author gave a test article (about 20 pages long) to an indexer, who came up with 7 or 8 search terms describing the index (the indexer did not produce a complete index to the article). The author compares his computer program, which is full of detailed instructions, plus the necessary human tweaking of the computer search results, with an indexer who was given no instructions at all.
>
> It is patently obvious that any indexer told to "index this article as if it were a book chapter" would produce a much deeper, well thought out index than the seven search terms the author received for his "test" indexer.
>
> In addition, because a computer program was used to produce this book's own index, there are a number of occasions where words are listed in the index simply because they show up on a particular page, not because they are an important topic on the page. While the books presents an interesting description of computer indexing and makes some important points about including users in the process, its analyses of human indexers display a total lack of the value added service and intellectual decisions that good indexers produce on a regular basis. It is also obvious that the author knows little about indexing, as he otherwise would have known that a list of 7 subject descriptors does not an index make.

Review 2

Reviewer—Virginia A. Lingle for the *Journal of the Medical Library Association*, January 2005:

> . . . Each of the three books discusses the topic of indexing and abstracting with a different emphasis. Lancaster addresses more of the theory and basic principles; O'Connor looks at the topic from a technical viewpoint; while the Clevelands write with a practical slant giving useful examples and suggestions. The three works together provide very comprehensive coverage of the subject. Each would be useful to students in library or information science, those working in

indexing and abstracting services, or persons seeking careers in the information and computer industries.

Review 3

Reviewer—Carol A. Hert for the *Journal of the American Society for Information Science*, March 1997:

> . . . Unfortunately the book's strengths are balanced by equivalent weaknesses. *Exploration*'s strengths are the result of O'Connor's view of indexing and abstracting, a view shaped by training in the special problems of visual librarianship. At the same time, my traditional indexer within was unhappy much of the time. I wanted more of the material placed within the traditions of indexing and abstracting; I wanted more recognition of existing solutions to the problems O'Connor posits; and yes, I wanted more references. There was a lack of links to other indexing literature, so I could not explore areas that were new to me. The bibliography had too few entries, and those were too obvious for experienced indexers.
>
> The index is another matter entirely. I believe that an indexing book's index should be held to the highest standard. Unfortunately the index of *Explorations in Indexing and Abstracting* is not up to the task. On page 173, O'Connor writes, "There is a certain irony in putting together a static paper index to a work on dynamic and user centered access." Maybe, but *Explorations* . . . is a book. What other kind of index would make sense? Continuing, O'Connor writes that the index was created by heavily editing the result of a word extraction program. Since he includes a significant number of subentries, heavy editing included pre-coordination. This is ironic at the least.
>
> There are two other weaknesses in *Explorations*. First is a lack of material about abstracts and abstracting. This common failing in books about indexing and abstracting is severe in this book. A collection of important words, which O'Connor says is adequate, is not an abstract. Finally, O'Connor also has the standard faith that computers (or other automata) can do indexing work. In a book emphasizing the intellectual work of representation, this assertion seems out of place to me.
>
> In summary, O'Connor attempted to examine the territory covered in *Challenges in Indexing Electronic Text and Images* (Fidel, Hahn, Rasmussen, & Smith, 1994), but that book remains the seminal book about providing subject access to non-print material. *Explorations in Indexing and Abstracting* simply does not have the breadth of subject matter or authority.

> Lastly, I must reemphasize the confounding character of *Explorations in Indexing and Abstracting*. The focus on information-bearing object representation and the concept of information as sign plus code are great strengths which O'Connor's almost metaphorical language only weakens.

There are three themes that float near the surfaces of these reviews: an insufficient index ironically ending a book on indexing; O'Connor's focus on computer generated indexing terms; and a disregard for traditional indexing guidelines. (We do not even know how to approach comments that references used were "too obvious for experienced indexers," except that the book was written expressly for those seeking a new approach to representation, that is, an approach that might improve access to information. Is that not our ultimate purpose?)

WHAT WOULD WILSON SAY? WILSONIAN VISION OF INTERPRETING AND UNDERSTANDING INFORMATION

Patrick Wilson is at the philosophical heart of our work. We take to heart his pragmatic ways of thinking about issues of doing things with information. We are fortunate to have his comments on *Explorations in Indexing and Abstracting* and have used them as a foundation stone in generating this book.

In 1960, Patrick Garland Wilson came to Dr. Paul Edwards with a few notes on a philosophical debate on interpretation and understanding for a proposed dissertation. How do we know when we understand someone? How can one understand information when information is open for interpretation by each who finds it and then uses it to an advantageous generation or regeneration of knowledge? Perhaps we think too hard about ways to use information and to develop the perfect system of limitationless access to information. We must refocus. Wilson knew it at least as early as 1960: before one can provide access, gain access, and control access to information, one must understand and interpret information from every individual viewpoint of all possible users and until we do, all access fails us. We have made utilitarian attempts to formulate ecumenical access: maximizing satisfaction with the greatest decent access for the greatest common denominator of users for the greatest number of access attempts, or at least until someone else complains about it. What actually has caused our failure is our general misunderstandings of understanding and our misinterpretations of interpretation. With a simple refocusing of Wilson's dissertation provocations coupled with a modern application of an old-fashioned mathematical equation for calculating entropy, we might bring access—but first representation—of information into renewed light.

After he proposed his idea, Wilson retreated for six months. When he resurfaced, he had completed the visionary piece of literature that rocks the foundation of library and information sciences still today, though many—two generations later—have only vague awareness at best where these thoughts originated. It is only fitting that we not only find a place for Wilson's genuine work in our library schools, but that we also remove our information beer goggles and refocus Wilsonian vision into contemporary information functionality.

Beauty is in the eye of the beer holder. It's a popular pun among pub goers who have experienced the degree of attractiveness of the man or woman across the bar increasing with the consumption of each additional pint. Once the metaphorical beer goggles are removed with the onset of sobriety, it is then clear that the temporary impairment of one's judgment made one blind to imperfections. The same is true of information—representation and access. Intoxicating updates and advances in any system create the beer-goggle effect. The faster the system retrieves information, the larger the recall of hits, the more vast the depository of facts, the more attractive the system seems. Additions, advances, more complex algorithms are merely blinding information seekers to the sobering reality that a system's accuracy depends on accurate representations of the data it intends to retrieve for me, and yet the system engineer, the mathematician who formulated the underlying search algorithm, nor the librarian who composes a book index did not ask me what I need for the system to work for me, personally. So, the system fails me, and it fails all who seek flawless information retrieval. "Good enough" should not be good enough. Once the beer goggles come off, what's left is the dissatisfying reality that we were attracted to imperfection in the first place. "Just as we may, through an appalled realization that we were unaware of what was going on in the mind of one we thought we knew, come to wonder how we ever know what another person is thinking or feeling, so too we may, having on some occasion wanted badly to understand and having clearly failed, come to wonder how we ever manage to understand, and how we know that we have succeeded" (Wilson, 1960, page 1). Perhaps "beer goggles" is a colloquialism more recent than the completion of his dissertation, but Wilson defines it succinctly.

"Information is meant to be predictive, not reactive." A Central Intelligence Agent speaks of information and intelligence gathering in a National Spy Museum film. It is effortless to extend this definition to information retrieval systems whose designs are intended to represent user needs based on best-guess predictions of those needs. Reality of such systems is not so perfect once we focus on sobering reactions to failed connection or communication of information. Systems are still requiring information seekers to express in keywords what they do not know and then the system offers to find a book or an article that might—by that particular algorithm's closest calculation—represent what the patron was asked to express of his or her knowledge gap. *If I knew what*

I don't know, then I wouldn't need to ask your system for help. Reactivity is an absolute response to information gathering. What the CIA foreshadows, we suppose, is that reaction should not be shocking, or surprising, or scandalous, but that reaction should be satisfactory, or boring, or predictable. Their expectations, like the expectations of minions of allegorically flawed information representation, are likely about avoiding high entropy returns: no surprises, no complications, no beer goggles. And so should ours be.

Kearns and O'Connor (2004) have shown that measurements of structure or form of video documents can match perceptions of the intended viewing audience, in that case, children. We are saying that expressing what a user perceives might be shown as a numerical representation without necessarily having to ask each possible user if she or he enjoyed the film. Why do we not use physiological and emotional reactions to documents as tools to improve access? Trained indexers can prepare sufficient book indexes, true, we are merely suggesting to look beyond a book index, abstracted ideas that form a simplified surrogate, and a library catalogue record, so that we may form more robust representations that reflect the user's perceptions, for all media, and for all users.

Representations should not yield surprising results; rather, we propose that the more complete we make the representation, the more predictive information seekers' paths to answers should be. In this respect, our goal as surrogate engineers should be to design low entropy systems of access.

If there is a flaw in Wilson's dissertation, it is that structural communication is overlooked in his description (though expressly stated in his chosen sentence structure), when Shannon & Weaver (1947), Watt (1978), Kearns & O'Connor (2004), Anderson, O'Connor, and Kearns (2007) clearly demonstrate that message structure is comparably important to message meaning. Meaning and method are not completely separate. We assert in this piece that the very nature of the document itself is a functional message.

Even Pope Pius XII warned us:

> What is the literal sense of a passage is not always as obvious in the speeches and writings of the ancient authors of the East, as it is in the works of our own time. For what they wished to express is not to be determined by the rules of grammar and philology alone, nor solely by the context; the interpreter must, as it were, go back wholly in spirit to those remote centuries of the East and with the aid of history, archaeology, ethnology, and other sciences, accurately determine what modes of writing, so to speak, the authors of that ancient period would be likely to use, and in fact did use. For the ancient peoples of the East, in order to express their ideas, did not always employ those forms or kinds of speech which we use today;

> but rather those used by the men of their times and countries. What those exactly were the commentator cannot determine as it were in advance, but only after a careful examination of the ancient literature of the East. (*Divino Afflante Spiritu*, 35–36).

In *Dancing with Entropy* (Kearns & O'Connor, 2004), this communication is described as a dance, because "appropriate and functional representation depends on knowledgeable partners" (p. 146). Designing surrogates is like dancing with entropy since the creator assumes to know something about the user and the user about the creator. At very least, they assume to speak the same language, the designer assumes knowledge of a set of possible information needs, and the user assumes the designer will point to the path that will solve the need. Without the assumed knowledge of the other, as in the caveat of Pope Pius XII, information retrieval cannot be a channel of clear communication (Blair, 1990).

In Claude Shannon's model of communication (1946), the communication channel can become noisy or dirty. We express the communication "noise" as all of the items on the designer's template of understanding that do not match items on the user's template of understanding. That is to say that structural information of the message does not change even when the user changes, but may be perceived by different users as having different meaning. Surrogate designers should recognize that some users might possess more of the code for understanding the message. In addition, when the surrogate engineer increases the number of representational points (human indexer generated index, plus computer-generated index, plus physiological data gathered, plus community memory interface information gathered (rating stars and reviews of amazon.com, allow user to insert search terms, etc., measurements of film structures, and so on) the predictability of the search increases too, that is, entropy decreases, which is our goal for access for all information seekers.

In brief, Wilsonian notions influence us to remain open-mindedly motivated to remember the very definitions of "information representation" as we build surrogates. Wilson described "information" as "anything I can forget" (personal communication with Brian O'Connor) and "representation" as "meaning the same" (Wilson, 1960, page 8), which should tell us that anything one can forget can be similarly expressed so that more people might follow the most personally meaningful path of access. Wilson does not tell us that we cannot use pictures to describe books no more than we should not use words to describe pictures, but that we should continue to exhaust all possible re-expressions, abstractions of each document, considering relevance to the smallest granularities of both document meanings and structures, assuming ordinary elements for you are extraordinary access tools for one user. Until then, we have not done our jobs as indexers, abstractors, cataloguers, indeed, as surrogate engineers.

ACKNOWLEDGMENTS

HUMBLING IS PERHAPS the most appropriate description for the experience of constructing a text for publication. Working to make our research accessible and meaningful to readers is a privilege and a challenge. "You've gotta teach to learn" is a line from a blues song, which reminds us that each attempt to make our ideas clear has afforded us the opportunity to learn more ourselves. We offer our deep appreciation to the students in our various courses, who have given us feedback, challenged us to clarify, and accompanied us during our explorations.

The mentors and researchers whose efforts are the foundation for our work deserve our deep appreciation. To Theodora Hodges, Patrick Wilson, M. E. Maron, William Cooper, Bertrand Augst, and Jesus Rosales-Ruiz, we say thanks for demonstrating the concern for fundamental problems and for firing passion for the multifaceted entity of human representation and discourse. To the many researchers in mathematics, management, philosophy, behavior analysis, computer science, and art (from whom we have drawn quite liberally), we say, "Thank you." To our mentors and the researchers, both known and unknown, we offer apologies for drawing bits and pieces and cobbling them together, in sometimes rather rough ways. We can only hope that the final product will speak well for us. We are honored to stand on your shoulders, if hesitantly, and gladly acknowledge that any mistakes and misrepresentations are our own.

Many people take part in the construction of a text. Author statements should probably include "prompted, goaded, spellchecked, critiqued, and suffered by . . . " The fine people at Libraries Unlimited were most gracious in their accommodation of our idiosyncrasies, and extraordinarily capable in their own tasks. Sue Easun has been an especially capable muse and taskmaster and deserves more gratitude than can ever be stated. Andrew O'Connor read the manuscript thoroughly, pointed out flaws in logic, offered kind words, and polished the presentation. Mary Keeney O'Connor gave conceptual advice, and abundant tolerance and encouragement. Yuka Koremura and Patrick McLeod, Barbra and Richard Anderson, Herbert Achleitner, Roger Wyatt, and Charlotte Russell provided inspiration and support. Guillermo Oyarce critiqued notions of indexing and provided access to retrieval software, which he has in development. Brian Bagatto provided a biologist's perspective and encouragement. We thank you all.

CHAPTER ONE

BACKGROUND CONCEPTS AND MODELS

BASIC MODELS

WE MIGHT SAY that for most people the preferred state is to have no particular need to seek information. If information is required, the first move is usually to consult nearby sources: a neighbor, a friend with some expertise, or the instruction book that came with that appliance that is not working. If these are not satisfactory in resolving the need, then a collection of recorded information is a possible solution. We must remember, though, that (even in an era of easy and nearly ubiquitous Web access) it is a solution with a price. Even under the best circumstances of searching, there is an investment in time and, probably, an investment of intellectual energy to construct a search then analyze and synthesize the new material.

In its simplest form, as in Figure 1.1, the model of a user approaching a document collection in hopes of filling an information gap has only two elements—a person with some requirement for information and a collection of documents.

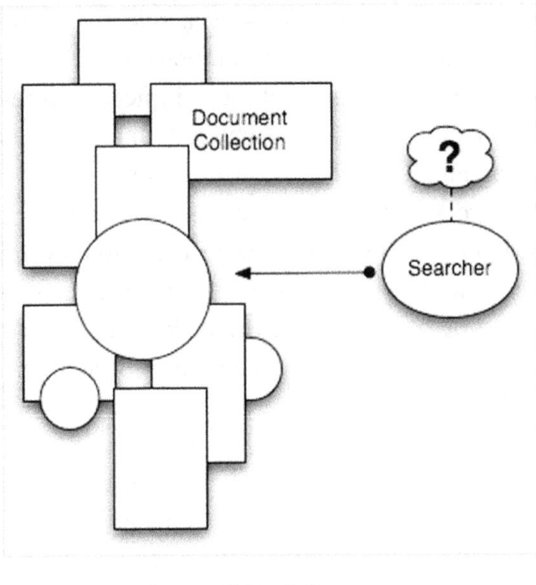

Figure 1.1. General Model.

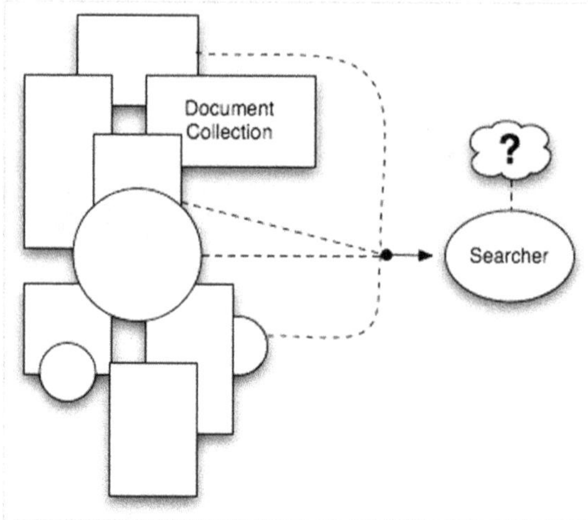

Figure 1.2. Searcher and Document Collection.

Unless the collection is very small and very specialized so that every document in the collection happens to be a good response, the user may have to make some selection from among the documents. A representation or sample of the collection is required. That is, some works are chosen or extracted, while others are left behind. Even in the unlikely event of a collection in which every document is a good response, available time may compel the user to take a smaller subset of the documents.

This selection could be made by going through all of the documents and selecting those that meet the appropriate criteria, as in Figure 1.2. This assumes that the person knows what those criteria are; that good responses can be recognized; and that time and other resources are available to conduct such a search.

A solution to the dilemma of making a selection within a reasonable amount of time is to make use of representations of the documents. Indexing and abstracting are systems of representation. Typically, representations of the whole collection are made, stating: "the materials on a particular topic are to be found here, those on another topic, over there." Indexing by subject headings points to clusters of works. At the same time, representations are made of each work, so that a searcher need read or view or listen to only a small document. Abstracting reduces each work to its essence, making a secondary document to stand in place of the original. Then, individual documents often have their own indexing (back-of-book index, table of contents) to point the way to regions containing particular concepts.

We have said nothing yet about the mechanisms of making the representations, or what the rules are, or who constructs the rules, whether the representations are made ad hoc, a priori, on the fly, by humans or by machines. At this point we are looking only at the general model, as modeled in Figure 1.3,

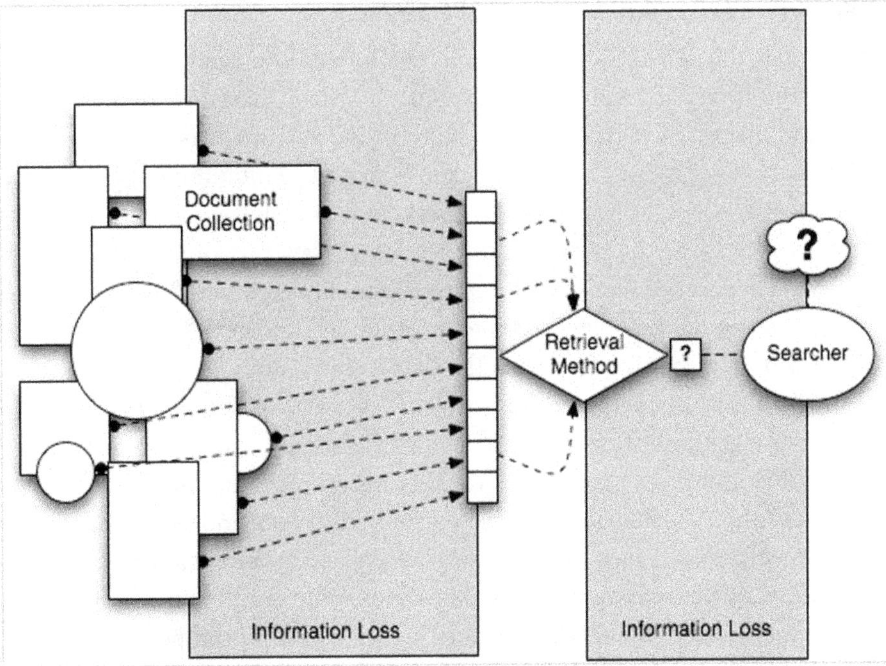

Figure 1.3. Information Loss.

in which representations of documents and representations of questions are compared in some manner. The results of that comparison will be a set of documents (or citations to documents).

Patrons cannot yet simply put their heads down onto a reference desk, or a keyboard, or a card catalog, or a cell phone keypad and have the system know the nature of their information needs. The technology is not yet in place and our understanding of the nature of question states is still crude. Thus, issues of representation of questions and documents are central to our concerns with bringing together people with questions and resources that might resolve those questions. Indexing and abstracting have traditionally been at the heart of such concerns.

Linked closely to issues of representation are issues of the system used to compare questions with documents. The mechanisms for making use of representations to put the most appropriate set of documents at the patron's disposal must also be central to our explorations of doing things with information.

Information loss is one of the most important elements of the general model. Representation, by definition, means there will be some information left behind, as suggested in Figure 1.3. Ensuring that the necessary loss of information is not fatal to the search effort is one of the crucial tasks of representing documents and questions. We might say that our task is to decide which information is expendable.

SEARCH TIME AND SEARCH SPACE

We can call the set of all the available documents the search space and we can call the time a user spends in the search space the search time. We can say that at one end of a spectrum of search time and space is the instance of having to do no searching at all. A person who has no requirement for outside information sources will not have to spend any time and will not look at any documents. Similarly, a person who has been given a title or the location of a work may have to spend a little bit of time actually getting the work, but will not have to spend any time searching for which work to get.

Search time that is too great is the flaw in the search method at the other end of the spectrum. In some ways it would be very reasonable to say to the person coming into a document collection with an information requirement: "Start at document one; go all the way through it; move to document two; go all the way through it; continue this process until you find what you need." Unfortunately, this makes some assumptions that cannot always be assumed. The least worrisome assumption is that the person would actually recognize the document or documents that would be right. Would the person have the critical and conceptual abilities necessary to recognize documents? Would a more elementary work have to be encountered first in order for the appropriate document to be sensible? Would the passage of time during the search change what would be the best response or even the validity of the question?

Time is the more vexing assumption. Even if we were to reduce the number of documents from all those available in one language to just those in a modest academic library, time would remain a problem. If we assume 500,000 documents in a modest academic collection, and if we grant that a person could read or view or listen to 10 each day, 135 years would pass before all the documents had been seen. Clearly this is not suitable.

Of course, it might be that good materials would be found well before the end of the collection had been reached. Yet the numbers remain instructive. For most users of document collections there have to be means for trimming down the search time and the search space. There must be means for looking at only some portion of the collection. There must also be means for examining that small portion more quickly than by reading each and every document in its entirety.

Indexing reduces search space. Abstracting reduces evaluation time. Together, indexing and abstracting reduce search time. Sophisticated and appropriate means of reducing search time and search space are required if people are to make full use of accumulated recorded knowledge.

CONTEXT

We must now establish a context for our considerations of doing things with information, of indexing and abstracting as the means of reducing search space and search time. We will sketch the intellectual discipline within which these modes of representation are studied. Then it will be useful to establish some touchstone definitions for foundational terms. The physical environment within which documents are sought will be established as a significant element. Models of primary issues and relationships will be proposed. A metaphor will set the stage for our investigations.

Theory of the organization of information is the common term for the discipline within which we find the study of representing document and questions. Looking into the catalog of a doctoral program for an outline of the field, we might find something such as:

- Fundamental Concepts
  - information
  - aboutness
  - relevance
  - closeness of meaning
- Basic Design Concepts
  - document identification
  - indexing
  - abstracting
  - classification
  - search languages
  - query formulation
- Automated Systems Techniques
  - associative search techniques
  - clustering
  - automatic extraction
  - full text retrieval
  - genetic algorithms
- Evaluation
  - system performance
  - user satisfaction
- Advanced Design Principles
  - vector space model
  - probabilistic indexing
  - utility theoretic indexing
  - community memory construction
  - inductive searches
- Knowledge Representation
  - formal logic
  - relational calculi
  - artificial intelligence
  - neurophysiological insights

Such an outline situates the concepts of doing things with information within a robust theoretical framework. (*Doctoral Digest*, 1991). This provides us with avenues of exploration, evaluation, and speculation. The outline summarizes, in no particular order, questions such as:

- Just what do we mean by "information"?
- How does somebody know what a document is "about"?
- Is the same work "about" the same thing to different people?
- What makes a document significant or "relevant" for somebody?
- Just what do we mean by indexing and abstracting?
- How do we do indexing and abstracting?
- How do we make a question?
- What do we have to tell a computer to have it index or abstract?
- What do we have to know about documents and questions?
- What does efficiency mean?
- Just what is good indexing or good abstracting?
- How do people get all those things into their minds?
- How can we embody questions and concepts for manipulation?

These sorts of questions will be raised and elaborated upon in the following chapters. Case studies and discussions together with bibliographic essays will frame possible responses or, at least, paths for exploration. The complex web of relations that mark the territory can be sketched as in Figure 1.4.

This map is an elaboration of the models in Figures 1.1, 1.2, and 1.3. It hints at the numerous subtle yet crucial distinctions that must be made when discussing documents and their users (Pai, 1995). For example, both the author of a work and a user exist within a knowledge framework and within some situation that compels the authoring of a work or the seeking of a work. The degree of similarity between the settings will likely determine, to some degree, the utility of a particular document to a particular user.

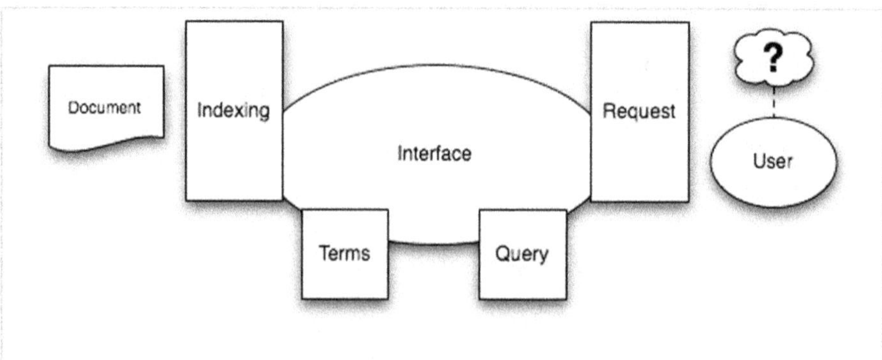

Traditional conceptual schematic of an information retrieval system.

Figure 1.4. Schematic of Retrieval System.

Similarly, a user may have a need for information, but be capable of expressing it only partially; thus, there would be a difference between the "need" and the "request." Also, the request may not be in terms useful to the search system, so there might have to be a translation from the user's request to the actual "query" put to the system.

DEFINITION OF TERMS

Consensus is lacking on concise definitions for many of the terms fundamental to discussions of indexing and abstracting. Differing camps within disciplines ranging from philosophy to artificial intelligence are still puzzling and arguing over the mechanisms of knowing, understanding, and reasoning. Therefore, it is not possible to give simple, unambiguous, widely accepted explanations of:

- data
- information
- knowledge
- wisdom
- indexing
- abstracting
- classification
- reasoning
- representation
- organization

However, it is necessary that we have some common vocabulary for our subsequent explorations. Working definitions of the preceding terms will be presented here, then refined, adjusted, and elaborated upon as we consider specific problems and issues.

Data, information, knowledge, and wisdom are generally related in some sort of hierarchical way, each one being more refined, advanced, or rare. Even within any one set of definitions the boundaries are not solid and well established.

We might argue that **stimuli** are the beginning point; all the input that we learn to ignore or attend. These are the impacts on all our senses. **Data** is here taken as the beginning of the progression of representation, of reduction. The word "data" is actually the plural form of a Latin word meaning "something which is given." Dictionary definitions tend to be of this sort:

- *fact[s], proposition[s], etc., granted or known, from which other facts are to be deduced*
- *something given or admitted, especially as a basis for reasoning or inference*

Yet note the confusion that arises in the Oxford American Dictionary:

> *facts or* ***information*** *[emphasis added] to be used as a basis for discussing or deciding something...*

For our purposes data will be considered **input that has not yet been evaluated or given a context**. There is a comedy routine that gives us a good example:

> **News broadcaster**: "And now for some football scores: 23, 17, 6, 42, and 12."

Without a context, these are just numbers. We may recognize them as being within the ordinary range of scores in a football game, but we can gain little more from this string of data. We do not know if any of these are to be taken in pairs, if they are just the winning scores from each of five games, if they are scores from today's games, or if they even have any relation to any real games at all. The numbers are simply data.

Similarly, seeing a thermometer reading of 37 degrees is data that is only made useful or meaningful if given a context. Is it that temperature here? Now? Am I going outside? Is this a lot colder or warmer than it has been lately?

Information is probably the term on our list with the most diffuse set of definitions. The word comes from two Latin words, "in" and "forma," which suggest the form or shape inside. Definitions in the literature range from statistical measures of the degree of uncertainty in a system; to anything one can forget; to changes in the mental maps by which we operate in the world; (Belkin et al., 1982) to Wheeler's "the quantum presents us with physics as information"(Wheeler, 1990).

Ordinary dictionary definitions do little to resolve the issue. *[I]ntelligence gathered or communicated*... simply adds another term for which there is no simple definition. *[C]ommunication or reception of knowledge or intelligence*... adds two more terms, one of which (knowledge) jumps ahead in our taxonomy. It also implies that communication is a one-way event, an assumption that we will soon abandon. *Facts told, heard, or discovered*... adds the term "facts," yet another term for our list.

What we can see in the terms "intelligence," "knowledge," and "facts" is an acknowledgment that "information" has a connotation of evaluation, context, and consensus. Data have been reduced, modeled, and tested within some accepted framework. We establish much of our consideration on Shannon's work on uncertainty and entropy. For our current purposes, we will suggest that information is the reduction and synthesis of data for use in reasoning (Hayes, 1993; Bates, 2000).

Both **knowledge** and **wisdom** remain beyond easy definition. Each implies a greater degree of reduction, synthesis, and analysis of data, together with community agreement about the means of reduction and the value of the resulting outputs. In our present taxonomy we might find it useful to make a distinction between "information" and "knowledge" based on concepts from evolutionary epistemology.

Plotkin suggests that knowledge is what gives our lives order and that "knowing is living and surviving" (Plotkin, 1994). We might say that **information** is an **acceptable internal picture of the world**, while **knowledge** is the successful use of internal pictures. Generally we think of these as occurring locally, within an individual, yet they could also be taken to happen to groups over years or generations. Both ideas and physical adaptations are generated, tested, and regenerated. We could say that knowledge is the set of ideas and adaptations that is working at the time. This suggests the possibility that knowledge may change, may have to change, as environments change.

It is important to note that wisdom need not be seen as universal. The counsel that seems wise in one group of people may seem utterly ridiculous to another group that holds to a different paradigm. Rock and roll music was the expressive force and metaphor for some lives, yet was ignored, vilified, and condemned by others. To those who held to an Earth-centered view of the universe, Galileo and Copernicus were raving lunatics, yet they are now heroes in our textbooks. To some, Darwinian explanations of the workings of the world are of little value, yet to others they are powerful explanatory tools.

While it will be necessary for us to consider what any individual user of an information system considers knowledge, there is probably no need for us to posit a formal definition beyond the concept of both knowledge and wisdom being, to varying degrees, **information evaluated and accepted by some group**.

Indexing is considered here in just brief and general terms since it is a primary topic of our explorations and will be refined and expanded as we encounter a variety of situations requiring some form of indexing. Index is a term derived from a Greek word meaning "to point." Whether we are speaking of a back-of-the-book index, a classification scheme, or a subject index to a whole collection of works, the elements of the index serve as signs pointing to some smaller subset of a whole.

We must be careful not to be unduly influenced by any particular concepts of the term that we hold from tradition and practice. The general idea of signs pointing toward a subset of information may well manifest itself in very different ways, especially in the newly developing digital environment.

Abstracting comes from Latin words meaning "drag out"; indeed, we get the word "tractor" from the same root. Samuel Johnson offers a powerful and poetic definition: **a smaller quantity containing the virtue and power of a greater** (*Oxford English Dictionary*). The operative definitions within the practice of abstracting stem from the American National Standards Institute. They speak to the "smaller quantity" by suggesting a numerical value (generally one-tenth to one-twentieth the length of the original) and to the means of achieving that size. The nature of "virtue and power" are not addressed so expressly.

In a sense, virtue and power suggest that we are speaking of the heart of the matter, of the most fundamental aspect of something. This runs counter to the daily use of the term "abstract," which suggests an ethereal nature that is hard to grasp. If one thinks of the military context within which the term abstract was once used, another issue arises. Abstract was apparently used by Roman armies as a term for pillaging conquered cities. To some, the virtue and power resided in the beautiful women; to others, in the strong men; to others, in the jewels and other riches; to yet others, in the religious objects. The saying "one person's trash is another's treasure" is apt here. To abstract is to pull out the virtue and power of some larger entity or set of entities, but these could well be different for different people.

As with indexing, we must be careful not to be constrained by our current notions of abstracting. Can we design systems that can detect the treasure for each user? Can we abstract multimedia documents? Must abstracts be constructed a priori, or might we design systems for ad hoc construction of custom-designed abstracts.

Figure 1.5 shows the general relationship between indexing, abstracting, and a document collection. Indexing points to areas of likely utility, while abstracting provides smaller, secondary documents for inspection. Indexing and abstracting of some sort are absolute necessities for navigating through the sea of information in which we find ourselves today. However, they must be accomplished in ways hospitable to and compatible with those who make use of them.

Classification is another concept closely tied to the reduction of search time. The Latin term "classis" meant a group called to military service or, more generally, a social group. This became extended to the idea of any **group of things sharing some common attribute or set of attributes**. Generally there will be fewer groups of things than there will be individual entities; thus, less examination is required to find a desired entity. What we must remember is that there are many instances in which a single entity can hold membership within several groups and that there are groups that have less than strict membership rules. We may think of classification as **putting like with like**, but we must remember to ask what we mean by "like" (Minsky, 1986; Smith & Medin, 1981).

Putting things in groups helps us to act rapidly. In can be argued that classification is a survival skill. If we had to compute the threat quotient or the food quotient of every single animal we encountered in the wild, we would not survive for long. Knowing that most instances of "large plus sharp teeth plus claws" mean fight or flight is more efficient than having to assess the consequences of size and the potential of sharp teeth and claws when they act on the human body for each instance.

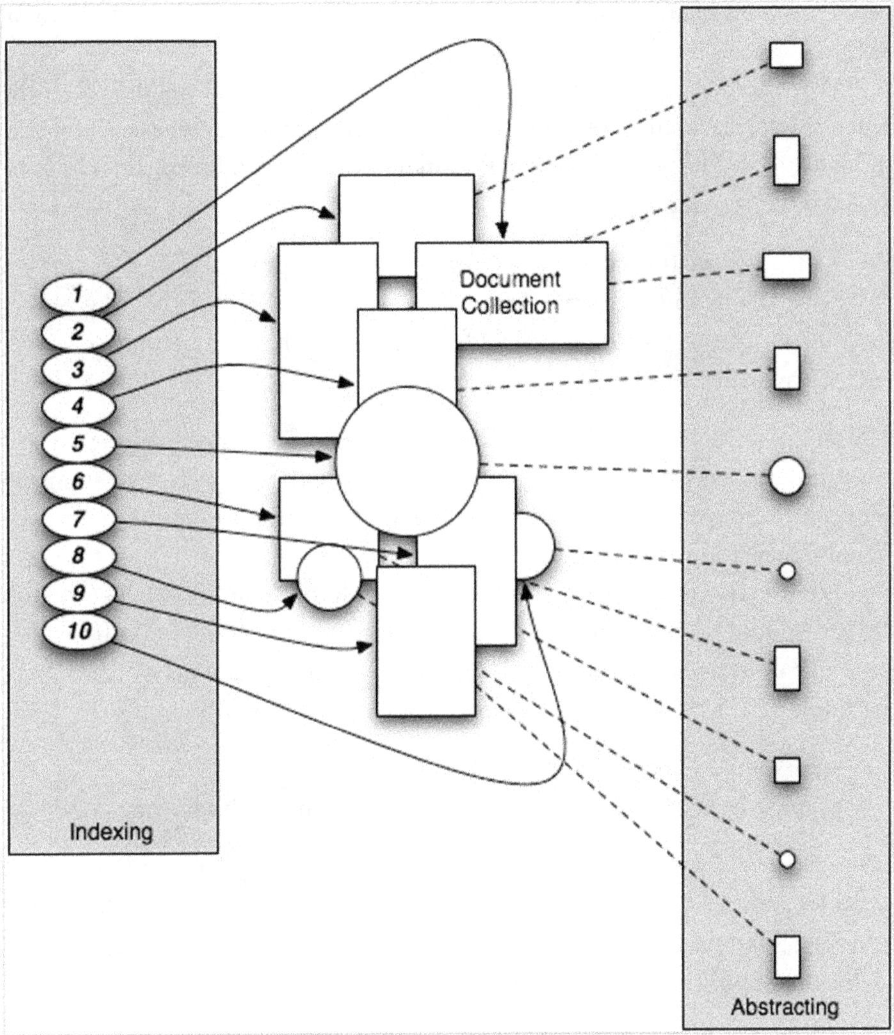

Figure 1.5. Indexing and Abstracting As Search Tools.

Of course, such classification can easily become what we disparagingly call stereotyping. The inappropriate attribution of characteristics and the subsequent inappropriate actions can cause difficulties. Similar difficulties can arise whether we are talking about encountering animals, dealing with people, or organizing documents.

Reasoning is closely linked with all of the concepts discussed so far. It is probably the subject of one of the longest-running debates in history, dating at least to the time of the major Greek philosophers and probably before. While this is not the arena for sorting out the various approaches to the nature of thought, we can say that information and the ways it is structured and utilized are fundamental to reasoning. Most of the efforts of the field of organization of information are focused on enhancing reasoning ability of people.

We will take reasoning in a very broad sense. We will include both the logico-sequential abilities we sometimes label left-brained, as well as the spatial and holistic abilities of right-brained thinking. Reason will be considered to be the faculties we use to:

- plan for the future by examining our past and present
- weigh differing possible actions
- make our way about in daily life based on all the data pouring in
- play with ideas and reshape them.

At this point we would do well to consider very briefly the characteristics of three primary sorts of reasoning. We do this because there is a close relationship between these sorts of reasoning and the changes in representation that the digital information environment may allow.

Deductive reasoning is the sort probably most often associated with "logical" thinking. It consists of rules for deriving true statements from preexisting true statements. One of the most common illustrations of this sort of reasoning is this construction about the Greek philosopher Socrates:

- All men are mortal [a true statement].
- Socrates is a man [a true statement with a link to the previous one].
- Therefore, Socrates is mortal.

Deductive reasoning seems to be at the heart of much of information retrieval apparatus developed over the past century. Whether because of philosophical compulsion or economic necessity, most systems have had:

- strictly defined and unitary placement of documents within a classification
- questions restricted to topic descriptions
- deductive links between a question, collection documents, and documents put into a user's hands.

Of course, there are many things in life that do not easily fit into such small packets of truth. Also, we often have to make decisions without complete data, so the issue of stringing all necessary truth statements into logical chains, as in deductive reasoning, is meaningless. Similarly, questions in an information system may not always be easily articulatable in precise terms.

Inductive reasoning is one method we use to cope with incomplete data and lack of time. Here we use the constraints that suggest a possible answer or set of answers and rule out some possible answers. A simple example can be used to demonstrate this sort of reasoning:

2, 4, 6, 8, —

If we now say, "Fill in the blank," there are many possible answers but only a few that are likely. These could be the digits of street addresses, so that 2, 4, 6, 9 would follow in the blank space. These could be digits in a repeating set—2, 4, 6, 8, 2, 4, 6, 8, 2, 4, 6, 8. . . . These could be the first few digits in a randomly selected group that just happened to fall into a sequence of incrementing by two—2, 4, 6, 8, 37, 92, 103, 54, 13, 27.

The more likely responses because of various combinations of what we are taught about numbers and what we are socially conditioned to do with numbers are:

> 2, 4, 6, 8, 10, 12, 14, 16, etc., adding two to each previous number
>
> or,
>
> "Who do we appreciate?!" using rhyme and meter for a chant.

Analogical reasoning seems to suit humans well. It could be said to be at the foundation of education, classification, and metaphor. Every time we think to ourselves or say to another: "It's like a . . . " or "It works just like a . . . " or "It's kind of like . . . " we are using analogical reasoning. We use what we know about one system or thing to understand or explain something that is not well-known.

A popular song had a phrase "My baby, he's like a freight train." Given the rest of the lyric, it was clear that the woman was not singing about a child under a year old. She was singing about her affection for an age-appropriate man. We use the term "baby" because the physiological responses and the accompanying feelings of devotion and tenderness most people feel for babies are similar to the feelings in a romantic relationship. The term baby makes clear the sort of feelings and their depth.

Clearly, the man is not made of steel, does not run on diesel fuel, does not weigh hundreds of tons, and does not spend his life on railroad tracks. He is not a freight train. However, he does have a habit of coming into town, staying only briefly, then leaving again. The emotional impact on the woman singing the song is one of devastation—as if she had been run over by a freight train. She has not been crushed, she is not bleeding and dying—she has not actually been run over by a train. She does feel incapable of conducting a normal life; chemical levels in the body have changed to induce some pain and inability to move; thoughts are too distracted to pursue daily affairs. The feelings and the consequences of the man leaving town as a freight train does are such that she might as well have been run over by the train.

Representation is the set of means by which one thing stands for another. The *Oxford English Dictionary* speaks of ". . . the fact of expressing or denoting by means of a figure or symbol," as well as ". . . to bring clearly and distinctly before the mind, . . . by description." It is a complex web of attributes of disparate objects and concepts, idiosyncratic and socially constructed codes and agreements, and neurological abilities. Paraphrasing Marr, we can say that representation is **a system for extracting or highlighting some characteristics of concepts or things, along with an explanation of the rules and reasons for that extraction** (Marr, 1982).

A representation is not just another instance of the original. It presents only some characteristics of the original. Generally it is shorter, smaller, or less time-consuming than the original. For some purposes it stands in place of the original. Two important points are implied by the definition. If someone does not know the rules and procedures for the representation, it may be of little or no use. We need only to look to the studies on catalog use or our own observations of card catalogs and on-line catalogs to see the importance of this aspect of the definition. The majority of users seem to have little understanding that:

- there is a sanctioned list of subject headings
- these are complex constructs
- they are applied at the level of generality of the whole document
- the odds of just guessing the same set of words as an indexer did are very low.

That is, they do not know the procedures for representing documents that we call Library of Congress Subject Headings, or Dewey Classification, or post-coordinate Boolean searches.

Also, if some things are highlighted, by definition some things are left behind. In an information environment, the decision of what can be left behind can be vexing. How can we know which parts of a book can be ignored or generalized into a broad subject heading? Can we really represent audio and video works just with words? Are patrons really concerned that the information in a library happens to come in segments of two or three hundred pages at a time? Can we really leave out levels of detail smaller than the book? Could we leave out a large percentage of the collection entirely and concentrate in detail on a small, representative set of documents?

Organization is where theory and practice meld. The word comes from a Greek term meaning "work." Organization puts to work all the elements we have discussed, as they relate to people seeking information. It enables those people to work productively.

If we look to the *Oxford English Dictionary* definition of "organization," we get the sense of **putting organs together into a vital system**. It may not be inappropriate to keep this biological metaphor. We seek to have systems that respond to differing needs and differing circumstances. The complexity of creatures with numerous organs suits them to survival in changing environments. Organization does not simply mean arranging things in some way. It implies that elements are put into play to facilitate some activity. **System** will be used for the results of "organizing—a set of connected . . . parts . . . that work together."

One term that is not in our list yet stands as a fundamental component of doing things with information is **question**. This is so fundamental that we devote somewhat more space here to this notion than we have devoted to the other concepts on our list. Note that we refer to "question" rather than "a question" or "the question." This is perhaps an awkward mechanism, but speaks to our concern that questions not always be taken as atomic packages.

QUESTION: WHERE ENTROPY, FUNCTION, AND MEANING CONVERGE

What is a question? The areas of study usually termed "Library & Information Science" are, in large part, concerned with helping people answer questions, yet there is precious little in the field on what constitutes a question. Just what are the problem states that require information of some sort for resolution? Again, just what is a question? While this question requires depth and breadth beyond the scope of our text, we feel it is critical to set out some of the components of a model of question states. There are at least three specificities one must recognize to understand *question*: entropy in document structure, the templates of meaning and function of a document (or a set of documents), and one's own template of understanding.

Entropy

Entropy is a measurement of document structures. Shannon and Weaver recognize that document content is a necessary part of the communication relationship between the sender and the receiver; they tell us that we communicate by both the content and the structure of a message (Shannon & Weaver, 1949). Their information theory measures structural communication elements. Entropy is a measure of the surprise in the structure of a message. If one is reading through a telephone directory, there is little surprise, since each entry is a name and number alphabetically arranged. If one is watching a movie trailer, there is likely to be a lot of surprise, since the plot is not known, the scenes are presented quickly and out of order, and a large number of images is likely to be presented in a very short time. If one is looking at a Power Point presentation that has a different font on every slide and a sound effect and animation on every slide, there may be too much surprise. Entropy is normally expressed in a range of zero to one, with zero being very low and one being total unpredictability. Message designers generally strive for a good mix of novelty and familiarity, or mid-level entropy, as suggested in Figure 1.6. When entropy is high, then, the amount of surprise, confusion, unpredictability or the likelihood of surprise, confusion, and unpredictability is greater. Likewise, when entropy is low, likelihood of predictability is higher.

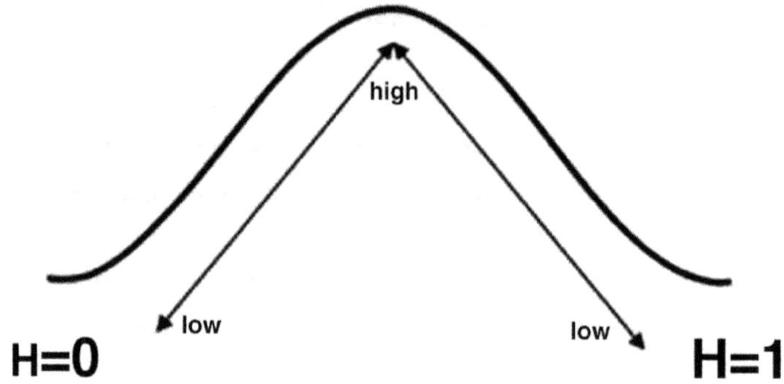

Figure 1.6. Perceived Entropy.

Document Templates of Meaning and Function

A document's template of meaning and function can be expressed similarly to articulations of traditional document aboutness practices. Every document offers a template of all possible meanings and functions. Every user may not be interested in or able to decode the same template items. Included in a template of meaning and function for a book might, for example, be topics, references, table of contents, index, language, availability in the library, color information, pictures included, computer-generated list of word frequencies, level of education required to read and understand the concepts, and so on. A kindergartener may read Dr. Seuss's *Hop on Pop* and for that child, the relevant pieces of the document's template of meaning may simply be several lists of rhyming words and functionality may corrollarily be practice reading. For that child's parent, the relevant template elements may also include a piece of Americana and interesting Seussisms in image and word, and functionality may be the tool by which her child learns to read. For an adult whose second language is English, a Dr. Seuss book in the English translation may offer no functionality at all. In all of these examples, the document's template of meaning is the same even when only small pieces of that template have meaning for one user, and entirely different meaning and function for another.

Consider another example. Patrick Wilson's *Public Knowledge Private Ignorance* is shown in Figure 1.7, with the Library of Congress MARC record. This MARC record is part of this document's aboutness, so it must appear on its template of meaning and function. This MARC record has meaning and function for most librarians and library students. How much meaning would it have for a high school math teacher, or an attorney? Probably less. In addition to every statement made in Wilson's book and the official MARC record, this document's template of meaning and function also includes the author's intentions, reader reactions, amazon.com reviews, keywords extracted by human indexers and computer-generated word counting programs. It includes every scribble made in the margins of every copy ever sold, and read, and on every

000 00928pam a2200265 i 450
001 2708572
005 19770805000000.0
008 770329s1977 ctu b 001 0 eng
035 __ |9 (DLC) 76052327
906 __ |a 7 |b cbc |c orignew |d 1 |e ocip |f 19 |g y-gencatlg
010 __ |a 76052327
020 __ |a 0837194857 : |c $13.50
040 __ |a DLC |c DLC |d DLC
050 00 |a Z665 |b .W76
082 00 |a 020
100 1_ |a Wilson, Patrick, |d 1927-
245 10 |a Public knowledge, private ignorance : |b toward a library and information policy / |c Patrick Wilson.
260 __ |a Westport, Conn. : |b Greenwood Press, |c 1977.
300 __ |a viii, 156 p. ; |c 22 cm.
440 _0 |a Contributions in librarianship and information science ; |v no. 10
504 __ |a Includes bibliographical references and index.
650 _0 |a Libraries.
650 _0 |a Knowledge, Sociology of.
650 _0 |a Information science.
991 __ |b c-GenColl |h Z665 |i .W76 |p 00013842437 |t Copy 1 |w BOOKS

Figure 1.7. MARC Record and Book Cover.

Xeroxed copy ever distributed to every student. It includes the contents of the congratulatory phone call this author may have received from his former major professor, and every confused look on readers' faces. It is the precise offering of this template of meaning and function from which readers will finally extract meaning and function.

At this point in this discussion, we are reminded of an ongoing conversation we've been entertaining about who gets to decide a document's meaning and function. We are certain that meaning and function can be determined only by the person who is searching for meaning and function, though we in the library and information sciences have means to eliminate some of the steps so that this person might find meaning quicker. One single library record does not hold the key to understanding the document. We have uncovered a phenomenon that interferes with the generation of complete templates of meaning: we call it information arrogance. We have observed information arrogance in at least the following ways to date:

- the assumption that document content is more important than document structure;
- the assumption that document structure is more important than document content;
- the documenter's assumption that all users will have the complete code to understanding the message;
- the user's assumption that she or he understands the documenter's intended message;

- the user's assumption that meaning and function are static;
- the user's assumption that hers or his is the only interpretation or the correct interpretation of the message; and,
- the user's assumption that document representation is complete, and that the indexer has selected the only important pieces of the document to represent it.

Wilson used the word "transintentionality" to describe meaning, because meaning—even with the direction we in the information professions offer—cannot be determined by anyone but the user (Wilson, 1960). Surrogate engineers can intentionally select representation points of access and interest, per se, but the job of completely representing each document's template of meaning is an extension beyond intentional direction (and arrogance of misdirection by omission) of meaning if every document has a template of possibly infinite meanings and functions.

User Templates of Meaning

A person's template of understanding is quite a simple concept to express, though each template is construed by a complex network of experiences, ideas, images, emotions, and knowledge. Figure 1.8 presents one such template.

It is by one's own template of understanding that meaning and function can be extracted from a document. Consider an example of a contemporary popular song in Afghanistan. If I heard it, it is likely that I would have few elements in my template that would lead me to extract any more than a pittance of meaning from this message. Perhaps I recognize that it might be a Middle Eastern language. A nurse with the International Red Cross-Red Crescent Society who had been stationed for six months in Jalalalbad would likely have a template loaded with more tools for understanding that this is an Afghani artist. Perhaps she can even recognize and sing along to parts of the song, because her Afghani interpreter listened to the song regularly on his iPod and shared the song with her. The interpreter's template of understanding for this particular message has all the relevant elements for him to extract meaning in the document. Every person's template is different, though many items on many templates overlap. Those whose template items overlap with yours are the people you call friends and colleagues. Those things a user does not know do not entirely fall outside her or his template of understanding, because she or he still knows enough to recognize the possible functionality of the elusive document, that is, her or his template of understanding provides a foundation (a template) such that the user knows enough to, at least, recognize that she or he should learn more, or should try to assimilate more, of that document's template of meaning. It is a process.

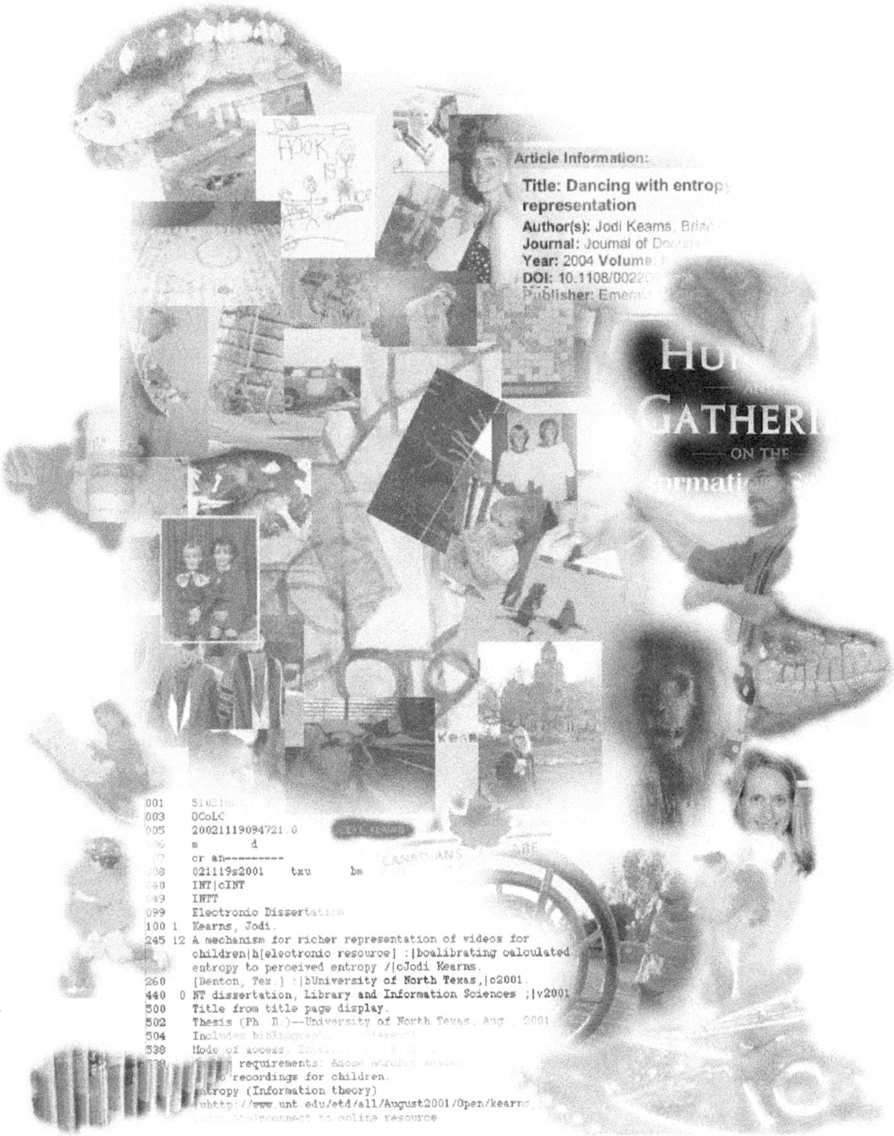

Figure 1.8. Kearns Template.

Question

It would be irreverent to not mention Belkin's Anomalous State of Knowledge while we are defining question, for it is the discontinuity in thought that becomes the question, yet we assert that question is a continuum, not a singular, finite expression of anomaly, because information is not static (Belkin, 1980). Document function and meaning change depending on the depth of the question and on the depth of the perception of the questioner.

Since situational function of the document is highest—or most obvious—at low-entropy (predictable, nonconfusing) document structures, and where items overlap in the document template of meaning and function and the user's personal template of understanding, meaning is achieved where overlapping items blend into reminders, enhancers, and extenders of knowledge. One can only ask a question about what one can formulate in some fashion.

Question, then, is the field of intersection of high entropy document information and the document meanings that do not match or fail to assimilate with an information seeker's template of understanding. Question is, representationally, here. Question is not always a simple concept to represent. Figure 1.9 simply presents one way to begin mapping a part of our explorations.

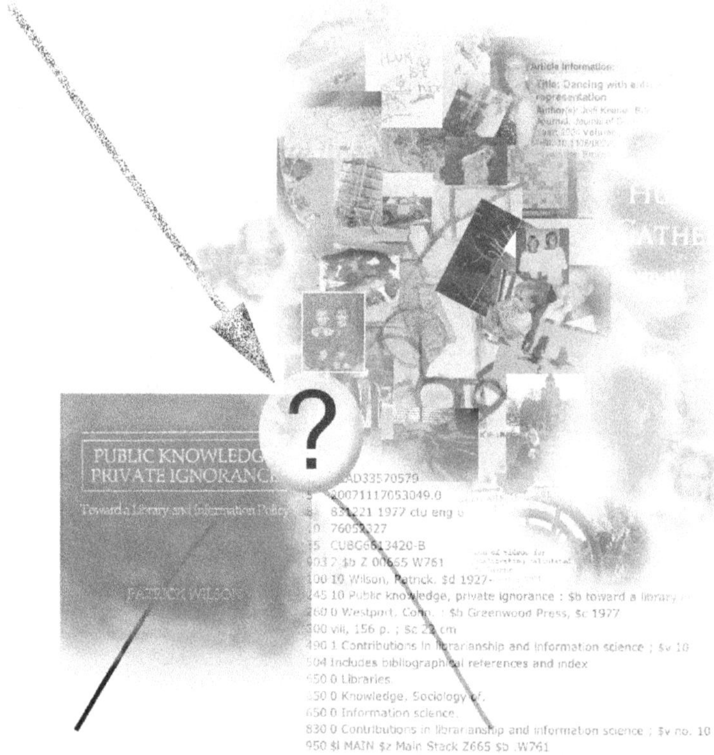

Figure 1.9. Question is Here.

CHAPTER TWO

CONSIDERATIONS OF REPRESENTATION

FUNDAMENTAL CONCEPT

REPRESENTATION is a concept fundamental to doing things with information. It is the ability to make one thing stand for another that enables humans to make sense of records, documents, signs that stand in place of direct experience; indeed, even the body's engagement with the environment depends on representation. In order to raise questions such as how we might best represent questions or needs, how documents put pictures and sounds and ideas into the heads of other people, how people decode information to use it, or how we might best help people engage useful information, it will be informative to spend some time considering representation. We must consider representation because we cannot as yet simply be in the presence of an information retrieval system and have it know what we want, as the seemingly silly Figure 2.1 suggests.

Figure 2.1. Interface with Systems Still Require More than Thought Projection.

Figure 2.2. Illustration for "What Is This?" Exercise.

Representation has already been defined as a system for extracting or highlighting some aspects of an original concept or object, together with some explanation of how the system does this. That is, we have some form of sign (in its broadest sense) that is generated from some original referent, by means of some code. In a general sense, we can say that there is no sign without a code. There may have been a code at the time of the sign's generation, but if any individual encountering the sign doesn't know the code, there is, in that instance, no sign (for example, Eco, 1976).

We can put our definition into terms of entities and attributes. Entities are the things being represented and attributes are the characteristics of the entities. Any object or concept can be termed an entity. The entity can be described as the sum of all its attributes or characteristics. The purpose of the representation will strongly influence just which attributes will be highlighted or selected as representative.

The subtleties of the mechanisms of representation remain elusive. Neurologists and artificial intelligence researchers ponder the physical embodiment of information in symbolic forms for use. Philosophers and artists, too, puzzle and argue over how one thing can stand for another. The two exercises below by no means exhaust considerations of the nature of representation. They are intended to demonstrate two broad forms of representation.

"What Is This?" Exercise

What will be said if we present Figure 2.2 and ask: "What is this?"

Most people will likely answer "a buffalo" or "a bison." Some will say "a buffalo in a zoo." Clearly, however, it is not a bison. If an actual bison were to inhabit these pages, reading this book could be a real adventure. A "real" bison weighs much more than this entire book; it exists in space and time; it needs food; it has an odor; it breathes and makes sounds; so Figure 2.2 is not a

Figure 2.3. A Photograph of a Portion of the Hieroglyph Segment on the Rosetta Stone.

bison but a reproduction of a photograph of a bison. Similarly, what if we ask of Figure 2.3 "What is this?"

Viewers who had gone through the above exercise might now say, "It's a photograph of some old writing," or "It's a representation of hieroglyphics," or "It's a picture of a stone with writing carved into it." Again, it is not a real stone with carved figures; it is a reproduction of a photograph of a stone with carved figures.

What if we ask a different question, such as "What does it mean?" or "What is it about?" or "What can I do with it?" Some might truthfully answer: "It doesn't mean much," or "It's some nice carving." Typically, though, most respondents say something similar to "I don't know" or "I don't know how to read the text."

Even if we add the Greek translation to the hieroglyphics, as in Figure 2.4, most people will answer "I still can't read it," or "It's Greek to me!" or "Isn't that the Rosetta Stone?" Adding the Greek translation of the Egyptian text enabled translation by scholars, but does not make the text any more evident to the untrained reader.

Direct Presentation of Attributes

The bison image is an example of representation by direct extraction of some attributes of the original. Direct extraction of some of the physical attributes enables the making of a sign that stands in the place of a bison. If we wished to show people in a classroom what a bison looks like, we could get a trailer, herd a bison into the trailer, and transport it to the classroom. This might be a valuable classroom experience, but it is not always practical or possible.

If we take some of the animal's attributes, such as color, the two-dimensional shape, the relative sizes of various body parts and scale those down

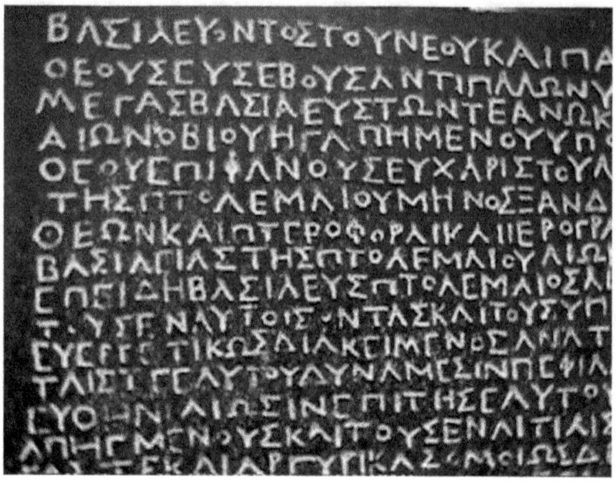

Figure 2.4. A Photograph of a Portion of the Rosetta Stone with the Greek Segment Shown.

to a manageable size, we can bring the essence of bison into the classroom. Essence here is defined only in terms of the requirements for the classroom. The essence for a Native American on the Great Plains or a modern-day buffalo rancher would be quite a different matter. Essence might then be in terms of resources available from the animal for food, clothing, spiritual values, or profit margin.

The representation highlights those characteristics suited to the classroom, while leaving out movement in time, size, smell—those characteristics that would be inconvenient in a classroom. Of course, a real but dead and stuffed bison might be convenient for some classroom experiences. Yet, even a stuffed animal is a representation of the living animal; it no longer has organs, or the quality of movement, or the ability to eat.

Regardless of the actual neural mechanisms, this direct extraction method of representation can be said to be a combination of a sufficient subset of attributes and some form of knowledge that a representation is at work. This combination enables reasoning about the original object or concept and, if necessary, filling in some of the missing attributes.

One term for such representation is isomorphic, derived from Greek roots meaning same shape. Realistic paintings and photographs are prime examples of isomorphic representations. They present two-dimensional projections of the myriad data of an object at one moment in time (usually). Figure 2.5 presents another example of isomorphic representation, with the rule for highlighting (extracting) made explicit.

In information retrieval systems, we make isomorphic representations when we provide a small photograph of an art object or a frame from a movie; when we enable patrons to hear samples of a musical selection; when we copy the title as it appears on the title page; or when we put a few works from the

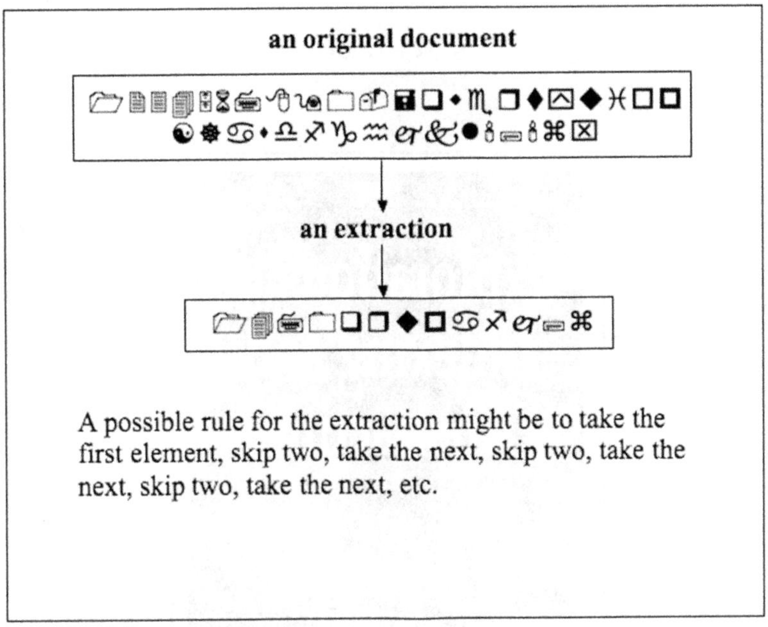

Figure 2.5. Example of Isomorphic Representation.

collection into a patron's hands. Abstracts that present salient points in words extracted directly from the original article are isomorphic representations. So too are previews for movies and keyword search systems. Photographs and fingerprints in a police database are isomorphic representations, as are audio recordings of speech and music. Of course, there are some subtleties here that should not be overlooked. The cover photograph of the *Explorations in Indexing and Abstracting* is isomorphic with the cover of the book in a way that is slightly different from simply typing the same words that appear on the cover. Note in Figure 2.6 that the title that appears on the publisher's web page is not in the same font and color as what is on the book cover, rather it is a Verdana font and light blue.

The tag cloud concordance shown in Figure 2.7 is another useful form of representation. The form of concordance in which the size of a word is a function of its frequency within the text extracts actual words and presents an attribute (frequency) but not by presenting each of thirty-seven instances of the word "document," but by coding that number into a second physical attribute—size. This, the concordance, could still be said to be an isomorphic representation of the first edition of this text.

Such a blended representation leads us to discussion of a closely related form of representation that can be termed indexical. Here the sign is in some way a direct result of interaction with the referent of the representation.

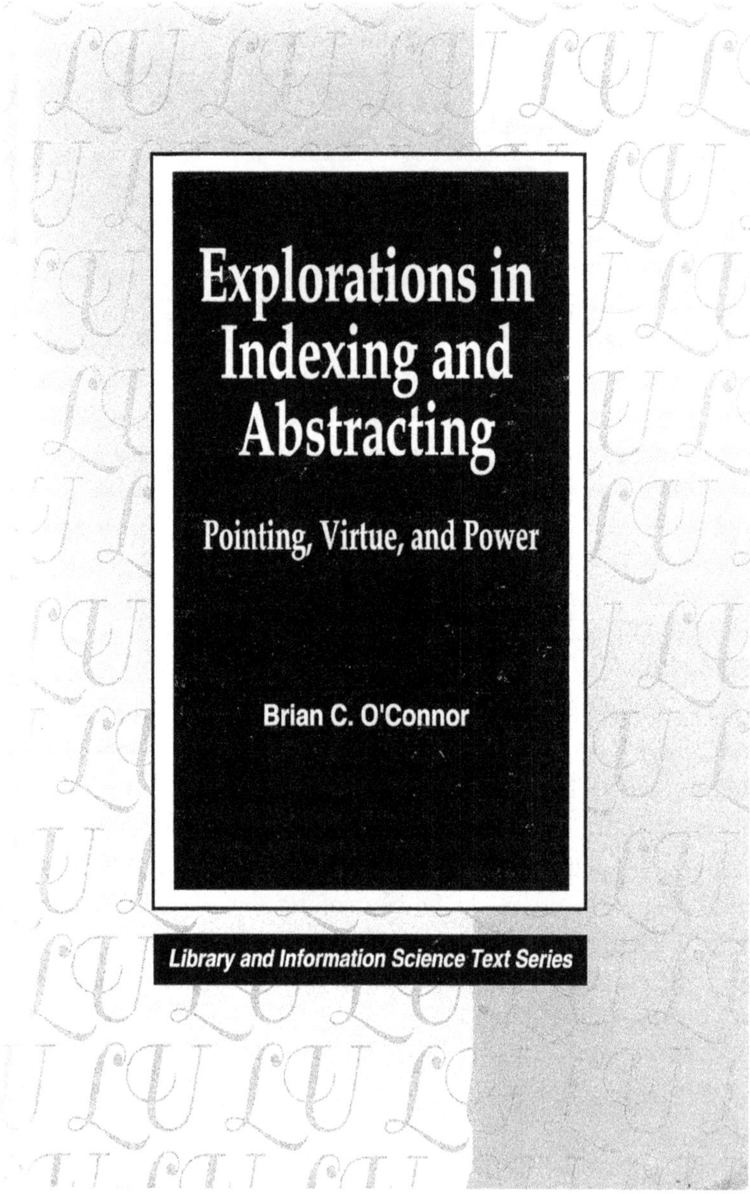

Figure 2.6. Cover as Representation.

Perhaps one of the best examples is a thermometer. The rate of movement of air molecules directly impacts a colored liquid in a tube causing it to rise or fall in direct proportion to the molecular movement. The liquid is not the air molecule movement, but we can tell the amount of movement by the position of the liquid. Other weather-related instruments provide additional examples: the direction of a weather vane, the speed of rotating cups or fins on an anemometer; the outstretched or limp flag on a post.

abilities abstracting access activity attributes author between book browsing chapter collection computer concept connection course data depth descriptors different document does elements environment evaluation even example fig figure find form general group headings however images indexing individual information issues know knowledge level library likely list little look material may means method might model must nature need new number part particular patron people pictures point possible present process questions representation retrieval rules sampling say scholar search searcher searching set should sign size sort subject system take terms text though time title topic two use used useful user value words work yet

Figure 2.7. Tag Cloud Concordance as Representation.

A bar graph or a pie chart presents a size in direct proportion to the size of some set of numbers or elements, as in Figure 2.8. Pebbles used for counting sheep, laps run around a track, or almost anything numerical can be said to be indexical because each one represents a set number of items. Even computers use the counting pebble method, when they print a dot on the screen for every "so many" operations in decompressing a file, search a database, or some similar activity.

The direct relationship between an object and a photographic representation of that object is modeled in Figure 2.9. A man stands against a tree and someone with a camera comes along. Light bounces off the man into the lens and onto the recording medium. While the picture will be two-dimensional and probably not the same height as the man (though there is no technical reason this could not be so), the same relative shapes and gradations of lighting will hold in the representation as in the original. Discoverable and repeatable relations will hold between the original, the original recording, and secondary images such as computer images, and paper prints.

Photographs can be said to be indexical, in the sense that light bounces off an object, travels through the various mechanisms of a camera, then directly interacts with a photosensitive emulsion or a magnetic oxide emulsion. This,

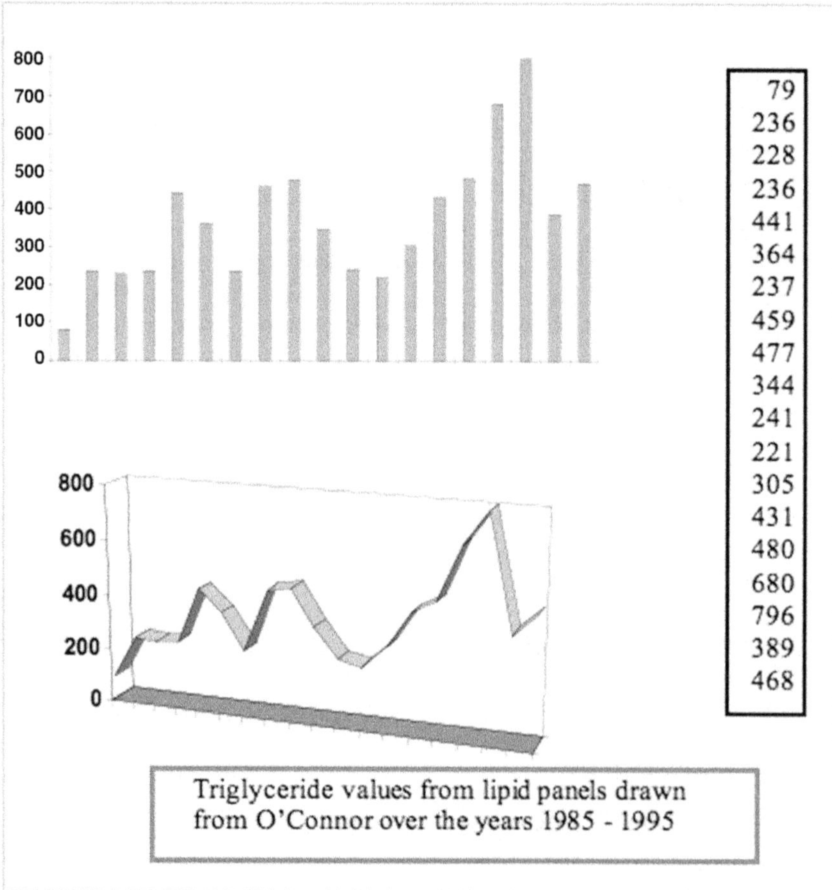

Figure 2.8. Isomorphic Representation—Size Varies in Direct Proportion to the Numeric Values.

of course, demonstrates that there is not a distinct boundary between isomorphic and indexical representation. It must also be remembered that the direct participation of some object does not necessarily mean a "true" representation. An actor may be made up to look like someone else, or the image may have been manipulated.

Indirect Presentation of Attributes

Both isomorphic and indexical representations are specific. That is, they are based on individual instances of an object or a concept. Another category of representation forms can be termed general because they are based on classes of entities and attributes. They highlight attributes indirectly. Again, we must be careful to remember that the boundaries are not hard and fast between the specific and the general.

A representation may start out based on an individual instance, and then become generalized. The photograph of the flag raising on Iwo Jima is, in one

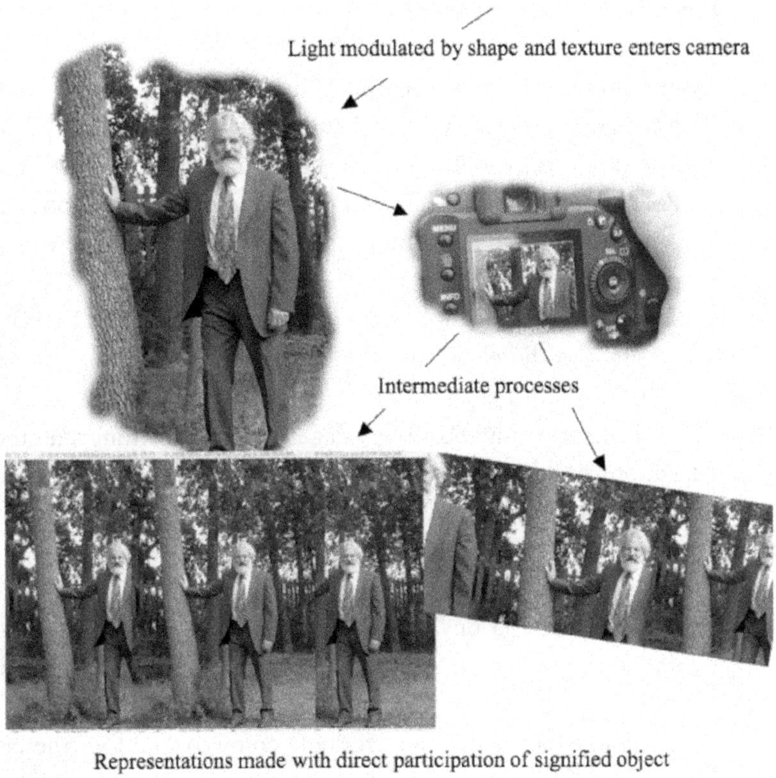

Figure 2.9. Representation Made with Direct Participation of the Subject.

sense, just a representation of a few specific men at a specific moment in raising a stick with a piece of cloth on it. Yet for many, it is generalized into a representation of the concept of valorous and determined patriotism. The single image of soldiers at one particular moment in history has come to stand for all valorous military acts. A part is used to stand for the whole. Such an image can be called iconic; it acts as a reminder or a touchstone for a greater web.

Other specific images have come to stand for some larger number of events or concepts. Both the image of an anti-war protester in the 1960s putting a flower into a soldier's rifle barrel and the image of a single man standing in the path of a tank in Tienamen Square have come to symbolize resistance to tyranny. The picture of John Kennedy's son watching his father's funeral procession evokes all the emotions of the passing of an era.

Of course, the greater meanings are not inherent in the images. They are community constructs. Different communities may well regard the meaning of the images differently. Anti-war protesters might regard the Iwo Jima image as a sad or revolting commentary on blind allegiance to a cause. Many people find the image of the war protester with his flower a symbol of cowardice or treason. It is also likely that many images that are held by some group to be meaningful beyond the particular instance have no greater meaning at all for other groups.

Photographs are by no means the only sort of iconic sign. Two perpendicular lines (†) have greater meaning than just two lines for millions of people. This structure and several variations were used in Roman times to execute thousands of people. One execution is held by many to be emblematic of a set of theological constructs. The instrument of one crucifixion out of thousands now stands for Christianity in all its variant forms.

National flags are just pieces of cloth, yet people will give up their lives to keep one from falling to the earth in a battle. People who protest the actions of a country will often burn that country's flag. Burning a piece of cloth, in and of itself, has little meaning; burning a flag is taken as a strong statement of "I dislike the actions and beliefs of your group!" During the 1960s, protesters were reviled for wearing flags upside down or with a peace symbol in place of the stars. The image of Abby Hoffman was censored on the Johnny Carson Show when he wore a shirt made of a flag, yet one can now go to a sports store at the time of this writing and buy a jacket or shirt printed like a flag. We see that the meaning of the same data set can be different for different groups and at different times.

Some brand names for consumer products come to stand for the class of products. Regardless of the actual brand name or manufacturer's name, facial tissue paper is often called Kleenex. Likewise, many people go to their Lanier, or Canon, or Minolta copying machine to do some "Xeroxing." Most people also have iconic images or materials of their own, images or materials for which the greater meaning is known only to themselves or some close group. A rock seen by anybody else would just be a rock with all its general possibilities for meaning—paperweight, sturdy, throwing object, and so on. Yet for the individual who picked up the rock during a hike in the mountains with a loved one, the rock can stand for the entire delightful experience surrounding the circumstance of the picking up of the rock. A minuscule part of the event can bring back the sights, sounds, smells, physical sensations, and emotions of the entire event.

Arbitrary Trace

Moving along a spectrum of the sign's distance from the original, we come next to the arbitrary trace or what we might call a sign by agreement. In the picture of Hawthorne in Figure 2.10, we have a sign standing for a man that was made by the direct participation of a particular man. Without going into various linguistic theories, we can say that there is little or no direct connection between the lines MAN and some individual male member of the group "homo sapiens." We have agreed that a certain sound will stand for the general concept "man" and that we can have certain signs stand for that sound and concept.

Figure 2.10. Photograph of Nathaniel Hawthorne and His Signature.

Different groups may develop different signs for the same (or similar) concept. Andros, homo, man, and homme are different sets of lines used by different sets of people to stand for the same concept.

Even when we label specific elements of a group, there is no direct connection between the sign and its referent. The man in the image above is the author, Nathaniel Hawthorne. There is not anything about the shape or size of these letters that stand for his name that derives from that individual.

Even in the case of the individual writing his or her own name, for example, Hawthorne's signature in Figure 2.10, the only connection is that that person physically made the trace – the handwritten signature. This may make the item with the signature on it valuable or more meaningful for some people, but it does not mean that the signature actually resembles the person any more than the typeset version of the name.

The signature, just as the photograph, is a representation generated with the direct participation of the signified object. However, it is mediated by a code that removes it from any resemblance to a direct experience of the object.

Wittgenstein suggests that groups create verbal tools for use in conducting their lives (Blair, 1990). People living where it snows frequently will have numerous terms for different types of snow, whereas people in equatorial regions may have no term at all for snow. This makes sense. Whether you are hunting for food, devising shelter and clothing, operating a ski resort, or planning to travel by car you want to know if the snow is light and fluffy, dense, mixed with sleet, or hard packed. In an area where there are earthquakes people will have concerns for the distance from the epicenter, the type of ground motion, the time separating the component waves, the soil type in various locations, and the time of day. To those watching television news in another state, "a moderate earthquake struck the San Fernando Valley today" will be sufficient.

Let us return for a moment to our earlier work, *Explorations in Indexing and Abstracting*. Recall that the cover of the book looks something like Figure 2.11 (though somewhat larger and three-dimensional). We can say that

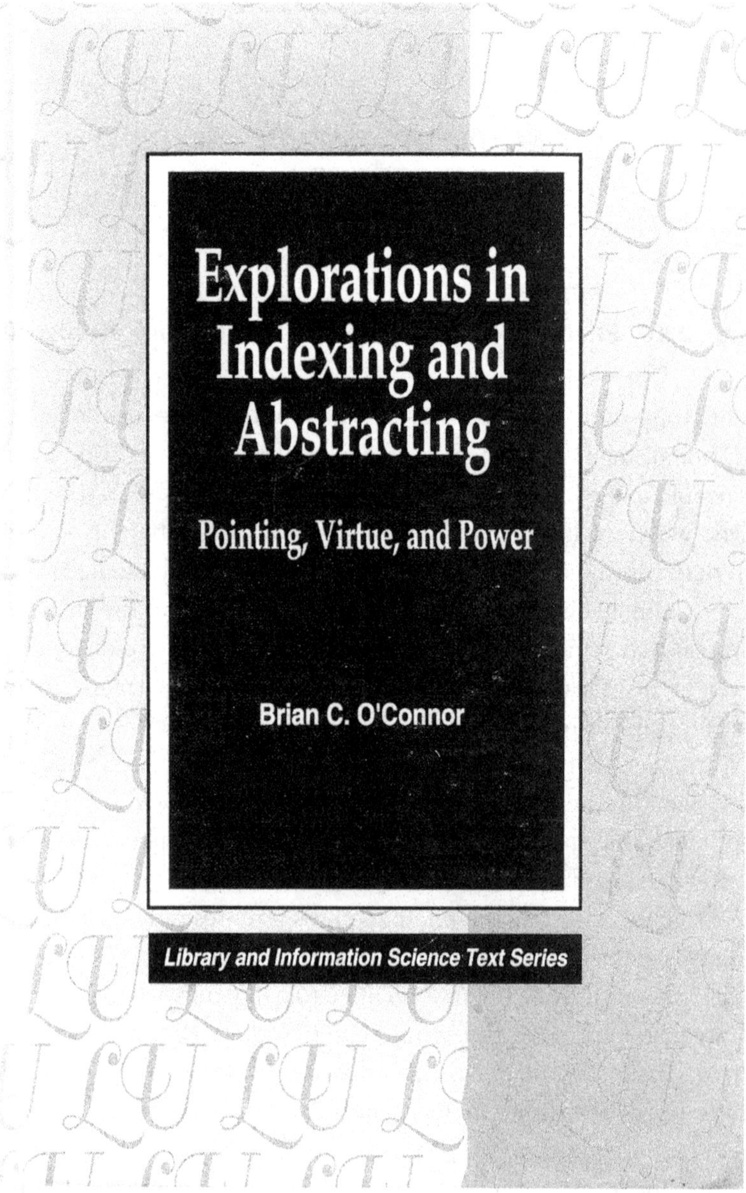

Figure 2.11. Indexical Representation of Book Cover for Comparison with Z695.9 026.

the photographic representation bears an indexical relationship to the original book. Z695.9 .O26 1996 is the Library of Congress representation of that very same entity. Even if one is facile with the Library of Congress system and the representation provides an adequate representation of the book, there is essentially no sense in which the representation could be said to be indexical. The trace is arbitrary in the sense that there is no one-to-one correspondence between the attributes of the document and the representation.

The important thing to realize about the arbitrary trace in terms of information retrieval is that, in Wittgenstein's terms, the map is not the territory. People need to know the agreed upon sign system, otherwise, "It's Greek to me" will be the feeling. Also, different people will likely make different uses of the map. A book in French given to a person who does not read French will be no response to a question, regardless of how appropriate the concepts in the document might be. Even a document in the patron's native tongue will be of only little utility if it assumes knowledge of a discipline or literary style that the patron does not have.

For our concerns with indexing and abstracting there are three aspects of representation with which we must be especially concerned:

- purpose influences mode of representation
- no representation without a code
- synchronic and diachronic attributes.

REPRESENTATION HISTORY OF A FAMILIAR ENTITY

An interesting progression from a specific representation to general representation we use everyday can be started with the image of an ox in Figure 2.12. Suppose we lived some three thousand years ago in the cradle of civilization and had reason to transport the idea of an ox – for which we would be using the word *aleph* – to some distant place; perhaps to the royal accountants. As with the bison in the classroom above, we could bring the real beast or we could bring some representation that would be adequate to the needs of the accountants. Suppose the king wished to know just how much wealth he held, as measured in cattle. It is worth noting that we still use this very notion, as the words pecuniary (and peculiar) are derived from "pecus" Latin for cattle. Bringing all the cattle in the kingdom would be one way to discover the extent of the wealth; yet the very act would likely decrease the wealth, since travel requires calories and entails risks of injury. There would also be the issue of housing and feeding all the cattle once they were at the royal establishment.

It might be easier, in one sense, to cut off the head or tail of each head of cattle and cart just the pieces to the palace. Of course, the consequences for stability of the wealth would be significant. Another approach would be to

Figure 2.12. Photograph of Oxen at Work.

make a little statue of each head of cattle. This would preserve the health of the cattle and, thus, the wealth; yet training craftsman to make the statues might require significant resources. Perhaps having counters go throughout the land and putting one stone or one stick for each head of cattle would work, at least until there was a need to count sheep and jars of wine and containers of honey. Perhaps it would work to return to the statue idea, but with a representational shift.

Suppose counters were sent out across the land making two-dimensional projections of part of each individual head of cattle. Perhaps a drawing of the head, as in Figure 2.13.

We have here the roughly triangular shape of head and snout, two small shapes jutting out where ears would be, and projecting arcs where horns would be. The rest of the body is left out, the color is left out, odor is left out, and movement is left out; yet the remaining parts will suffice to carry the idea of an ox.

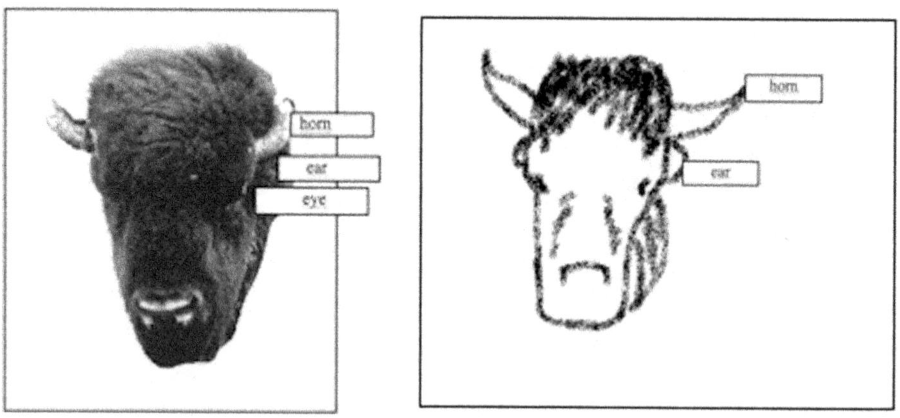

Figure 2.13. Sketch of Ox Head with Outline of Basic Shape and Parts.

Suppose now that we have to make an image for each one of a hundred or more oxen. It might seem reasonable to reduce the number of strokes and to simplify the remaining strokes. An image such as that in Figure 2.14 still has the basic shape of head and snout, ears, and horns; but the irregular contour has been simplified to three simple arcs.

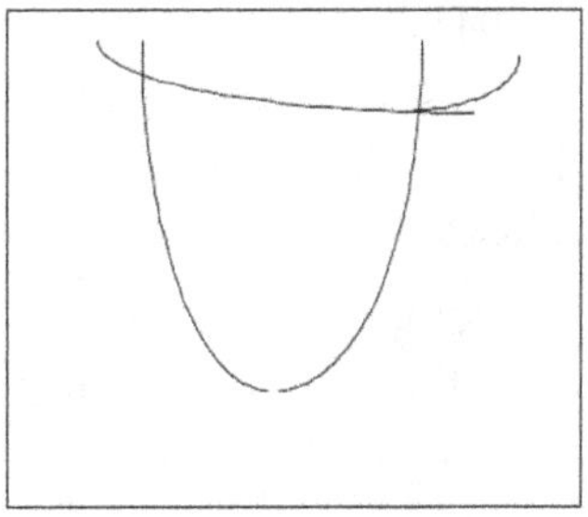

Figure 2.14. Simplified Drawing of an Ox Head.

An increased need for speed or simplicity could yield a sign such as Figure 2.15. Here the head, ears, horns have been reduced to straight lines forming a triangle with projections of the line segments. The basic shapes and orientations of parts remain the same. The general concept of an ox remains.

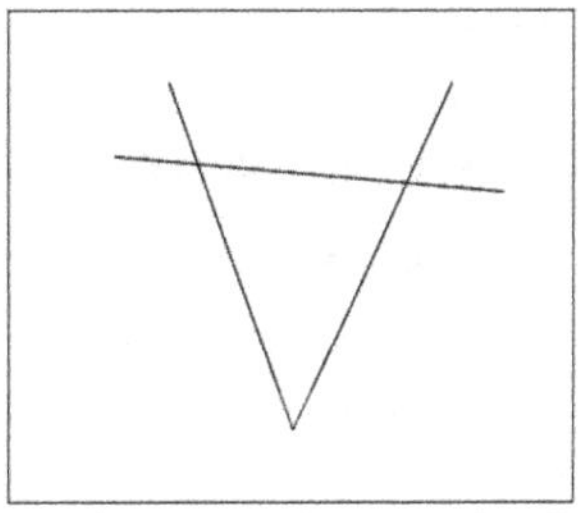

Figure 2.15. More Simplified Sketch of an Ox Head.

Over time others may wish to use the representation we have developed for ox, but they may not be so careful in their design construction, and just orient the basic shape in some other manner, as in Figure 2.16. They may also come to regularize the production of the shape as in Figure 2.17. Also, they may just want to use our sign for ox to remind them of the sound of our word for ox. They don't need to convey the idea of a whole ox, but they want to remember sounds, perhaps for a religious ceremony.

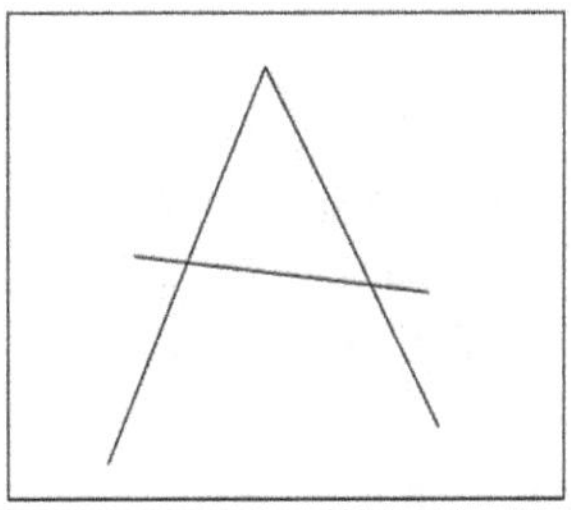

Figure 2.16. More Simplified Sketch of Ox Head.

In a crude retelling, this is the development of our letter "A." The letter "A" in the Roman alphabet (here in a Times New Roman font) still retains the hint of essence of ox, even if upside down. The progression from a specific representation of an animal or other object to a letter parallels the progression from orality, through the occasional use of signs for a few specific purposes, to a general alphabet. The alphabet is a simple code system capable of great complexity in its output. Both the simplicity and the consequent complexity are the result of generality. It is no longer required that there be an individual sign for each and every object or concept or even class of objects or concepts.

Figure 2.17. Romanized Version of the Greek Version of an Ox Head Sketch.

The actual nature of the progression from crude marks, to signs, to letters is still under debate. Did Mesopotamian accountants and other officials develop the ideas over a long time period and keep the secrets to themselves? Did the idea arise essentially full-blown and spread rapidly among a large group? The scanty evidence is tantalizingly adequate to support either direction of theorizing, but inadequate to prove either. Whichever way the progression took place, it is interesting to note our direct linguistic ties to the animals of the Mesopotamian region. The term for ox from that region is "aleph." When that was transformed by the Greeks into the sign for the sound we recognize as "A." the word was slightly transformed into "alpha," from which we derive "alphabet" (Drucker, 1995; Schmandt-Besserat, 1997).

The Evolutionary Nature of Representation

Lineage: A continuous line of descent; a series of organisms, populations, cells, or genes connected by ancestor/descendent relationships (from http://evolution.berkeley.edu/evolibrary/glossary/glossary.php?start=g&end=m—UC, Berkeley—Understanding Evolution).

What we see in the evolution of the letter "A" propels us into a broader model of documents, representation, and use. Denise Schmandt Besserat notes that over several thousand years farmers in the fertile crescent made use of tokens to keep track of the accounting function: how many sheaves of wheat do you owe me at harvest? How many cows do we own? These tokens evolved in a very short time into an alphabet, a way of recording human ideas. Schmandt Besserat suggests the tokens and the alphabets to which they are ancestors constitute a mechanism of cognitive (cultural) evolution.

We would like to cast the notions of representation and use of documents into an evolutionary construct that reflects the power and concepts behind the alphabet. We take the construction of some original text, the uses of the resulting document, the index, the abstract, the bibliography, reviews, critiques, subject headings, Dewey Decimal numbers, user comments on amazon.com, etc. as descendents in a textual lineage. Indeed, we would push the idea of lineage backward as well. For example, much of the material in our earlier book was derived from lectures and exercises for two courses. After a while the collection of notes was something handy to give to those who wanted the background material for thinking about organization of information. When the opportunity to publish a book in the area of organization of information made itself available, the constraints of the requirements of publication (size of the document, writing and citing conventions, intended audience, for example) yielded a different version of those lectures with some additional material. This package was an adaptation of the lectures, which had, in themselves been adaptations of earlier research and lecturing.

If there were not very many documents in a collection and there were unlimited time to sit by a fire on a snowy day in New England throughout which to read, there would be little need for an index, an abstract, or a bibliography. The environmental constraints of numerous documents, little time, and the limitations of human memory (among many others) set the conditions for adaptations of the document. An index is such an adaptation. It serves the purpose of (re)presenting some part of the content of the original in a form better adapted to serve as a pointer. A review is another adaptation providing an evaluative component, why one should or should not spend time with a particular document.

SIGN AND MEANING AND FUNCTION

Meaning and function are at times essentially synonymous in the realm of documents. A well-written book on cosmology enables a mind to model the universe; an Alfred Hitchcock film may take a viewer to world that is exciting because it is both imaginable and troubling; a well-illustrated handbook enables the owner of a 1968 Chevrolet to make repairs and alterations; a snapshot mentally transports the viewer to a distant time; a graph of frame to frame differences in the red, green, and blue components of the colors in movie frames makes visible subtle relationships in the film; and an airline Web site tells whether a flight is on time and at which gate it will arrive. What if the book on cosmology requires more mathematics and physics than the reader knows; what if the editing pace of a Hitchcock film is just too slow for modern audiences; what if three pages are missing from the automobile manual and the user does not read the language in which the manual is written; what if a user does not know that a semi-log graph is a means of presenting data that change with an exponential function; what a person headed to the airport is already in a car and does not have a web-enabled phone to access the airline website? It should be evident from these few examples that there are at least two elements at play in the functionality of a document, by which we mean there is the physically present document and there is the ability to decode the document. The meaning, the functionality does not inhere in the document, to be distilled and made useful with a good shake of the document.

In a behavior analytic system, there is little distinction between a set of documents returned as the result of a user asking a question in an Information Retrieval context and the delivery of food to a pigeon in an operant chamber as a result of the pigeon pecking a response key. Both the food and the returned document set change the behavior of the behaving organism. If one were looking simply at function, the food and the document set are functionally equivalent. Although one can find a common, shared tradition between radical behaviorism and information science, the assertion that the behavior of a pigeon pecking a key in an operant chamber is equivalent to a person seeking information is, perhaps, too large of a conceptual leap and offers little practical utility to a discipline focused, as Buckland and Liu (1995) suggest, on "documents and messages that are created for use by humans" (p. 385). We have begun the discussion of just what a document is so that we can lay the foundation for a functional model for using information.

Document as Binary System of Structure and Function

Anthropologist John Tooby comments:

> [W]e spent hundreds of thousands of years as hunter-gatherers without police, without hospitals, and without agriculture. During all that long period of time, slowly, this process of natural selection built or engineered a set of designs that are structured for surviving the challenges of being a hunter-gatherer (Bingham, 1995).

O'Connor, Copeland, and Kearns (2003) later note that "we are hunter-gatherers; there has not been enough time for the hunter-gatherer brain to have changed." Human beings have been seeking, consuming, and producing information far longer then they have been building libraries and producing documents. We will be constructing a function-based model of doing things with information throughout the text. This functional ontology construct (FOC) document model proposed here could apply as easily to analyzing the expression on a person's face or analyzing a group of clouds to determine the chance that a thunderstorm is approaching as it is applied to more traditional notions of a document such as ***Moby Dick*** or ***The Birds***.

While there are a number of ways the term "information" is used in Information Science (see Belkin, 1978; Hayes, 1993; and Buckland, 1991 for reviews of the different meanings of the term information), the term will be used in a manner consistent with Shannon and Weaver's (1949) technical definition of the term. Weaver states in the introduction to Shannon and Weaver's (1949) *The Mathematical Theory of Communication*:

> The word information, in this theory, is used in a special sense that must not be confused with its ordinary usage. In particular information must not be confused with meaning.
>
> The concept of information developed in this theory at first seems disappointing and bizarre—disappointing because it has nothing to do with meaning, and bizarre because it deals not with a single message but rather with the statistical character of a whole ensemble of messages, bizarre also because in these statistical terms the two words information and uncertainty find themselves to be partners (p. 8).

Shannon and Weaver's definition of information is expressed mathematically as a logarithmic function of the number of choices for a given message.

Shannon's work was conducted in the context of engineering telecommunication systems. In this context, the semantic aspects of a given message are secondary to the structural aspects of the message.

Shannon and Weaver's model is a binary system. The structure of the message has a degree of independence from the semantic meaning of the message. This is similar in concept to other ways of conceptualizing meaning such as semiotic theory (Eco, 1976; Chandler, 2004; Wittgenstein's "language games"; and the behavior analytic account of verbal behavior (Skinner, 1957). Eco (1976) states that semiotics is "concerned with everything that can be taken as a sign (p. 7)." Semiotics breaks meaningful phenomena into a dyadic or binary system between signifier, the structure of the sign, and signified, the concept associated with the sign (Chandler, 2004).

Like *Information Theory and Semiotics*, Wittgenstein's (1953) concept of "language games" is a binary system of structure and meaning. Meaning emerges from the relationship between the participants in the conversation. Wittgenstein puts greater emphasis on meaning than on the structure of the message. In a sense, it is the inverse of Shannon and Weaver's (1949) focus on the message independently of the message's intended meaning. Wittgenstein's concept of language games is similar to Skinner's (1957) system of verbal behavior (Day & Liegland, 1992). The main difference between the two systems is the analytic nature of Skinner's system. Wittgenstein asserts that there are as many types of language games are there are conversations or instances of language games. In a somewhat different but compatible vein, Dawkins' (1982) notion of memes and memetic phenotypes is also a binary system of function and structure where memes are a unit of meaning and the memetic phenotype or vehicle is the physical expression or container for the meme. Dawkins (1982) describes the relationship between memes and memetic phenotypes in the following way:

> The phenotypic effects of a meme may be in the form of words, music, visual images, styles of clothes, facial or hand gestures, skills such as opening milk bottles in tits, or panning wheat in Japanese macaques. They are outward and visible (audible, etc.) manifestations of the memes within the brain. They may be perceived by the sense organs of other individuals, and they may so imprint themselves on the brains of receiving individuals that a copy (not necessarily exact) of the original meme is then in a position to broadcast its phenotypic effects, with the result that further copies of itself may be made in yet other brains (p. 109).

The model of the document used in the functional ontology construction approach is similar in principle to Dawkins' concept of the meme. The document is a bundle of signals that have behavioral function.

Sign and Code in Document Retrieval

There is no sign without a code. We have mentioned this concept earlier and we have seen in our exercise that in the absence of a code we are left to guessing. It is common in discussions of this concept to mention sign systems from cultures of some other time or place. "It's Greek to me!" means we do not have the code and can make no more sense of the sign than that it is intended as a sign.

Until the Rosetta Stone with its Greek translation of hieroglyphs was discovered, the Egyptian writing was just so many squiggles, even to Egyptologists. Painted and carved marks on stones in the American Southwest are obviously the work of humans, but in most cases we do not have the code and cannot decipher a meaning.

Libraries present a more immediately vexing example of the concept "no sign without a code." It is quite likely that success will elude the patron who does not know that the Library of Congress Subject Headings are a mode of representation; that they are applied at the level of the document; that questions must be translated into these terms. The code for tagging concepts is not made explicit. Even well-educated frequent users of the library are often unaware that there is a system of subject headings.

Again, perhaps more troubling is the idea that we do not make explicit to users of information systems just how the salient concepts were determined. Especially in those systems where only two or three concepts are selected to represent the whole document, this failure presents a major roadblock to successful searching. Even the patron who is familiar with the subject headings or classification scheme in use in a particular setting has no way of knowing how some other person extracted the "main" concepts of the document.

Even in machine indexing environments the patron can be at a considerable disadvantage if the rules for extraction or ranking are not made known; if the contents of a stop list (those words considered meaningless and, therefore, not ranked) are not made known; if any uses of synonymy or translation or generalization are not explained.

If the means by which the system accomplishes its highlighting are not made known, the representation is not complete. If the concept tagging system is not made known, the representation is not complete. The patron is left in a position of having signs without a code. However, the situation is more insidious than that of the archaeologist faced with squiggles from another time and place. The patron is hampered by the "illusion of knowledge" (Weisburd, 1987). The system is not obvious in its lackings. Indeed, it may even work well with sufficient frequency so that the patron who cannot find something assumes that the library just does not have anything that would be an appropriate response. In reality, a document might well exist in the collection, but the patron lacked sufficient knowledge of the code used to represent that document.

Synchronic and Diachronic Attributes

Attributes of document entities are the focal point of a related course of discussion. As we pointed out in the archaeological exercise, descriptions of an object usually include both the observable physical attributes and purpose of the object. We can link this to two broad categories of attributes:

> diachronic—those that remain the same across time synchronic—those that may change with time and place.

These are closely linked to the concepts of:

> message ("physical text" in *Explorations Indexing and Abstracting*—the squiggles, whether on paper, stone, or video tape meaning ("conceptual text" in *Explorations Indexing and Abstracting* —the concepts generated in any individual user by the squiggles

Hamlet will always have been written by Shakespeare. "I can't get no satisfaction" will always be a phrase in the song "**Satisfaction**" by Richards and Jagger. "Arma virumque cano" will always be the opening of the **Aeneid**. Instruments playing a Beethoven symphony or Stravinsky's "Rite of Spring" will always set air waves into motion in the same way. These are diachronic attributes, the physically present text.

Not everyone will understand all the concepts within Hamlet with the facility of a Shakespeare scholar or a theatergoer of the author's time. Many parents, teachers, and clergy were upset with the sexual innuendo and rock music of "Satisfaction," while many people delighted in both the music and the expression of sexuality. Years later the song seems simplistic in its orchestration and tame by comparison in its sexual expression.

"Arma virumque cano" was the opening of an important and compelling work in its time; today, relatively few people pick it up to read and those who know of it often have dreadful memories of high school Latin class. Beethoven and Stravinsky were not always held in high regard. The Paris opening of "**Rite of Spring**" evoked considerable revulsion. These differences in reaction to the same squiggles are the synchronic attributes, the conceptual texts.

Not long ago, one could not say "pregnant" on television; today many sexual topics and practices are presented on network programming. Words for which Lenny Bruce was ostensibly harassed by authorities are common fare on cable comedy shows. Less dramatic but just as exemplary are all the gender-specific pronouns in works created well into the 1970s. Even scholarly works would frequently say "How is a man to . . . ?", or "If anyone . . . , he . . . " For many readers and viewers today, though certainly not all, these cause a hesitation in the use of the document. The worth of the document may not be significantly diminished, but the question arises, "How could the author say that?"

In older movies horses were tripped with wires in stunt scenes; in a time when animals were regarded as expendable, this was acceptable to audiences. Now films with animals often carry a statement of compliance with regulations for humane treatment. In nineteenth century art and writing it was popular with men and women to display women as ethereal and saintly by virtue of illness and victimization; today this is not acceptable to many.

The number of examples of changes in synchronic attributes is large indeed. It would be an interesting exercise to take a few moments and jot down more examples of changes. Changes in the way television commercials are produced, or editing pace in movies of twenty years ago, or music enjoyed by different groups of people, or reactions to documents by people of different political persuasions, are but a few of the areas to be explored. We might also list tattoos, men's hair styles, what counts as offensive language on television, and even the value of a dollar.

In the field of library and information management we have become quite good at making use of the diachronic attributes. If a patron can supply a title, or author, or publisher, or even a date, we can do a good job of retrieval. However, we have not been good at providing access by means of utility, especially concept as defined or evaluated by each patron. This is not to say that this does not exist at all. Reference librarians or readers' guide librarians often give evaluative representations of documents based not only on their own beliefs but also on the reactions of other patrons to the documents. There is also the practice of putting some sample of works into a patron's hands, saying: "here are some things that might work for you," then going to find more like those the patron has found most useful.

We would not be in error, though, saying that information retrieval is still based largely on the diachronic attributes of documents. We do not account for the author's stance or "slant" on a topic; we do not account for the reactions of various groups of patrons; we do not account for current validity of the data, assumptions, or conclusions; we do not account for the knowledge base required to make use of the text.

Also, we do not often inform the patrons that we do not account for the synchronic attributes. We do not tell them that indexing is not usually tailored to individual or small group requirements, perhaps with the exception of special libraries and research collections. Again, by not presenting a major aspect of how the system accomplishes it's highlighting, we are compromising the integrity and utility of the representation.

People coming to the document collection with information requirements don't know something. This means that they may well have difficulty formulating the "proper" signs to express concepts. If I hear some sort of a scrunching sound when I release the brakes in my car I am in a difficult position because I don't know anything about calipers, and idler arms, and all the other arcana of automobiles that might relate to a "scrunching sound." I seek out a mechanic who is good at asking me to imitate the sounds and their source.

If I go into a furniture store looking for a chair to go with a particular look I have in mind but I have no knowledge of the technical terms for types of chairs or names for different periods, all I can say is "I need a chair." Then the sales person will have to conduct an interview and perhaps show me some samples to narrow down the size of the category "chair."

If I move from an urban area in California to a small town in Kansas and go to the ranch store to buy winter clothes, I may be faced with a bewildering array of boots and "cold weather gear." It all looks "Western" and it all looks substantial, but I have little idea of what sort of boots are intended for what sort of use. I may not want to appear ignorant or out of place, so I puzzle in solitude over heel shapes and sizes, toe shapes, type of leather and insulation, as well as the construction and appearance of coats and coveralls.

WHERE DO WE STAND?

Let us take a moment to summarize what we have explored and consider some of the basic concepts and relations we have proposed. We present here a bulleted list of eight points and a figure bringing together fundamental aspects of messages, information, and meaning together with how we might achieve more functional connections.

- Structure is a phenomenon that is physical in nature.
- Function is a phenomenon that is behavioral in nature.
- Meaning is a phenomenon that is cultural in nature.
- Structure, function, and meaning are not independent of one another; however, they can be viewed independently.
- Structure is the information content of the message, the diachronic attributes of the message, and those attributes of the message that can be physically measured.
- Function describes the relationship between the message and the behavior of the individuals who interact with the message. Function can be measured in terms of operant contingencies and the products or accomplishments that arise due to the individual's interaction with the message and the environmental context where and when that interaction takes place.
- Meaning describes the relationship between the document and the cultural context in which the document and individual examining the document exist. Meaning can be measured in terms of the collective behavior of individuals or the products and accomplishments of the collective behavior of individuals.

- Structure (see Petroski's work), Function (see Behavior Analytic work), and Meaning (see Marvin Harris, Richard Dawkins, David Hull, Sigrid Glenn, the book on Moby Dick, etc.) are things that can change over time and are subject to a process of selection or "evolution."

Evolution of Tools in Search Space

Our purpose, the codes with which we are familiar, and the situation in which we find ourselves, all work together to determine how we come to find and to understand signs. These may be spoken language, objects in our surroundings, or documents in a collection. It is vital that we account for these attributes of a user who comes to a retrieval system. Presenting the diachronic attributes—the physical text—or even the synchronic attributes of one person—the indexer or abstractor—at one particular point in time may not be sufficient to the user's needs.

Representations act as the tools to reduce search time and search space. If the tools are to be useful, they must be suited to the task. We wouldn't use a sledgehammer to drive in carpet tacks and we wouldn't use a carpenter's hammer to crack sections of a concrete sidewalk. A garden hose is useful for watering plants, washing the car, and cooling off children in the summer. It can be used for brushing teeth or putting out a house fire, but only with great difficulty.

Our considerations of representation are intended to aid in the construction of suites of tools capable of providing each patron with an appropriate level of engagement with the document collection. In order to fashion such tools, we have to consider the nature of the tasks to be accomplished. We must examine:

- the nature of documents and their use
- the relationships between users and authors
- the concept of a subject of a work
- the components available to construct tools suited to individual purposes.

Indexing and abstracting have been the primary tools for accomplishing the goals we are considering. We will examine the components of such representations and consider how they might be adjusted and refashioned to be the most useful tools possible.

CHAPTER THREE

REPRESENTATION, FUNCTION, AND UTILITY

CONTEXT FOR REPRESENTATION OF DOCUMENTS AND QUESTIONS

IN *Explorations Indexing and Abstracting* we used this model as a scaffold for discussing relationships between those seeking to resolve some issue and those who constructed or made available packages of information. We used what was a distillation of semiotic and engineering notions to consider how representation can be situated within the context of recorded documents and their use, as in Figure 3.1. We said at that time that such a context indicates the numerous points at which issues of representation enter into the relationship between an individual with an information requirement and an individual document. We want to discuss the same model as an early instance of the new model we present later in this text. We have presented some basic concepts and have considered representation; we will now begin to weave concepts together; we will present different examples of doing things with information; then we will weave all these threads into a comprehensive construct.

OBJECT/EVENT SPACE

Setting aside some of the intricacies of physics and philosophical considerations of just how we experience the world around us, we can posit an object/event space. All the particles in the universe are subject to certain forces and, thus, hold certain relationships to one another. As Democritus (Δημόκριτος) noted: "All the Universe is atoms and void; all the rest is opinion (though he probably made his comments about atoms and void in Greek—*περι ατόμων και κενου*—rather than in English.) Segments of this set of relationships can be termed objects. These relationships may change over time. Changes in the relationships among the particles over time we will call events. This is especially the case for changes viewed by an aggregate of particles that would commonly be considered a sentient being.

Of course, different viewers may choose to select different chunks of particles and name and use those chunks differently. The same viewer at different times may choose to select a different configuration of particles holding some

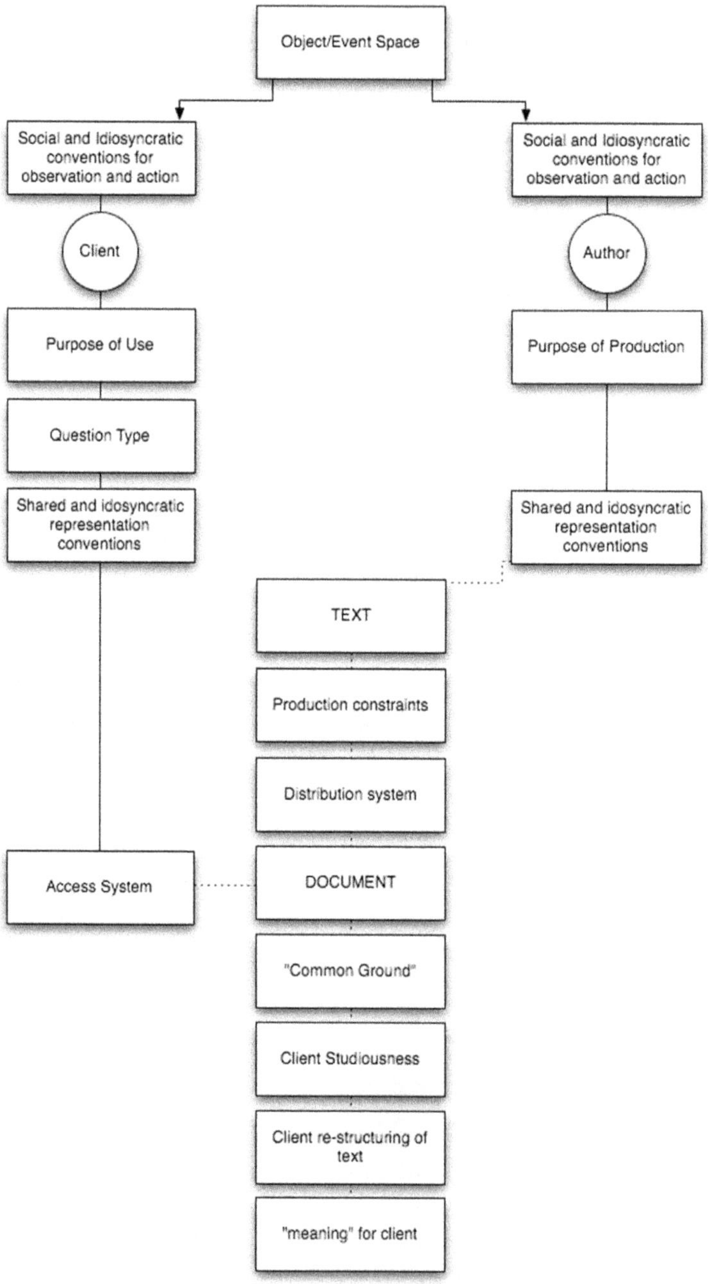

Figure 3.1. Functional Representation Web.

subset of an earlier group and use a different name. A quote attributed to Buddha suggests this chunking for use: *In the sky there is no east and west. People create distinctions out of their own mind and believe them to be true.*

Similarly, artificial intelligence pioneer Marvin Minsky notes that humans are quite capable of making more than one use of the same chunk:

> *How would you classify a porcelain duck? A pretty toy? Is it a kind* of bird? Is it an animal? Or is it a lifeless piece of clay? It makes no sense to argue about . . . we frequently use two or more classifications at the same time (Minsky, 1988).

Regardless of how any individual or group cluster the elements of the universe and make use of them and regardless of how we might say we know the universe about us, we can say that we each deal with the world on a daily basis and throughout our lives. Each of us operates within many arenas and many roles. The range of our activities is great, as we:

- contemplate the morality of actions toward others
- change diapers
- drive to work
- view the stars overhead
- mow the lawn
- compose music
- weed the garden
- consider humanity and its place in the cosmos
- generate models of land mass movement
- practice dribbling a basketball
- smoke bees from the hive and gather honey
- worry about a date for the prom
- write stories about the San Francisco earthquake
- consider electronic funds transfer across borders
- worry about budget cuts
- look for the car keys
- panic over lost files in the computer
- seek a physician for our child's pain
- decide where to eat lunch
- give aid to those who have no lunch
- examine data from Voyager for clues to the nature of the universe
- buy smoke detectors
- write books and make movies
- take the dog for a walk
- wonder if sentences are too long
- stretch skin on a kayak frame
- decide to buy a cell phone with a camera
- advise Ph.D. students on research methods
- fly to Patagonia to do some fly fishing
- test the strength of a piece of rope
- make a chocolate mousee

- rush to get grades in
- wash the car.

All of our actions and interactions, both realized and potential, we will here call the object/event space.

CONVENTIONS OF OBSERVATION AND ACTION

Each person grows up within a web of beliefs, customs, language structure, political and philosophical paradigms, and circumstances requiring action. The education system, of whatever sort, shapes each person's way of viewing the world. Yet individual circumstances may lead to individual variation. That is, we each bring a similar physiological set of tools to our observations, but there are small variations in our abilities and experiences that may yield significant differences. Also, each of us experiences group situations such as school in different ways. Each of us has abilities to consider and remodel those things that we have learned in social settings. We can critique, compare, judge, and contemplate alternatives.

Authors and users of their works each have a set of conventions. If the author of a work and a potential user share backgrounds, their conventions are likely to have significant overlap; if they do not share backgrounds, the degree of overlap will be smaller, perhaps approaching very little or none.

For a message to have meaning, we might say that it has to have both familiarity and novelty. There must be enough that is already known for it to make sense to the receiver; and there must be enough that is new so that it is not just a repeat. If I read a book on indexing and abstracting written by someone who studied with some of the same mentors that I had, then the familiarity is high. Of course, if the level of familiarity is very high, then I might not want to take the time to engage the book, since I likely know most of the material. If I read a book on evolutionary epistemology by a British author, then the familiarity with the topic is modest but the language conventions are reasonably familiar. If I read a French treatise on semiotics, then language conventions stand in the way of my full engagement if I don't read French fluently.

If I read the works of Homer with a dictionary, then I can gain some of the insights from a time long since past. However, I can have only a halting understanding of what it would have been like to be a part of Attic Greek culture, to feel the necessity of the oral poetry, the belief system, or the political environment. I can study cultural artifacts and make assumptions that help me increase my common ground with the author, but it will never be really high.

Author and Client

Author here is taken to be anyone who causes a recorded message to flourish. This might be a writer, painter, filmmaker, composer, editor, publisher, librarian, teacher, or programmer, among others. Certainly, there authors of more ephemeral messages, but the primary material of our field is the recorded message. Client is taken in a generic sense for anyone who comes to any document collection seeking to resolve a knowledge gap. Payment, position, time spent in the collection, and level of system help required have nothing to do with the definition. Other terms are used more or less synonymously—user, seeker, patron).

In the model above, Figure 3.1, the author and the client are shown to make their separate observations of the world about them. These two views are compared in the common ground stage near the bottom of the model. Here the degree of congruence between the author and the user is presented. The client may make a decision as to whether the overlap is adequate. Such a decision may well depend on the urgency of the information need. If the document is to satisfy casual interest, then it is unlikely that finding a translator or immersion in a different culture will be contemplated. If, on the other hand, it is necessary to know a work in a foreign tongue in order to complete a doctoral dissertation, then time and energy simply must be made available.

Purpose

Some of the decision about the adequacy of the common ground, then, is dependent on purpose. Pratt suggests that the majority of reasons for constructing a document or for consulting a document can be summed up in the four subheadings:

- motivation—try to get the reader / viewer / listener excited about an idea or cause
- articulation—try to make evident the workings of a concept
- education—try to pass on useful skills or methods of thinking and doing
- felicitation—try to entertain (Pratt, 1982).

Of course, these are not necessarily distinct categories. The same user may seek two or more at the same time. The same document may be able to serve different purposes for different users. This may be the point for discussion of the nature of questions

Question Type

Also linked to the determination of adequacy is the question type with which the client comes to the system. Broadly, we may distinguish between data and topical or functional requirements. Data requirements are those that can be met by a single (or small set) of responses about which there would be little or no doubt. This does not necessarily mean that finding a response to a data requirement will be easy or that such questions are in trivial. However, the evaluation of "rightness" and "completeness" is simpler.

Table 3.1. Matrix of Question Types

Matrix of Question Types				
	Look Up	Deductive	Inductive	Conversational
Articulated				
Vague Awareness				
Monitoring				
Browsing				

Data requirements are easily defined and results are evaluated simply. If I need to know the name of the wife of the fifth President of the United States, I can be reasonably certain that there is a "correct" response. If I need to know the mean distance between the Earth and the Moon, then I can be reasonably certain that there is only one figure. If I need to know the species of birds generally seen in Kansas, then I would expect a list with quite a few names. However, this would be shorter than the list of all birds. It might be that some such lists would be a little longer or a little shorter than others. These differences would be the result of differences in observation practices or constraints of time, money, or space on the production of the list. They would not likely be because of fundamental differences in how to define a bird that is seen in Kansas. See Table 3.1 for a question type matrix.

We might say (as Blair suggests) that there is a deterministic relationship that holds between a data request and response to the data request (Blair, 1990). The request is a precise statement of requirements; while the response is a precise set of attributes that map directly and explicitly to the attributes of the request. As William Cooper mentioned during a lecture on relational databases in 1980, atomic questions and atomic responses are well-suited to many sorts of information requirements, "but much of the world is too squishy to be served by atomic representation." Most systems of document retrieval are well-suited to the upper left quadrant of the table of question types, where precise attributes are more likely and ease of determination of rightness are simpler.

Topical and functional requirements relate to more ill-defined regions of a patron's cognitive maps. Searching and evaluation are required. The time and place and paradigmatic foundations of a work come into play. As an extreme example, we might say that few astronauts today would want to base their trip to the Moon on a pre-Copernican text of the solar system. We could, though, imagine that while there is a great deal of literature on post-Darwinian concepts of the animal world, there are many people who base their relationships to animals on a pre-Darwinian model.

Within this more diffuse form of information requirement, we can identify different types of questions. Clearly articulated questions are those in which the patron knows what is needed, though its exact nature may not be describable. We can imagine:

- I need just enough about the Gulf War to give a talk at the Kiwanis club next week
- I need to know how to build a deck onto the back of my house
- I want to visit sites painted by French Impressionists
- I need information to help me decide when to have my first baby.

These are not trivial retrieval tasks, but the judgment as to utility is reasonably easy to make.

More difficult to operationalize is the vague awareness that there is a need for information. Questions of this sort constitute a form of seeking in which the patron says: "I am not sure what I want, but I'd know it if I saw it." We may have to bring together pieces of information from numerous disparate sources to satisfy questions such as:

- I am having difficulty relating to my teenage son. Where should I look for information?
- I am not satisfied with my financial situation. How do I go about making changes?
- What do I need to know if I have to determine mainstreaming policies for autistic kids?
- Why should we preserve documents?
- What should I read to understand the possibilities of expert systems for reference?

Monitoring the information environment and shaking up the knowledge store (Overhage, 1965) both acknowledge a different form of information requirement. They are activities carried out by those who say, "I know I don't know everything." Professional people, artists, and scholars know that there is information being generated constantly and some of it may be useful or vital, even though it is not nominally within a particular discipline or topical subject heading.

Monitoring the information environment ranges from checking tables of content in a wide variety of journals, to surfing the Internet, to browsing the new book shelves in the library. There is no stated goal, only a reasonable likelihood that something useful will be recognized if seen.

Shaking up the knowledge store is a term coined by the Intrex conference to refer to all those activities in which a person goes looking in no particular place for something that will put a new twist on an idea, bring two distant ideas together, or stimulate a new train of thought. This may take such forms as random browsing; or finding a license plate number and using it as a starting point in a classification scheme; or purposely going to a section of a collection which has nothing to do with one's own ideas, job, or discipline.

We might conceptualize the array of question types rather like Table 3.1 that is a weaving together of notions of question types from the seeker or client side as suggested in the earlier edition of this work on the vertical axis with a distillation of question types from the system side as suggested by Maron, Levien, and Cooper in various venues (see Kearns's *Foraging for Relevance*, in O'Connor, Copeland, & Kearns, 2003). Note that the well-articulated inquiry that can be fulfilled by a single response or small set of responses occupies only a small portion of the conceptual real estate. We will return to more discussion of questions shortly.

CONVENTIONS FOR REPRESENTATION

Just as people have conventions for observation and action, so too they have shared and idiosyncratic conventions for representation. These include not just language, but also the use of language: epic poetry or personal narrative; political oratory or talking blues; encyclopedia entries or historical fiction. It might well be argued that the necessary "rightness" that the novel once held has been taken over by film and video; that the making of one's own music has been supplanted by DVDs, MP3 players, and multifunction cell phones; that children's fiction making has been dislodged by easy access to DVDs for repeated viewings.

We can look to the television commercials of the 1960s and see not only peculiar fashions and products, but also "crude" production techniques. Films that seemed compellingly new and different in the 1970s now often seem ordinary or passé because their production techniques were incorporated into mainstream production and then surpassed.

Of course, we can also look to those circumstances in which there is little sharing of conventions for insights. Again, "It's Greek to me" comes to mind. We do not have the convention of either oral poetry (with such exceptions as talking blues, rap, books-on-tape, and story hour) or the Greek poetic language. Few of us today would sit through the dozens of hours required to recite the *Iliad*.

We can, though, sense a little of the strain between differing conventions of representation. The complaints of what seem to be every generation's parents over the raucous noise that children call music "these days." The difference in camera angles, editing pace, and lighting between *Miracle on 34th Street* or *Dr. Zhivago*, and *Live Free* or *Die Hard*, or the Peter Jackson version of *King Kong* is in a similar vein.

Such differences in representation codes are always an issue for authors, regardless of medium. The balance of the familiar and the novel is always crucial. Does one throw caution to the wind and throw something totally new at the audience, say *Rite of Spring* or performance art in the grocery store; or does one just push the edges a little bit, so that the larger audience is likely to go along?

These differences are also of importance in our considerations of information retrieval. The patron who has to struggle with the mode of presentation may not feel the effort is warranted, or may misunderstand the text, or may make the effort only to find out that there is little of value in the document. On the other hand, of course, it is possible that an unfamiliar method of representation will prove to be terribly compelling and revelatory for a patron. The very mode of presentation may make the material all the more evident.

Text and Document

Somehow an author makes a decision on what slice of the object/event space to consider and for what purpose and by what means. While there is still considerable dispute on the nature of authorship, text, and reader, there are some generalities of importance. We must first think of the difference between what the author (again, regardless of the medium) has in mind—here called text—and what actually ends up in the hands of the patron—here called document.

The author may have a great idea, but not have the money to realize it. The author may have a great idea, but simply not have the craft to mold the chosen medium to realize the idea. The author may have a great idea and skill and money, but not have time or access to needed material. We may refer to these as production constraints.

There also constraints established by the distribution system. Just what topics are considered "salable" or "appropriate" can determine whether a document, regardless of its potential value to some individual, ever makes it to market. The decision to distribute the work in a different medium from the original can restrict or increase the distribution. Here we might also include the reviewers and the competitions and promotions by which recommendations and purchase decisions are made.

We can also include in the distribution system any decisions by a library or bookstore or video store on how to display and promote a product. Wear and tear on documents as they are used by more and more people is an aspect of distribution that must be considered. Some of these issues are eased within the digital environment, while others such as resolution (e.g., large screen to cell phone repurposing) come to the fore. We might also include the information workers such as producers, publishers, who decide not to purchase certain works or to purchase large numbers of certain works. We can also include any direct manipulation of the work, such as putting labels on the working part of a diskette, or cutting out pictures of nudes from magazines, or accidental ripping of pages, or purposeful corruption of a file. We might also want to include among these, the bodies that rate movies and video games and thereby either cut off portions of potential audiences or cause an author or production company to dilute some aspect of the original intention (text) of the work.

Such actions can mean that the piece that ends up in the hands of the patron is not a robust reproduction or re-presentation of the author's original concept. It is from this document that issues of common ground will be decided. It is from this document that the patron will gain whatever is to be gained.

Common Ground

Common ground may be said to be another term for shared ontological contexts. We are referring here to how much overlap is to be found between the local environment of the client, receiver, reader, and the author. The overlap may be "actual" in the sense that both lived at the same time and within the same culture; or it may be "second hand" in the sense that someone might learn to read ancient Greek and study the religion and politics of the time and then be able to read Homer's *Iliad* and not have to say in despair: "It's Greek to me!" Of course there are more subtle differences that will require attention. An author and message recipient living at the same time and in the same culture may hold very different political or philosophical values; a lovely philosophical work from the 1970s might seem occasionally annoying because gender-neutral pronouns were not yet in use; the fact that Sean Connery starred in early James Bond films might make it difficult for some viewers to accept him as a credible Brother William in *The Name of the Rose* (Eco, 1983). If we look to the Shannon & Weaver (1949) notion of a message and its complementary relationship with meaning, we might say that the "common ground" is the degree to which the message maker and the message recipient share message making conventions or codes and share context.

Studiousness

Studiousness speaks to the resources of time, intellectual effort, and physical effort a patron is willing to commit to finding a satisfactory resolution to the information requirement (Wilson, 1977). The desirable solution might be seen as never having a need to go to a document collection in the first place. Next to this ideal, being shown the one or few works that will suit the need well seems to be desirable—low studiousness. Generally, it is only the person with a compelling problem or a professional position dependent on information who is willing to do a great deal of searching and evaluation. Even within a single work a user may seek only certain portions rather than engaging the entire piece.

This is, of course, quite reasonable in some circumstances. A work may be of use only in part, why should one expend additional resources. We may say that the user participates in constructing the meaning of a work by restructuring the work. If you subscribe to a weekly news magazine, such as *Time*, *Newsweek*, or *U.S News and World Report*, it is unlikely that you read each and every word of each and every page in sequence from beginning to end. You have favorite segments and other segments you generally skip over entirely, and others you check on occasion. Probably you read an editorial or cartoons or letters and then go on to other regions.

We must also consider here just what sort of knowledge gap is in need of resolution. If I just want to see some action adventure movie or video game, I may just go see what happens to be playing at the local cinema and enjoy whatever is presented without critiquing and come out satisfied. If, on the other hand, I am writing a critical essay on the role of action films in setting the political climate, I may well make deeply considered selections of titles and attend to each of them with a critical eye and likely watch each more than once. One might put the former viewing experience on the low end of a scale of studiousness and the latter on the high end without attaching an evaluative judgment. That is, not every encounter with information need be of high studiousness to be perfectly (or even adequately) satisfactory.

Meaning and Utility

As we have suggested earlier, in keeping with Shannon, semiotics, and Skinner, information (the sculpted substrate of a message, for our purposes) has a binary relationship with meaning. That is, meaning does not inhere in the message; rather, meaning is a result of what the receiver, viewer, reader, or the listener brings to the decoding of the message. We would assert here that meaning is more or less synonymous with function. What a receiver can do with a message is its meaning for the receiver. That function may or may not have close correspondence with what the original author intended, but that is irrelevant.

All of the interactions, conventions, and considerations presented in the rough model at the opening of this chapter come together at the point where the user derives some meaning from a document. The word meaning is even more diffuse than many of the others we have considered. We might simply say that meaning is the change or reinforcement made to a user's set of models of the world after engaging a document.

In the first edition of this work we asserted that: "Indexing and abstracting help a patron to locate meaningful documents." While that still holds, we would like to broaden the assertion and suggest that indexing and abstracting are only a subset of the tools that are available to and used by someone seeking resolution of some knowledge gap. Some of the tools are internally generated or learned, while others are external and come from outside the realm of indexing and abstracting, at least in the common sense of the words.

Just as the meaning of documents depends on conventions and codes, purpose and studiousness, so to do indexing and abstracting and all the other personal and external tools for doing things with information. It is difficult to overemphasize the importance of the concept that meaning and utility depend on the coding system and a user's decoding ability. We will take some time now to work through another example form and utility.

If purpose drives the selection of attributes for a representation, then it is reasonable to assume that a particular form of representation determines what one can do with that representation. Our purpose, of course, is to maximize the utility of question and document representations. However, a simpler example may serve to make clear the notion of utility of a representation (Marr, 1982).

If I had some horses and wanted to let somebody else know how many I had, I could pick up a rock or stick for each horse, or I might draw a line or dot for each one.

* * * * * * * * * * * * * * * * *

This is reasonably convenient, so long as I do not have more than some few dozen animals. If I do have a larger number of animals, I need a sign system that reduces data. I need a system that provides a single sign (or at least some reduced number of elements) for some larger number. One example of such a system is Roman numerals. These give me a short-hand system for constructing large numbers.

XVII

Here the X stands for ten; the V stands for five; and each I stands for one. The sign for our number is more compact. However, there is a significant problem with this method of representing numbers. The absence of a place value system makes manipulation of numbers difficult, if not impossible. There is no convenient and systematic method for multiplying or dividing. Once a number is known, it can be represented; but there is no inherent method for calculating a number.

The introduction of a place value system and a zero to stand for the empty place enabled complex manipulation of numbers. In the common decimal system, ten digits are used over and over in positions that multiply the digits by some power of ten. This results in the "ones, tens, hundreds, thousands" system learned in elementary school. In such a system we can represent our number of horses with economy of pen strokes: 17

We can also determine a profit margin if we have 17 horses which cost \$7.13 each for feed and shelter for a month and after six months eight new horses have been born and at the end of two years we sell all but two at \$535 each. Elementary school level activities can calculate the profit of \$8369.24 in this rather idealized example.

We could make seventeen piles of pebbles, each with 713 pebbles to stand for the number of pennies required to provide for the original group for one month. We could then duplicate this five times for a total of six groups of seventeen piles each with 713 pebbles. The same sort of process could then be repeated for the twenty-five horses over eighteen months. We could then make twenty-three piles to represent the twenty-three horses sold. Each of these piles would have fifty three thousand five hundred pebbles. Then we could take away all the pebbles in the cost pile one by one, at the same time taking from the profit pile an equivalent number of pebbles. The remainder of the profit pile would represent our gain in pennies. Roman numerals would offer only a marginal improvement. We could label each small pile and each larger pile, but we would still have to do the counting.

Computers use only two states to perform functions—off and on. This means that a ten-digit system or a system of any other number of digits (except two) would not be suited to implementation in a computer. A binary system will work, though. Here "1" and "0" represent the "on" and "off" states. Place values are still a part of the representation, with each position representing a power of two. Our sample number * * * * * * * * * * * * * * * * *, XVII, 17, would look like this:

10001

That is, reading from right to left:

- there is a "ones" (2^0) value of "1"
- there is a "twos" (2^1) value of "0"
- there is a "fours" (2^2) value of "0"
- there is an "eights" (2^3) value of "0"
- there is a "sixteens" (2^4) value of "1."

1 times 1 = 1; 2 times 0 = 0; 4 times 0 = 0; 8 times 0 = 0; 16 times 1 = 16;
1 times 1 = 1; 16 times 1 = 16

TOTAL = 17, * * * * * * * * * * * * * * * * * *, XVII

If I wish to indicate the sounds associated with our number I can type SEVENTEEN, seventeen, or Seventeen or I can handwrite the equivalent letters. In Figure 3.2, we can see that a binary code—American Standard Code for Information Interchange (ASCII)—enables a computer to represent the alphabetic seventeen, as well as the numeric concept.

So, pebbles or other items used for a one to one correspondence, are convenient and still have utility, even in a digital environment. A system such

Alphabetic	Decimal	Binary Place Values						
		64	32	16	8	4	2	1
S	83	1	0	1	0	0	1	1
E	69	1	0	0	0	1	0	1
V	86	1	0	1	0	1	1	0
E	69	1	0	0	0	1	0	1
N	78	1	0	0	1	1	1	0
T	84	1	0	1	0	1	0	0
E	69	1	0	0	0	1	0	1
E	69	1	0	0	0	1	0	1
N	78	1	0	0	1	1	1	0
space	32	0	1	0	0	0	0	0
s	115	1	1	1	0	0	1	1
e	101	1	1	0	0	1	0	1
v	118	1	1	1	0	1	1	0
e	101	1	1	0	0	1	0	1
n	110	1	1	0	1	1	1	0
t	116	1	1	1	0	1	0	0
e	101	1	1	0	0	1	0	1
e	101	1	1	0	0	1	0	1
n	110	1	1	0	1	1	1	0

Figure 3.2. Decimal and Binary Representations of the Word Form of "17."

as Roman numerals enables reduced time in representation and looks good on statues and other formal objects (according to some people). A system such as Arabic numerals maintains economy and adds manipulability. Ones and zeros require sacrificing some economy in representation, but in an electronic environment they enable rapidity of manipulation well beyond human capability. Visual representation of the associated sounds works well in formal writing and looks good to some people on a magazine cover.

FORM OF REPRESENTATION IN INFORMATION RETRIEVAL

The context web for representation is of fundamental importance to indexing and abstracting because, ultimately, the success or failure of a search may hinge on one representation. The user will have only the tool that is offered as the interface between a knowledge gap and a collection of documents. If that tool does not account for the elements of the context web as they relate to a particular patron, the representation has a high probability of being useless.

The utility of a form of representation is a crucial element of information retrieval. Just as in the example based on the number seventeen, the form of representation determines what sort of tasks can be accomplished using the representation. Title representations are, in a sense, analogous to the use of stones to stand for the number of items in a group. The title is extracted directly from the document. It stands for the whole document. It may or may not give an immediately evident clue to the contents. If a patron knows the title of a work, the search is a data search presenting little, if any, difficulty. If a patron does not know the title of a work that would answer the information requirement, that title is of no use to that particular patron for finding that document. If the patron can guess a title word and the title word is reflective of the contents and the patron has access to an electronic environment or a knowledgeable reference librarian, the title may well be of use. If the user applies a term to the information requirement that is a synonym of the title word, in many cases, the title is of little use.

Subject headings stand for concepts, while not necessarily using the elements of any particular document to represent the concepts. This brings together similar documents that may use differing elements of expression. This collocation can be useful to many patrons; yet, it is achieved at the expense of requiring knowledge of a secondary code. The patron must translate the query concept into system terms, that is, the same subject heading that was applied by the system. Elements, such as keywords, extracted directly from the document offer a search tool made of native elements. A patron need not translate the query; yet works using synonymous elements can easily be missed, unless an additional layer of representation (e.g., a thesaurus) is included in the system.

The level of generality from which the representation is drawn will also determine the utility of the representation for any user. Representation at the level of the whole document will hide smaller but still significant components from users. On the other hand, either the patron or the system must expend additional resources if representation is carried out at deeper levels of generality. Patrons looking for works "largely about" a particular topic do not want to have to wade through a lot of details.

Utility and the Code

We might say that a representation only works to the degree that any user knows the code and to the degree that the code is capable of embodying useful elements and procedures. Again, there is no sign without a code. Utility of a sign depends on the coding system coding something worthwhile. That is, just because a patron knows the coding system, does not mean that unimportant material properly coded will become useful.

Purposeful obfuscation by choice of representation offers another way of considering the utility of representations. It has been suggested that copyright dates on films were done in Roman numerals to make it more difficult to determine when copyright would have expired. Leonardo Da Vinci, used mirror writing to enable the keeping of notes, while reducing theft of intellectual property. Spies and school students devise codes so that messages can be sent over distances and yet be of value only to those who have the code.

We can say that the type of representation chosen can clarify or obscure the message for certain readers. Perhaps these instances of the necessity for transmission of concepts are especially useful for getting to the heart of representation. Some set of symbols or traces is devised to stand in place of objects, concepts, and activities. For those who have the code, the objects, concepts, and activities are decipherable (the pictures are regenerated in the recipient's head). For those who do not have the code, the squiggles are meaningless. They are not signs; they are not representations.

Reconstructing the Model

Let us turn to weaving these elements into a model consistent with the comprehensive construct. One element of the relationship between documents and questions that we have sought is a symmetry or similarity between questions and documents. In other work we had proposed that documents are representations of authors' knowledge states and that questions are representations of users' knowledge states. This simplifies the task of bringing together documents and those who are seeking information by turning the task to one of finding a class or category that contains both the question and some document or set of documents. This approach has a certain parsimony to it, but also does not make explicit certain useful characteristics.

The model presented at the opening of this chapter has symmetry until the point where the "text" encounters production and distribution constraints and the "client" encounters the access system. This point in the model represents the ordinary situation of formally produced documents, such as books, journal articles, films, audio CDs, and the like. However, it does not fit some of the realities of newer document forms such as blogs and other interactive Web sites; and it does not explicitly include all those other forms of information production and seeking that occur in the lived life. Asking Mom about this different cough that the baby has; calling Jack from the coffee shop to find out the name of "that character in Harry Potter who . . . ;" talking with mentors over the wisdom of taking a position at a different university; sending an e-mail to Mark at the kayak supply store to find out if the new nylon material can be sewn with dental floss; googling "Honda driver door won't open" in order to do a home repair on your car; examining photos on Flickr.com to see if users of the camera I am thinking of buying make good pictures; asking Rich if the new Bruce Willis movie is worth seeing in the theater; calling your brother to discuss whether or not Mom and Dad would consider installing a home alarm system; posting a message on Craig's List to sell your old television; and numerous other information seeking activities, large and small, require sending and receiving of messages outside what is implied by "Text/Document" and "Access system" and "Production constraints." At this point is worth making the small observation that terms such as "client" or "user" or "information seeker" are all inadequately descriptive, while also sounding too formal; yet, simply using "folks" or "people just trying to make their way through problems" are likely not much more useful.

Our first thought upon reconsidering the model was that recasting the Object/Event Space as "reality" means we can eliminate it from the model. The concepts underlying the O/E space become simply the blank piece of paper that is the background for the model. This does not mean that the concepts disappear; rather, it means that they are so fundamental as not to require separate elaboration. Each individual behaves within an individual reality or object/event space together with all the contingencies that drive that person. Clients, seekers, and authors all exist within their own realities and have their own contingencies. Within the comprehensive model we are weaving, the "question type" on the client side is the client's verbal behavior or the product of the client's verbal behavior. Similarly, the "text" is the author's verbal behavior. Within our new model "studiousness" and "restructuring of the text" are client behaviors.

The comprehensive model requires more exploration of the ways in which people do things with information, philosophical foundations for doing such things, and some worked examples before its full explication. We present here, in Figure 3.3, the model in Figure 3.1 recast to present even greater symmetry between authors and seekers and to begin to elaborate on new ways to see the relationships holding between the parties and their products.

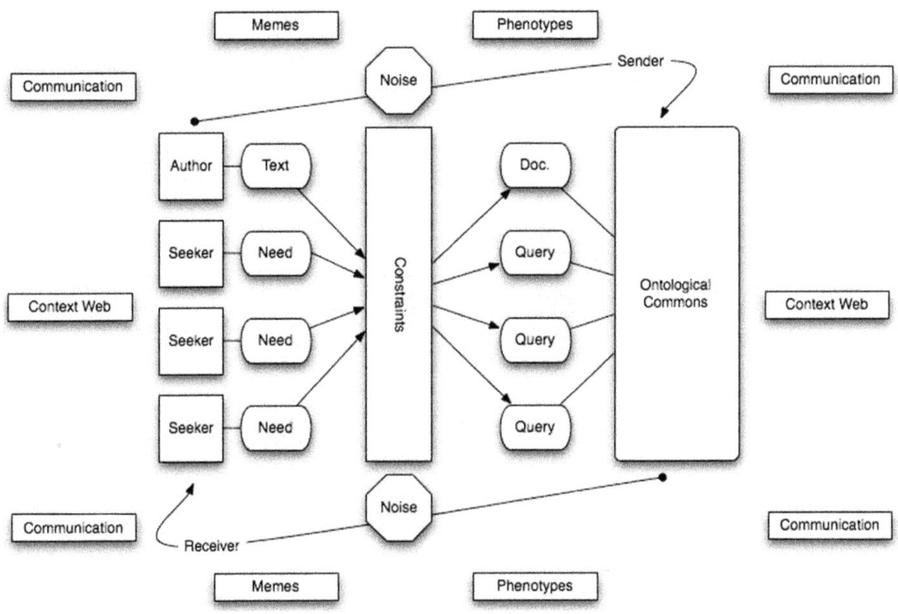

Figure 3.3. Updated Model.

CHAPTER FOUR

FAILURES OF REPRESENTATION: INDETERMINACY AND DEPTH

DOCUMENT STRUCTURE, INDETERMINACY, AND DEPTH

THE **subject** of a document is not some creature that inhabits the work. We cannot simply shake the document and have it drop out, self evident to all who gaze upon it. Milstead, in her review of *Explorations in Indexing and Abstracting*, asserts: "Most authorities would say that the subject of a document is inherent in the document" [*International Cataloguing & Bibliographic Control*, 26(2), 1997, p. 52]. Those making the statements on which our statement on the subject of a document was founded hold considerable authority in their respective fields. We would now point to Shannon's model of information and state emphatically that a complementary relationship between a message (information) and the subject (meaning) of the message, but that must not be taken to mean that information and meaning are the same.

At this point in our explorations of the representation of questions and documents we will enhance our critical perceptions by putting ourselves into the roles first of patron and then of indexer. We will build on what we have covered so far; we will also lay some of the groundwork for subsequent discussions of access models, which are responsive to individual requirements.

A few words about "document" and about "structure" are appropriate here. With the variety of media available, it is no longer appropriate to use just book or article to describe the majority of recorded messages. The word "document" has some of its own problems, but still serves reasonably well to refer to the general concept of recorded messages. Even within libraries, the formats of documents have expanded beyond books and journals to videos, audio CDs, prints, Web sites, and podcasts. The etymology of document points us to rather formal notions; the word has Latin roots meaning to teach" and, so, an example or a lesson, particularly one recorded in some fashion. Considerations of just how one might go about representing documents have been based largely on notions of formal works, generally constructed of words. Yet, a video clip might show how to tie a knot to hold a chine to the ribs of a kayak; indeed, a kayak might also present that information, along with much more on hydrodynamic principles and cultural assumptions. The locations of billboards may tell us as much or more than the words on the billboards. A series of GPS coordinates may tell us how to get from here to there.

Small portions of what we have traditionally called documents may tell us things not evident in the title or subject heading. Useful information from sources other than books or journals—the number of lanterns hanging in a church bell tower, or a stream of ones and zeros sent from the surface of one of the moons of Saturn. While we will still use the word "document," we would like to set it within the context of the word "message." Here we are using Shannon's theory of communication and using message to mean structured data. Information is a term relating structure; meaning is complementary to information, in the sense that (in human systems) the information arrives at a recipient, but decoding determines the impact. Shannon's notion of communication provides a robust means of describing and utilizing structure at the level of the bit (the individual binary digit) up to the whole message and even sets of messages.

We take the concept of document to be wide reaching and complex. We agree with Drucker's assertion: "The attempt to define a part of a document raises immediate questions about the 'whole' we assume." We suggest that using Shannon as a framework for studying what Buckland terms the "anatomy, physiology, and ecology of documents" (*A Document (Re)turn*, p. 332) enables us to make progress in studying and providing constructing means of access to "fields of shifting relations momentarily stabilized in an artifact that exists in a continuum of temporal and spatial and quantum dimensions, only constituted through the framing acts of intervention" (*A Document (Re)turn*, p. 51). It is the idea that the framing acts of intervention are so important to meaning that causes us to argue we must be able to represent questions and those who pose them with vigor and cleverness equal to that we cast upon documents.

When Cutter suggested representing a document at the level of the whole document, he may have assumed someone looked at the structure of the message, but he hinted at neither any form of algorithmic analysis of the parts of the document, nor at any opportunity for patron penetration to some smaller part of the document. That is, Cutter assumed that the structural elements of a message were subsumed in or entirely represented by the whole. No paragraph and no illustration that could not be guessed to be part of the whole was accessible. For some works, this may actually be the case; it is not, however, entirely the case.

With all these things said, we now set about thinking of what happens when systems fail to bring together a patron and a document that would have helped the patron. We begin with word-based documents since they are still the most familiar form, and since most retrieval practice is based on words.

EXERCISES IN SUBJECT REPRESENTATION

Exploring the sense of subject and the difficulties one may encounter by assuming a single **the** subject will be aided by engaging in two exercises. Each will put us into a role on one side of the actual representation. The first exercise has us confront the use of representations already generated by somebody else. The second has us generate representations with others in mind. In order to facilitate the conduct and analysis of the exercises, the procedures for both tasks are presented together. The analyses for both follow. It is strongly suggested that the exercises be conducted before reading the discussions.

Exercise One

Listed below are several questions for which there ought to be resources in a modest academic library or even a large public library. In a classroom setting it might be desirable to divide the questions—perhaps three to a person. A search period of one hour should be allocated. Obviously, if a patron desperately needed material, a search might be protracted beyond twenty minutes per question. Yet one hour for three questions is not an unreasonable approximation of the time that a patron or an intermediary would allocate to a first search.

A search form template is given after the questions, as Figure 4.1. This will facilitate discussion of strategies, results, and consequences. Making notes of false leads, seemingly good hits, which turn out to be marginal in value, and serendipitous findings is a valuable activity here. Keep in mind that Cutter suggests that an access system ought to enable a patron to know what materials a collection has on a certain subject.

Before you set off to do searching, you should note that these questions are asked in the manner that some real patrons might present them to a reference librarian or other search intermediary. They are all members of the class we called in the previous chapter "well articulated." The patrons are reasonably sure of what they want and there is not a great deal of ambiguity inherent in the majority of the questions. It is, however, possible that the questions are not "properly" stated. A question implies a lack of knowledge of some sort. Therefore, it is possible that the state of ignorance constrains the construction of the question.

Of course, some of these questions could become passé or responses to some of them may become common knowledge. It should be of no particular difficulty to generate more questions of a similar sort. Indeed, it would be a good secondary exercise to generate a set of similar questions and discuss the characteristics of the questions.

SEARCH FORM

Searcher name: **Date:**

Question:

Search strategies:

Terms:
initial:

revised:

Candidate works:

Works found (with evaluations):

Comments

Figure 4.1. Sample Search Form.

Search Requests

- My father-in-law was a world-class gymnast. He has a substantial lay interest in artificial intelligence. He is now wondering about robotics and gymnastics, particularly tumbling. What do you have available on tumbling robots?
- What information is available on the relationship between photography of the American West and the engravings by Remington on the West?
- Why do translations of Homer's works contain the phrase "wine dark sea"? Is this an error in translation? Does it have something to do with ancient Greek perceptions?
- What role did librarians play at CNN during the Gulf War?
- Where can I get detailed pictures of the inside of a space shuttle?

- I am interested in pilot training and I understand that there's a book about using trampolines to do some of the physical training of pilots. Where is that?
- Is there a video or part of a video portraying medieval troubadours?
- Are there any personal accounts of vacationing on any of the islands off the New England coast, particularly any associated with New Hampshire?
- I would be interested in contemporary accounts or project reports on machine systems for browsing developed in the 1950s or 1960s.
- I have a collection of antique glass lantern slides that I would like to put into a computer. Are there any magazine articles or books that could give me some hints about the techniques of actually getting them into the machine and, maybe, how to think about organizing them?
- What is available on radio as an art form?
- I've heard there is a good book on animal tracking written by a former hunter who is now a vegetarian. Can you help me get hold of that book?
- There is a lot of talk about paradigm shifts these days. Has anybody come up with an algorithm for determining when a paradigm shift took place or predicting when one will take place?
- Are there any articles on the difficulties of achieving sense of touch on the skin (other than fingers) in virtual reality?
- Where might I find accounts of prison life by first time, nonviolent offenders?
- With all the talk about space shuttles and space stations, I was thinking about all the pictures they must take. Are there any articles on automated process for indexing all these pictures?
- Every once in a while in the library school I hear the name Hipacia. Is this a place, an acronym, a company, or a person? Are there any books or videos about whatever it is?
- I need some examples of Carolingian manuscript.
- Are there any newspaper columns or anything like essays that were written by the woman who wrote, *Little House on the Prairie*?
- How did the Romans send messages and military dispatches around their Empire? Did they use anything like mirrors or fire or carrier pigeons?
- Do you know of any videos or parts of videos that demonstrate the method of casting type for printing?
- Since most physicians, until recently, were men, is there any misogyny in medical illustration, especially that before 1980?
- Is cold fusion still the subject of research anywhere?
- Where can I find some reviews of Blake's *Representation and Language for Information Management?*

- It would seem to me that with all this interest in artificial intelligence, somebody in philosophy or some area like that, must have given consideration to the potential for revitalizing epistemology. Can you be of any assistance to me?
- The movie *Desk Set* seems to have to do with the information profession. Is it possible that there is some information about the relationship this film has with actual librarians, database management workers, and other information professionals?
- Are there any speculations on what might have happened in the world if steam power had become prominent in transportation, communication, and computing?
- Where should I begin looking for material on representation as it relates to vision?
- What is a good text for learning about evolutionary epistemology?

Exercise Two

Simply find an article of modest length, say four to ten pages. Each person involved in the exercise should then index the article. To the question "What do you mean by indexing?" the answer should be "Indicate ideas in the article which you could imagine someone would be happy to find." There are no constraints on number of terms or form of presentation. The exercise should take only half an hour.

The article used as a sample here is "The Vindolanda Tablets" by Anthony Birley from ***Minerva***. Vindolanda is the site of a Roman fort with a

> . . . remarkable state of preservation of the finds, especially a collection of legible writing tablets which have provided a unique insight into the daily lives of soldiers in this Roman fort close to Hadrian's wall.

The article details the history of the fort, the excavation of the site in recent years, and the techniques of observation and preservation. Photographs present a collection of shoes, a woman's hairpiece, numerous writing styli, and actual written messages. Mention is made of birthday invitations and a contractor's invoice from the site. Quotations are given from letters dealing with daily life at the fort, including one with a curious familiarity:

> I have sent you . . . pairs of socks from Sattua, two pairs of sandals and two pairs of underpants . . . Best wishes to Tetricus and your messmates, with whom I hope you are living in the greatest happiness.

After indexing is complete it is most instructive to display all the terms devised by everyone engaged in the exercise.

DISCUSSION

Again, the **subject** of a document is not some creature that inhabits the work. Rather, the subject is a relationship that holds between each individual and the squiggles that comprise the document (Maron, 1982a). If the subject were a single self-evident entity, then subject representation would be only a slight challenge. We would need only to list the synonyms that reflected differences in terminology. In reality, most documents have a good many squiggles. The circumstances of the patron and the nature of the squiggles combine to generate a unique, user-dependent meaning for each engagement with each document.

Of course, the meanings that are generated will generally (but by no means always) likely be within bounds that are, to some degree, predictable. One would not expect to learn how to grow vegetables in Kansas from a book on evolutionary epistemology, nor how to make a mid-life job transition from a book on tiger sharks. Yet, there remains a large range of possibilities.

It is only an incidental consequence of packaging that the documents in a collection of any sort are individual entities of a particular size. So far as a patron is concerned all the data in a library or electronic database is one large document. Just where the information for a particular requirement resides is of little consequence. That we generally point to (index) or summarize (abstract) information at the level of the document is a matter of system convenience, not a reflection of minimum useful size of an information package.

Discussion of Exercise One

The difficulty of finding substantial and useful subjects embedded within larger documents is one of the primary points intended to be made by the first exercise. In a large collection of documents with a paper-based card catalog, the difficulties of filing and maintaining even a small number of cards for each book could be enormous. One reasonable solution has been to represent the document at the level of the whole document. That is, do not worry about the details; just represent the most general topic.

However, as should be evident from exercise one, there is a considerable wealth of material that may be hidden from users by not providing for topics at a greater level of detail. Several of the questions in the exercise were designed to make this point.

- Tumbling robots is the subject of chapters in an annual review of artificial intelligence from MIT. There is nothing in the title or the Library of Congress Subject Headings for the book that suggest tumbling or robots. In fact, there is no title of a chapter that mentions tumbling. The term "gymnastics" is the closest to tumbling. So, in order to find the chapters, one must generalize from tumbling to gymnastics; one must generalize from robot to artificial intelligence; then look for works on artificial intelligence that would be broad enough in coverage to include robots. Even then, one would have to go through the several works on artificial intelligence to find the specific topic of gymnastics. Alternatively, one could think of institutions where there is considerable activity in artificial intelligence and robotics and look for publications from those institutions, and then go sifting for gymnastic robots.

- There is a small section in Zajonc's ***Catching the Light*** that deals with Homer's use of "the wine dark sea." However, there is nothing in the subtitle, table of contents, or subject headings that points to Homer. To find this material by a subject-heading search one would have to generalize to the idea that color is an attribute of light and that philosophical or physiological considerations of light might be a subject under which to search. Then one would still have to go through the index of each work (at least) to check for Homer.
- The librarians at CNN are the subject of a small portion of General Perry Smith's book about CNN and the Gulf War. Again, there is nothing in the subtitle, subject headings, or table of contents to indicate that this material is to be found within.
- There is a Navy pilot training manual from the World War II era that has an extensive section on the use of trampolines for training pilots. Once again, there is nothing explicit in the standard forms of representation for access that would indicate that trampolines are discussed within. If one knew that Keeney, one of the authors, was an expert on trampolining, one might look for works with his name. This would be too much to expect of most searchers.
- James Burke's ***The Day the Universe Changed*** series contains a segment on the changes wrought by the printing press. Within that consideration there is a dramatization of troubadours as information transfer agents of their time. There is no evidence of this in the title. One could only guess that the time period likely to be covered by a consideration of printing would also include troubadours.
- ***Tracking and the Art of Seeing***, cited earlier in our exploration, is written by a former hunter turned vegetarian and wildlife photographer. (Rezendes, 1992). The only aspect of the document that mentions being vegetarian is the introductory material of the book.
- Personal accounts of prison life by first-time offenders can be found, among other sources, in a book about protesters during the Vietnam conflict era. Once again, one would have to generalize quite a bit to find this work. It is possible to find works on prison life through Library of Congress Subject Headings. However, this book is not entirely, or even largely, about prison life, so it does not have a subject heading reflecting prison life.

- Artificial intelligence and the revivification of epistemology is the topic of Gardner's ***The Mind's New Science*** (Gardner, 1995). Here, epistemology is not explicit in the representations, though one might expect that anyone who would ask such a question could connect the term "philosophy," which does occur, with epistemology.

Two of the questions in the list were designed to elicit consideration of the nature of a question, even when the information requirement can be articulated reasonably well. The question about Hipacia will not go very far in most systems because of the spelling. The patron has heard the word, but can only guess at the spelling. Just what sort of entity a hipacia might be is unclear, so the appropriate search paths are unclear. The more generally accepted spelling—Hypatia—would make things simpler. There are speculative novels about this woman, as well as some historical fragments. Perhaps the best retelling of her story is found embedded in a few lines of the Sagan work, ***Cosmos***. Here the name appears in the index, though it is not a subject heading for ***Cosmos***.

Similarly, the question regarding the book by Blake entitled ***Representation and Language for Information Management*** will cause problems for most systems. The patron has gotten the author's name confused and has muddled the title. If this were not the case, the search would be trivial. If the patron searches by author name or by title, then there will be no retrieval. If a reference librarian or a "what to do when there are zero hits" screen on an online catalog suggests trying alternate spellings for the author name, Blake could become Blair—perhaps. In an electronic environment there might be a suggestion to try a title word search, in which case "representation" and "language" would point to ***Language and Representation in Information Retrieval*** by Blair. Presumably, the patron would assume that this must have been the sought item. Yet that assumption is based on some sophisticated knowledge about human abilities to confuse spellings and word orders. It is also based on the patron knowing of the possibility that the original question might be stated incorrectly.

The question about steam power raises an issue about system representation of the collection as a whole. One of the most eloquent speculations on this topic is in the form of a novel—***Difference Engine***. Fiction works present a great deal of material that could serve to respond to information requirements; yet, access has generally been very limited. Usually author, title, and genre constitute the totality of access points.

Discussion of Exercise Two

A general pattern of response has arisen from several iterations of this exercise in the past. A major portion of those indexing compile lists of five to ten terms, while another group compiles a list of considerably greater length. Many who have worked in libraries or used them frequently will attempt to construct terms in the manner of Library of Congress subject headings. Several will ask "Can we use xxxx?" or "Is it all right to mention xxxx?"

Most notable about the exercise is the number of terms derived. Even with articles of four or five pages, there are generally fifty to one hundred terms in all. Remember that the instructions simply said to list elements that some user might be happy to find. Many elements of only minor consequence within the framework of the article might still be of considerable interest to someone. For example, if I were writing an article on women's hair fashions, I might be quite interested to know that the Vindolanda article mentions a hairpiece from nearly two thousand years ago and that a photograph is available. Perhaps, if I were preparing an advertisement for a word processor, I would be interested in Roman fountain pens that still worked. If I were writing a dissertation on handwriting and representation, I would surely want to know of early examples of daily communications.

The list of terms presented in Table 4.1 is typical of the results from conducting this exercise with the Vindolanda tablets article.

As we look at these typical results of a group exercise in indexing a single article we can see some questions implicit in the variety of terms. Within these questions, as listed below, the term "element" has been substituted for "word,"

Table 4.1. Descriptors for "Vindolanda" Article

Archaeology	Archaeology, Roman	Artifacts
Writing tablets	Britain, Roman	Soldiers
Fort	Hadrian's wall	Boots
Daily life of soldiers	Shoes and slippers	Hairpiece
Styli	Wattle and daub walls	Excavation
Preservation	Vindolanda	Coins
stable flies	Natural defenses	**All place names**
All personal names	Stone fort	Fort-village
Camp followers	Traders	Anaerobic conditions
Chamfron	Leather objects	Army tent
Handwriting	Handwriting, Roman	Vulgar Latin
Fort family life	"Little Brits"	Birthday party invitation
Roman army society	Roman army economy	Letter to soldier
Infrared photography	Garrison	Stylus tablet
Filing	Fountain pens	Conservation techniques
Site laboratory	Stylus tablet	Socks
Underpants	Sandals	**Photographs**
Army, ancient Rome	Papyrology	Roman soldiers
Conservation, leather	Writing utensils, history	Conservation, leather
Roman handwriting	Iron nib pens	Latin
Rome—1st century AD	Britain—1st century AD	Latin—vulgar
Pens, iron nib	Metal objects	Spear heads
Needles	Rings	Environments, ancient
Latin, use of	Roman clothing	Cohort of Tungrians
Horse chamfrons	Buildings, history, Roman	British heritage
Celts—history	Archaeology, sites, Britain	Rome—0–299 AD—forts
Historic ruins	Timber forts	Artifacts—restoring

so as not to exclude image and sound documents. What is made evident from the exercise with a word-based document might be applicable to documents in other media? The insights can be summarized as:

- Just how many elements should be extracted?
- Which elements should be extracted?
- Should the elements be extracted in their "natural form" or translated?
- Should the elements be in a natural order or a constructed order?
- Should generalization of individual concepts take place?
- What are the rules to guide extraction?

If the indexing is to be a representation, then we can say that not all the elements in the document will be used. Yet, beyond this limiting case, we must ask whether or not there is some ideal raw number or ideal percentage of the total number of elements in the document. Then we ought to refine this question by asking "ideal for whom"? If we speak of an ideal system for those who must manage it, perhaps one or two elements would be the most economical use of resources. However, if we mean ideal for the patron, we may have to assume a much larger number, at least in some circumstances (Maron, 1982b).

Closely associated with the number of elements to be extracted is the issue of just which elements. In word-based documents we might well say that words such as all forms of the verb "to be," most prepositions and articles, and pronouns should be considered to hold too little meaning potential to be included in the representation. What additional constraints could we add? Assuming we want to be liberal in providing access, we have to consider the balance between "enough" and "too much." That is, where is the balance between high utility and inordinate use of time. Is the balance point the same for all users? Is it a sliding point dependent on user requirements? Is there some golden mean available? (Meadow, 1988; van Rijsbergen, 1979) We must further consider just what the elements will look like when presented to the patron. Are they going to be salient elements from the document simply extracted and put into some useable order? This would seem to ensure the closest relationship between the document and the representation.

However, if the words are professional jargon or from an author from a different time or place, they may not be sufficiently familiar to be useful. The patron might not be able to guess that these would be the sought terms and might not understand them properly even if they are found. It is also possible that the author has used several disparate terms for subordinate concepts, but has not represented the more general concept well. One alternative to direct extraction is the use of a sanctioned list of terms through which all extracted terms are translated. This brings together synonyms and other disparate codings for similar concepts. Of course, one has to hope that differing concepts or differing levels of concepts are grouped together in an understandable and useful manner. The sanctioned list (such as the Library of Congress Subject Headings or the *ERIC Thesaurus*) must provide access to the accepted term from all the possible terms it translates.

An interesting variation of the indexing exercise involves the direct use of a thesaurus. Following the same beginning steps, restrict the terms that can be used to those found in a sanctioned list. Comparing the terms that are derived by all the various participants can be most instructive. Each person should explain the translation process from extracted term to the sanctioned term. If we are dealing with word-based documents, should we use natural word order or inverted word order for the representative terms? Should we argue that people typically want to find the general class first and then move down a tree of hierarchy to the specific concept they seek? Just which is the more general concept: Archaeology or Roman or Great Britain? If we seek anything "archaeological," then "Roman" and "Great Britain" are secondary partitions of the greater concept. If we seek any thing about Rome (poetry, politics, statuary, etc.), then "archaeology" is a subset. If we seek historical material or travel guide material about Great Britain, then "Roman" and "archaeology" are the detailing partitions. Should we provide for multiple configurations of the same set of concept tags?

If we choose to extract terms directly from the document, what then of higher and lower degrees of specificity? That is, do we depend on the elements of the document to present their own hierarchy of relationships of concepts in the document? Need we construct generalized or more specific terms if these are not provided? If we move beyond word-based-documents, can we even assume that individual elements will even be adequate to express levels of generality without some additional context? Finally, are there any real rules beyond, "Read the work and you'll know what the subject is"? Even if we say that an indexer is to use a certain number of terms and to think about what terms would be likely to be used by patrons who would be happy to find the work being indexed, can that be considered enough? Are there other rules that would ensure that any indexer looking at the same work would generate the same representation? If there were such rules, wouldn't machines be nicely suited to indexing? Are rules to ensure uniformity really what we would want if different users have different needs and decoding abilities?

Subject Representation

Our two exercises raise the possibility that there is frequently a wide gulf between the tools that are generally provided for access and the requirements of the people using those tools (Blair, 1986). The exercises present two primary questions:

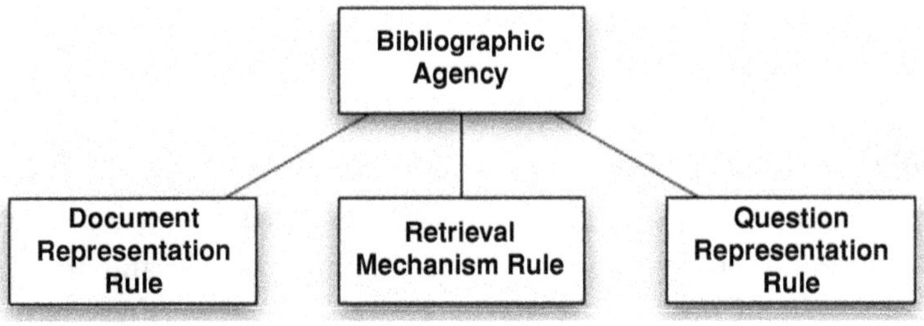

Figure 4.2. Typical Model of Representation by Agency.

- Why was it hard to find so many of the documents needed in the first exercise, when they were available?
- Which parts of a document does one choose and just how ought one to present them?

One significant part of a response is presented in Figure 4.2. It is not the necessary case, but it can be argued that it is a frequent case, and that the patron is largely or completely left out of the representation process. Some external party—here termed the "bibliographic agency"—establishes the rules by which documents are represented, the rules by which questions are represented, and the rules by which the two representations are compared. The individual patron does not have an opportunity to input what coding/decoding abilities he/she has. The patron does not get to specify the depth of penetration into the collection or into the individual documents. The patron is seldom told just what are the rules of highlighting in the system of representation being used.

Of course, most indexing and abstracting does not take place in total ignorance of or disregard for the likely patrons of the system. For example, if the language of the user community is English, then most of the documents will be in English and most of the representation will be in English. Academic libraries and specialized databases and special libraries will probably be staffed by people familiar with the content area and the specialized clientele. This may lead to closer attention to appropriate terminology and deeper levels of detail.

Yet, there remains the troubling issue that there is little in the way of formalization of inclusion of the patron into the representation process. If the system does not take account of the user's decoding abilities, then it cannot be said to use a code known to the user. Thus, it is only by chance that a proper sign, a true and useable representation, is generated.

The exercises helped us to elicit some of the difficulties posed by searching with the typical tools of the formal bibliographical apparatus. We will now consider formal models of those difficulties, giving special attention to the issues of representation. The discussions will use indexing as the focal activity, but, on the whole, they relate to most of the forms of representing questions and documents, such as indexing, abstracting, classification, reference interview, and database design.

The general model, presented as Figure 4.2, hints at the reasons for some major difficulties. There is nothing in the model that prohibits the bibliographical agency from providing ad hoc representation based on rules suited to the individual patron. However, such a system requires considerable resources and cleverness.

Representations that are going to stand as is for some time can only present the diachronic attributes of the document, those that do not change. Author, title, publisher, date, spine height, and length are attributes that can be extracted without any consideration of the patrons at all. Subject headings too can be constructed without consideration of the patrons. Simply tell the indexer to come up with a few terms that she/he feels describe the topic of the book. If these work for a patron, fine; if not, it cannot be helped. Of course, many people providing subject representations do try to take into account the general nature of the patrons using the system. Yet there is nothing formal in the rules requiring such consideration. Even if there were such rules, we might ask just how accommodation of the patron would actually work.

Let us step back for a moment and ponder indexing. There are basically three modes of indexing available:

- human examines document and extracts or applies terms;
- machine examines document and extracts or applies terms;
- machine makes preliminary pass; human refines terms.

Obviously, the machine is only following rules imbedded by humans, but the crucial point is that the human programmers had to make precise rules. The rules are followed for each and every document. One could expect that the same program running on several different machines would produce the same representation of the same document. Research shows that one cannot make the same assumption about human indexers. Indeed, one cannot even assume that the same indexer will represent the same document in the same way at two different times (Cooper, 1969).

This is because humans generally act on "gut feeling" or some assumption that if they read the work, they will "know what the topic is." There is even some evidence to suggest that humans attempting to follow an algorithm will not index in precisely the same way because of the vagueness and vagaries of language. We will discuss machine-assisted representation in Chapters Seven, Eight, and Nine. For now, we can say that a machine-based system of representation offers consistency in application of rules. Also, those rules, whether or not they are made evident to the user, are at least, available to the system managers. Of course, consistency in the application of the rules is only a positive attribute if the rules provide useful retrieval.

It has been suggested by Cooper that indexing consists of "great vagueness and much generality resting on a foundation of shifting quicksand." Those rules for representation that are typically used by human indexers speak only to diachronic attributes and only to structural aspects of the process of subject representation. For example:

- Use direct content—that is, index only what is "actually" in the document.
- Cutter's rule—index at the whole document's level of specificity.
- System constraint on depth of indexing—for example, use only three terms.

There is nothing inherently "wrong" with saying, "index only what is actually in the document." Indeed, a great deal can be gleaned from counting words. However, as our discussions of representation point out, "what is actually **in** the document," can be said to be a function **of** the document and the user.

Cutter's rule was an attempt at a rigorous process of representation. However, it took us only a few examples to show that it is not sufficiently rigorous to accommodate a heterogeneous user group (Wilson, 1983) In a sense, Cutter's rule can stand for the whole class of problems that come to pass when there is a discrepancy between the needs of the patron and the system's method of representation.

Subject indeterminacy is the phrase proposed by Blair to stand for this class of difficulties. We will examine Blair's model by first suggesting that within the general model presented in Figure 4.2 several implied assumptions must hold true for the system to provide satisfactory results. Subsequent figures will present various scenarios in which not all of the assumptions are valid.

The scenario modeled in Figure 4.3 is the ideal situation, in which all assumptions hold true. Here we are considering only one document. An individual patron has an information need that would, in fact, be satisfied by the document in question. When the person constructing the representation (e.g., indexer) examines the document, she/he must select the concept that will satisfy the user. This may be at a very general level or at a very specific level. The user may have no idea whether there is a whole document devoted to the information need, or just a paragraph or two. Whatever the circumstances, the concept that will help the patron must be the one selected by the indexer.

The user must be able to articulate the concept. The user must be able to put that articulated concept into system terms. That is, if the system is based on the Library of Congress Subject Headings, then the concept must be presented as a Library of Congress Subject Heading. This assumes that the patron has some level of facility with the system.

The person making the representation is, presumably, skilled in the use of the particular system for representation. However, it is quite possible that there

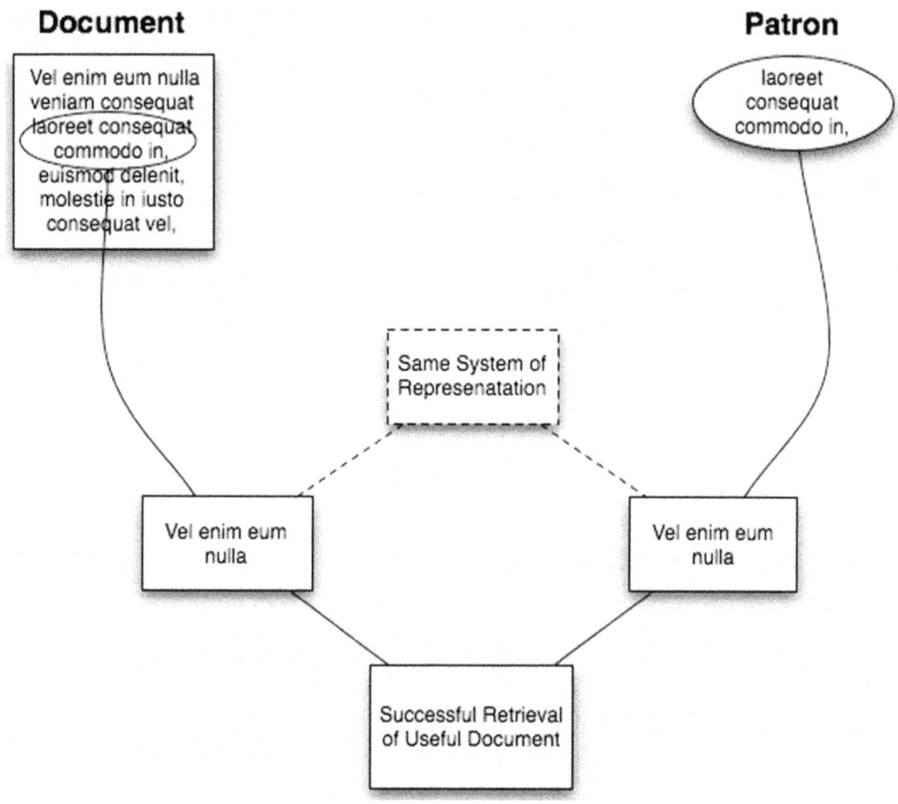

Figure 4.3. Ideal Situation for Successful Retrieval.

is more than one way to code a particular concept, even within a particular system. In many cases there will be links (such as "see" and "see also" references), but there is no guarantee that such links will exist. A person looking for information on the history of military installations in Great Britain might not immediately think of "Roman army—forts," for example. Of the candidate possibilities for the description of the target concept, both the patron and the indexer must select at least one in common.

It is quite possible to imagine that the indexer and the patron are both skilled in the same system of representation, but the indexer, constrained to select only some small number of concepts, selects one that will not satisfy the patron, as in Figure 4.4. The concept is in the document, but it is not highlighted. The patron depending on the representations in the system will bypass this document.

It may well be that another document will be found within the system. That document might have a reference to the bypassed document. In this case, the document can be found. However, in terms of the current search, the representation fails. Without user input at the time of representation, the system does not know what elements ought to be highlighted.

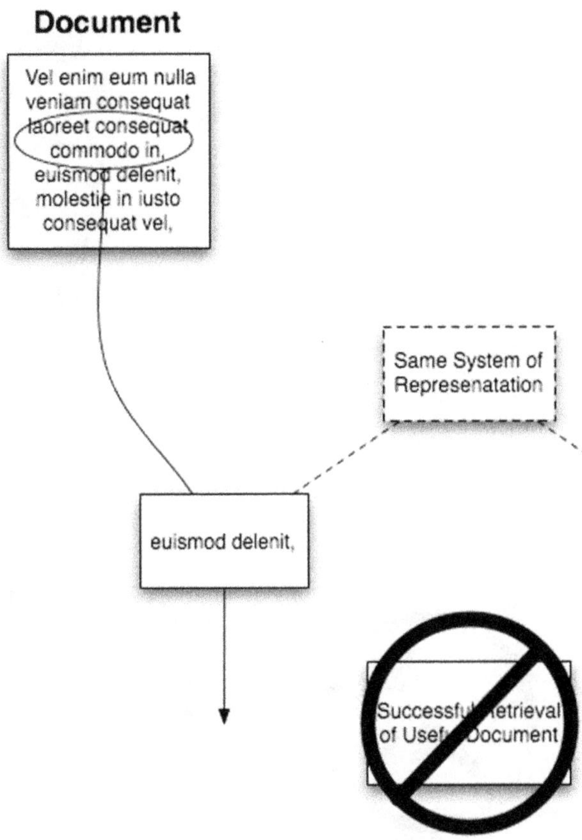

Figure 4.4. Failure Due to Difference in Concept Identification.

In Figure 4.5 we see another common scenario. Here the patron is not familiar with the system of representation being used by the system. It may be that the patron is familiar with some other system of representation. For example, a person accustomed to using a computer to search by key words in titles might have little idea of how to operate within a system using Library of Congress Subject Headings. In the former system the patron can just think of a word and see if there is a title containing that word. In LCSH the patron must guess at a complex string of words, which may have nothing to do with any word in the title. One can also imagine patrons accustomed to the way commercial audio retailers arrange Compact Discs, being unable to operate within a Dewey Decimal audio collection.

Even if the patron and the indexer identify the same concept, the representation will fail because the patron has not been made aware of the rules. Of course, if there is sufficient time and interest, the patron may receive some bibliographic instruction (or the equivalent in an electronic environment). It may also be that the patron would seek help from a system employee, essentially to translate from one terminological system to another. If the patron does

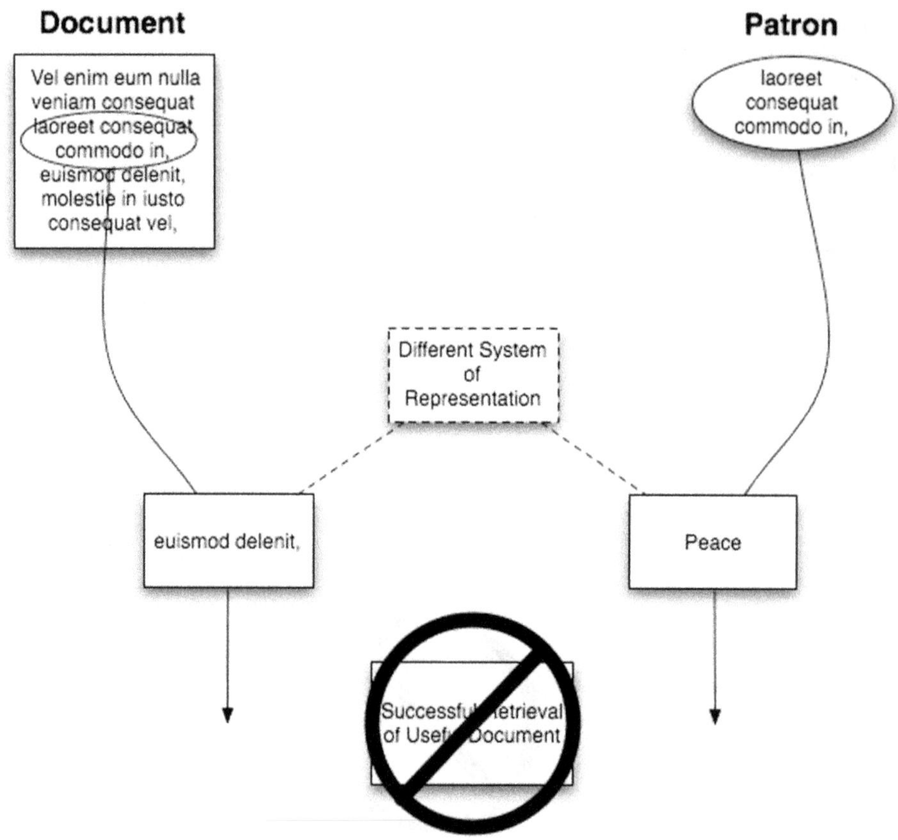

Figure 4.5. Failure Due to Differences in Representation Systems.

not know the coding system, there is, for that patron, no sign, no representation.

In the preceding scenarios there has been an assumption that the patron can give at least some vague idea of the information requirement to the system. However, what are we to make of the case of the artist or scholar attempting to generate new knowledge? The system cannot make even a guess at which concept in a document would be useful to some such a patron. This is because even the patron cannot give voice to the information requirement.

The generation of new knowledge requires, at some critical point, the finding of new connections, new twists, and new observations. If it is the "new" that is sought, then, by definition, it cannot have been identified yet. Therefore, it cannot be a subject heading. In such an instance, as in Figure 4.6, the very idea of the system providing representation is meaningless.

There may well be value to representing documents for other patrons, but the potential generator of new knowledge has no need of it. Later on in the process the formal bibliographic apparatus may come back into play to provide "more things like this." However, the nature of the search has changed then.

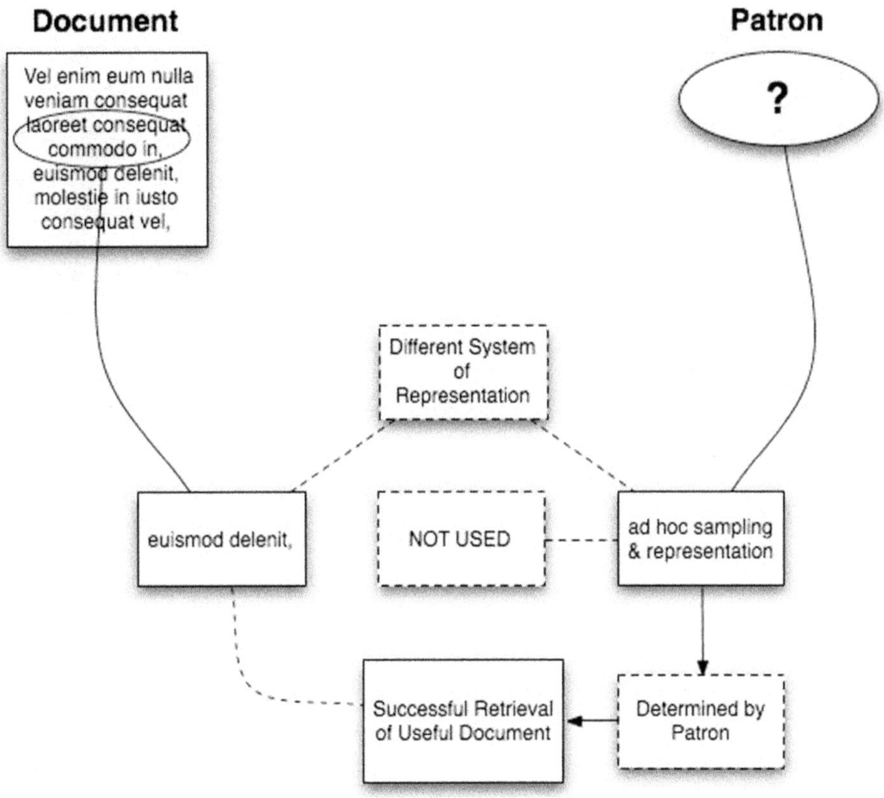

Figure 4.6. Successful Retrieval Despite Formal Representation System.

For decades academic librarians have puzzled over the fact that engineers, physical scientists, humanities scholars, and social scientists have made little use, if any, of the formal bibliographical apparatus. If we acknowledge that the apparatus is set up to answer topical queries and the scholars need functional information that they cannot articulate until it is seen, there is no mystery (O'Connor, 1993). If there is no way of stating which elements ought to be highlighted, then there is no way to design a representation system in advance of use.

Browsing is the activity or set of activities used by scholars to get around the difficulties of representing documents in advance of use by searchers with no clearly stated goal. We will consider browsing in greater depth in a subsequent chapter. For now we can say that browsing is a willful putting aside of the pointing and summarizing functions of indexing and abstracting. The wisdom of going through each and every document is recognized. Of course, such recognition does not generate more time for searching.

The browser takes a different approach to representation of the collection as a whole, as suggested in Figure 4.7. If there is no articulated question, then any and every document is just as likely to produce a useful response. The

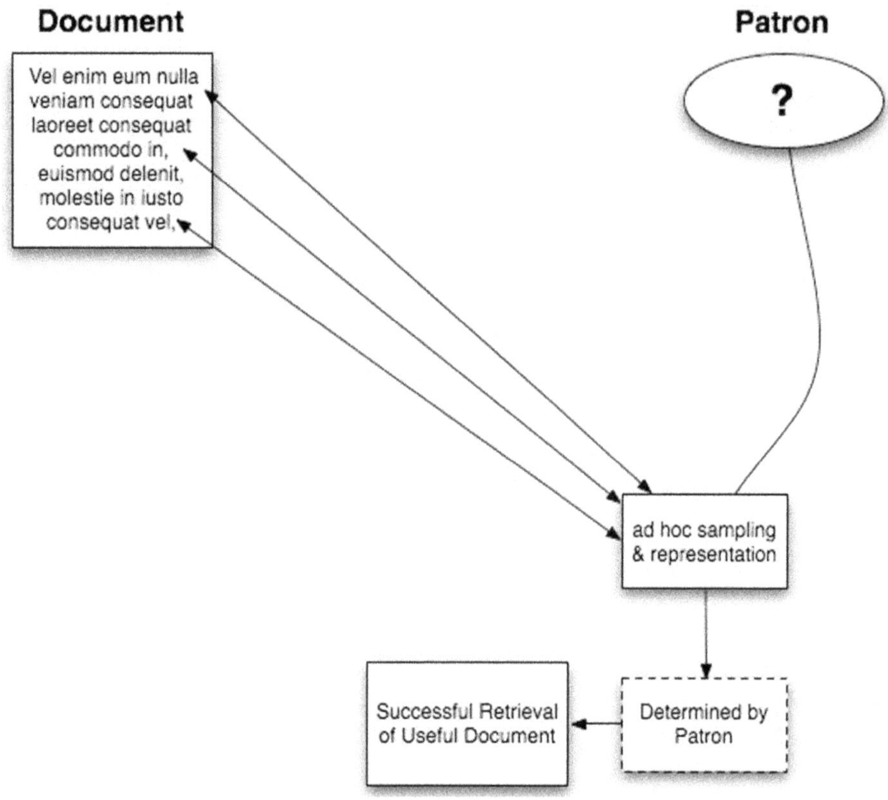

Figure 4.7. Successful Retrieval with No Regard to Formal System.

searcher might want to exclude documents that are already known, such as those normally associated with the searcher's discipline. Equal likelihood of satisfaction means that the browser can make random selection of documents. The rule for what to highlight is "anything," or "anything I have time and energy to put my hands on."

Once a document is found, the method of examination and subsequent moves both within the document and within the whole collection are determined by the browser. That is, once within some point in the collection, the representation changes from "anything" to "everything I know to any degree, in my terms of understanding."

DEPTH OF INDEXING

Closely related to the scenarios above is the concept of depth of indexing. Cutter suggested representing at the level of the whole document. There are, however, often useful elements at levels of greater specificity. There are two sorts of depth to be considered:

- the number of descriptors for any one document;
- the conceptual detail represented by the terms.

	useful	not useful	total
in patron's hands	A	B	A+B
not in patron's hands	C	D	C+D
total	A + C	B + D	A + B + C + D (Whole Collection)

$$PRECISION = \frac{A}{A+B} \qquad RECALL = \frac{A}{A+C}$$

Figure 4.8. Precision and Recall as Gems and Trash in or Not in Patron's Hands.

As an aspect of representation this should seem self-evident and worthy of rather little special attention. Essentially, we are talking about which elements to highlight and the ability of the descriptors to discriminate between concepts at the document level and within the document.

However, two other concepts related to depth have been made important measures of system performance. **Precision** and **recall** are numerical ways of stating the degree to which a search has succeeded. The concepts are useful, though in practice they are very difficult to achieve.

Precision is a measure of the gems to trash ratio. That is, of all the documents put into the patron's hands, how many are actually useful? Recall is a measure of just how many of the useful documents in the collection actually end up in the patron's hands. Both measures are usually expressed as a ratio or percentage. See Figure 4.8 for definitions.

Clearly, what we would like to see are high values for "A" (rightly put into patron's hands) and "D" (rightly left out of patron's hands). This implies that we would like to see low values for "B" (wrongly put into patron's hands) and "C" (wrongly left out of patron's hands), as demonstrated in Figure 4.9.

UUNU
NUUU

U = useful
N = not useful

$$\frac{6U}{6U+2N} = \frac{6}{8} = \frac{3}{4} = 75\% \text{ Precision}$$

or

NNUN
NUNN

U = useful
N = not useful

$$\frac{2U}{2U+6N} = \frac{2}{8} = \frac{1}{4} = 25\% \text{ Precision}$$

Figure 4.9. Precision as Ratio of Useful Documents to Total in Hand.

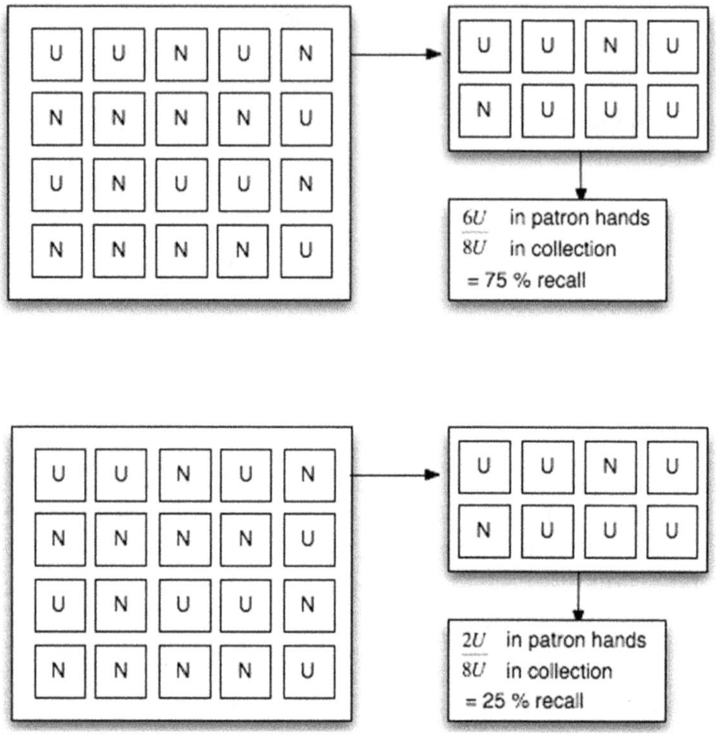

Figure 4.10. Recall as Ratio of Useful Works in Hand to Total Useful Works.

As the framework for some examples, let us assume that we have a collection of twenty documents, as in Figure 4.10, and that we have the means for knowing which documents satisfy the patron, as well as which of all the documents could have satisfied the patron.

If we put into the patron's hands eight documents and six of them are useful to the patron, then we have a figure of 75 percent for precision. If we put eight documents into the patron's hands and only two of them are useful, then we have a 25 percent precision figure.

If we know that of the twenty documents in the collection, eight are useful and six of those useful documents are put into the patron's hands, then we have a 75 percent recall. If we put into the hands of the patron only two of those eight documents, then we have only a 25 percent recall figure.

There is generally an inverse relationship between precision and recall. That is, if you cast a broad net to be sure you get everything you want (high recall), you are also likely to get a lot that is not useful (low precision). If, on the other hand, you aim to have very little useless material (high precision), you run the risk of missing out on useful material (low recall).

We must return to some of the difficulties with the concepts of precision and recall that diminish their utility as measurements of the representational capabilities of a system. To determine how many of the works in a patron's hands are useful is no great task. It may take some time for the patron to do sufficient analysis to make such a determination, but it is a relatively simple task. There are, of course, some circumstances under which the patron might not realize that a potentially useful work is so; or it might only be in retrospect after some time that the utility would be recognized. Yet, in general, the variables are knowable and the process simple—count what is in hand, count how many are useful, and calculate the ratio.

More troubling is the concept of recall, in terms of what is not known (or not easily knowable). How are we to know the total number of useful works in the collection? If we do not know the total of useful works, how can we calculate a ratio? If we know all the works that would be useful, why didn't we put them into the patron's hands?

If we leave the patron out of the loop and simply count subject headings in hand and compare those with subject heading numbers known for the collection, then we can deliver a number. However, we have to ask if we have measured anything useful. Maron and Blair have demonstrated the efficacy of a sophisticated statistical sampling and analysis technique for providing a well-educated guess about the total number of useful documents in a collection (Blair, 1986). However, the system resources and the time commitments required of the patron to do this would be prohibitive in most circumstances.

To distinguish only "useful" from "not useful" yields a binary system. This burdens the indexer with the task of being right on target for every user. In many instances a user will say: "This one was pretty good; this one was only good for the pictures; this one was a waste of time; this one was great." In other words, user satisfaction is rarely a binary entity.

If the indexer wants to satisfy every user who might be happy to find the document, even for just one photograph or three pages or two minutes of an hour-long video, she/he must construct a representation with many elements. However, this is likely to put a lot of trash into the hands of some patrons. The patron searching for material for a paper on Jeffersonian concepts of democracy in developing countries would not be happy to have a work in hand tagged with "democracy" because there is one paragraph about the role of postsecondary education in a democracy.

We return to considering depth of indexing with some questions:

- Is there an ideal set of indexing terms for each document?
- Is there an optimal depth of indexing?

Yes, but.... If we accept the notion that a patron's requirements and decoding abilities determine the level of specificity of elements highlighted and the mode of representation, then we must qualify our answers. Yes, but these are not single entities. Rather, the ideal is likely to be different for each different use of the system.

Let us look at the level of specificity that can be obtained by varying the breadth of distribution of the descriptive terms used in the collection. Using just a few terms to describe all the documents means large clumps put together under a few terms; using a larger number of descriptive terms means finer granularity of description. In our collection of twenty documents, if we had a total of one hundred terms applied to the collection, we could look at breadth in these ways:

- 100 terms in all applied/16 different terms used = breadth of 6.25
- 100 terms in all applied/27 different terms used = breadth of 3.7
- 100 terms in all applied/63 different terms used = breadth of 1.59.

If we have twenty documents and one hundred terms, we can assume that there is an average of five terms per document. If we have only sixteen terms from which to choose those five for each document, our choices are limited. As we increase the number of available terms to twenty-seven or sixty-three, we increase our choices for describing each document.

If we have twenty documents and one hundred terms, we can assume that there is an average of five terms per document. If we have only sixteen terms from which to choose those five for each document, our choices are limited. As we increase the number of available terms to twenty-seven or sixty-three, we increase our choices for describing each document. Once again, we are presented with a tradeoff. The more descriptive terms used, the more precisely we can make our first selection; but we may miss useful documents. Casting a wide net requires tossing out unwanted catches, while casting a narrow net misses some good catches.

In our samples above, we see that as our choices increase, the numerical representation of breadth decreases. We can think of this in terms of a given volume of liquid (say, one quart) in different containers. If the container has a large diameter (say, 6.25), the liquid will be shallow in the container. As the diameter decreases, the depth increases. Thus, a diameter of 3.7 yields a deeper body of liquid; and 1.59 yields a still deeper body. So, the lower the breadth number, the greater the breadth.

Intensional depth refers to the semantic detail available from the indexing vocabulary. We can define this as the total number of term assignments made in the collection divided by the total number of documents. In the example of differences in breadth, we said we had twenty documents and one hundred terms that yielded an average (intensional depth) of five. If we assume the same collection of twenty documents, we can see that the higher the resulting value, the greater the intensional depth:

- 100 terms assigned/20 documents = 5.
- 525 terms assigned/20 documents = 26.25.
- 917 terms assigned/20 documents = 45.85.

Table 4.2. Breadth and Specificity in Terms of Precision and Recall

Greater Breadth	High recall/Low precision
Less Breadth	Low recall/High precision
Greater Specificity	High precision/Low recall
Less Specificity	Low precision/High recall

Specificity is a term addressing two closely related concepts:

- Ability of the indexing language to describe documents precisely.
- Actual level of the documents which are represented.

There is a set of relationships that typically holds between precision and recall on the one hand, and breadth and specificity on the other. These relationships can be summarized as in Table 4.2.

These relationships present what might seem obvious: cast a wide net and get more of what you want along with more of what you don't want. The more broad terms we apply to each document, the more likely the patron is to get desirable materials (high recall), but at the cost of having more undesirable material through which to wade (low precision). The broad terms do not address the degree to which any particular document is "about" the term. Similarly, if we apply very specific terms to each document, we may well hide from the patron works that are closely related but described a little bit differently.

The bibliographic agency posited in the general model in Figure 4.2, generally sets the number of descriptive terms to be used. There is a countermodel that does not impose any particular level of description. Maron, Cooper, and Robertson posit a model that includes the patron in the representation (Maron, 1982). While the goal of putting into the hands of the patron all the documents that a patron would find useful and only those documents is not unique, the underlying assumption of the model represents a significant shift. Representation actively includes the user.

The basic model can be summarized as follows. For any given descriptive term and any single patron, we can ask "If the patron were to use this term to describe the information requirement, would she/he be happy to find this document?" If the answer is "yes," then apply the term as a descriptor; if it is "no," then do not. We can then extend the question to cover all patrons (or all likely patrons), either by asking the same question over and over with each patron in mind, or by keeping track of how many patrons are satisfied over time. The system, in effect, knows: "Of those who used this term in their search, 83 percent were happy with document A, 47 percent with document B, and 91 percent with document C."

The system could set a cutoff point, for example: "Any document rated over 90 percent will be shown to the patron." However, the system does not know how much material the user needs, or the purpose (if one is writing a critique of a field, the works not liked by others could be of great interest), or the time and interest level available. The solution is to simply make available the ranking of the collection. Thus, if a patron needs "just any good work or two on . . . ," she/he need only look to works in the top 5 or 10 percent. The patron writing a dissertation could check down to the 30 percent level or even less. The patron needing to write a brief report, but finding the items in the top 10 percent unavailable, could examine items in the 80 percent range.

There are numerous variations of the ranking model, but a key element in them is the concern for the user in the construction of (or, at least, control over) the representation. This enables a closer fit between the system and the user in terms of the elements selected for highlighting, as well as the coding system.

Earlier we asked the questions:

- Which elements should be extracted?
- How many elements should be extracted?
- What form should the descriptors have?

Our definition of representation suggests these answers:

- Extract whichever elements are useful to the patron.
- Extract however many elements are necessary for the patron.
- Employ whatever form is consistent with patron abilities and requirements.

We have begun to explore the concepts underlying the implementation of such answers. Depth and breadth of representation, together with precision and recall, are attempts to model the attributes of the collection that would enable a system to be constructed. The premises are flawed, however, if they do not include both the patron and the documents.

Our subsequent explorations will weave together additional theoretical constructs and case studies to illuminate the user/collection relationship. While we will examine means of refining system abilities to describe patron knowledge states and knowledge states represented by documents, we will not be approaching a single, "one size fits all," system. Rather, we will be suggesting the nature and the components of a vital organization capable of responding appropriately to varying conditions and requirements.

A NOTE ON STRUCTURE

While the depth of representation of any document or of the document collection may present additional options for access, depth says very little about the structure of a document. Knowing that the following nouns appear in a particular text gives little in the way of clues to the nature of the message: girls, manner, dress, dowels, rags, cow, guns, home, time, church, Sunday, hands, marbles, things, boys, cat, nite, moon, lessons [from "On Girls" in *English as She is Taught* in *The Complete Essays of Mark Twain*, edited and with an Introduction by Charles Neider, p. 47]. Even a list of co-occurring words does not tell us much about the nature of the message; we might not know whether we were being presented with a representation of a sonnet or a transcript of testimony in a trial (courting document or court document). In some ways the situation is similar to having place names, highway numbers, and elevations but no connecting material, the elements of a map, but no map.

CHAPTER FIVE

ABOUTNESS AND USER-GENERATED DESCRIPTORS

INTRODUCTORY COMMENT

IN OUR EARLIER book on indexing and abstracting aboutness and user-generated descriptors were discussed much later in the book. The chapter was written before the existence of social networking Web sites with tagging of photographs, such as flickr.com or del.icio.us. We have moved this material to this point so that it accompanies the other material on the disconnect between assigned verbal descriptors and the ways in which individuals seeking documents may think. Because words and images function differently, consideration of how images might be described by words serves as a useful probe. That is, photographic entities have very different attributes from those of verbal entities, so considering them takes us outside the centuries-old models on which notions of documents and their use have been based.

Here we present two initial explorations into the use of verbal descriptors for aboutness of image documents. In both instances we are assuming that verbal descriptors stand for the behavior of viewers of the images. Thus, instead of using a priori descriptions of documents that may inform behaviors by viewers, we have viewer behaviors describing image documents, and perhaps influencing behaviors by subsequent viewers.

DIFFICULTIES OF THE LITERARY METAPHOR

The fundamental differences between words and photographs urge closer scrutiny of the native elements of photographs and their possible roles in representation of photographs. At the same time, we must remember that people do use words to express at least some of their requirements for photographs, videos, music, and other messages not based on words (Maron, 1977). We might say people's use of words to describe nonword documents results from a distinction between subject and aboutness. This distinction is similar to Wilson's distinction between topic and function.

While noting the inappropriateness of words as descriptors of images because of the very different means by which the two sign systems operate, we can suggest that surely, no matter how a viewer interprets a photograph or a

- Old man
- 19th century clothes
- Walt Whitman
- Santa on vacation
- Caricature
- Nice beard
- Casual strength
- Serene

Figure 5.1a. Descriptors of Whitman Image Provided by Different Viewers.

- Exam week
- Laacoon group
- Great body
- Some Greek tragedy
- Frustration
- Tangled up
- Torsion
- Stressed out
- Agony

Figure 5.1b. Descriptors of Laocoon Group Provided by Different Viewers.

video document, she/he could say something about it. That something would likely be a reflection of the viewer's reaction. Thus, no matter what relationship that reaction bore to the author's intent or an indexer's conceptual tag, it could be said that that something represented the document's aboutness of that user.

The images in Figure 5.1 (a and b), together with their accompanying descriptions, point to a major problem in the representation of any sort of documents. Different users may well have very different notions of what the document is about (for example, Maron, 1977; Robertson, 1979; Wilson, 1968). This highlights the access problem for users who must depend on the judgment and coding of someone else.

Photographs Are Not Words

Photographic images are not words. Photographs are usually very specific representations made at particular moments, of particular objects. Words are general representations. Pictures are made more general by adding more pictures in a sequence or collage. Words are made more specific by grouping them with other words. Figure 5.2 illustrates this point.

We can say that photographs help to make document representation issues more obvious because of the very different ways in which pictures and words work. Word texts can be described with elements directly from the document

CAT

My young, rust color cat, Willie, peeking up over a toy horse in our yard in El Sobrante, Califomia in October 1986.

Figure 5.2. Word Representation and Photograph Representation of Pet.

and similar to daily speech acts. Thus the possibility for confusion of elements with topic and topic for aboutness runs high.

Likewise, word texts have clearly segmented elements set within rule-bound structures. We can, for example, say that a particular word is a noun and because of its place and the places of other words that noun is the subject of a sentence. At one level, then, we can determine topical characteristics of a text with some ease and surety. There are, of course, many caveats to such an approach. The meaning of a text for any particular user is heavily dependent on that user.

Image texts are not constructed in a manner that allows easy demarcation of elements or rules for extraction of a subject. Photographs are, in a sense, made by sampling a very broadband stream of data. They are analog representations with very fine gradations from light to dark. They present no easily discerned noun/verb analogs. There is no rule for translation of a whole image or any of its parts into words (Novitz, 1977). The old phrase "one picture is worth a thousand words" speaks well to the high bandwidth of communication that is possible with image texts. However, there is no saying just how many words or just which words are required to describe any individual picture. The word document has easily discernable units and clusters of units of meaning. Photographs do not.

Humans have brains that are uniquely suited to visual information. Nearly 50 percent of the neocortex, the "higher," primate portion of the brain, is devoted to visual processing (Fischler & Firschein, 1987). We seem to be very good at pattern recognition. So, when we say that pictures cannot easily be translated into words, there is no implication of inferiority of images as a representation medium. As multimedia systems burgeon in many fields, the issues of image representation become more vexing and more compelling.

Pictures represent the object/event space in a manner fundamentally different from words (O'Connor, 1985). In turn, representing pictures with words is a vexing challenge. Yet, people do, in fact, represent pictures with words. If you ask someone what a picture is about, they can usually say something. Reactions to the lanternslides pictured both above and below indicated that the "something" is often not just (or "even") the object or set of objects in the image. Variety of potential usage generated a variety of conceptual descriptions. Choices among synonymous terms or level of specificity are not the only issues.

Representation of images by words becomes even more problematic when we consider the issue of generalization. The words "elephant," "sheep," and "horse" can be generalized to "animals." We have verbal representations of taxanomic relations. What, though, would we do with a photograph of a horse, as in Figure 5.3a; a photograph of an elephant, as in Figure 5.3b; and a photograph of sheep, as in Figure 5.3c? Is it adequate to simply combine all the photographs into a collage, as in Figure 5.3d? Are combined pictures really a better solution

boy and horse

Figure 5.3a. Photograph of a horse.

elephant

Figure 5.3b. Photograph of an elephant.

sheep

Figure 5.3c. Photograph of sheep.

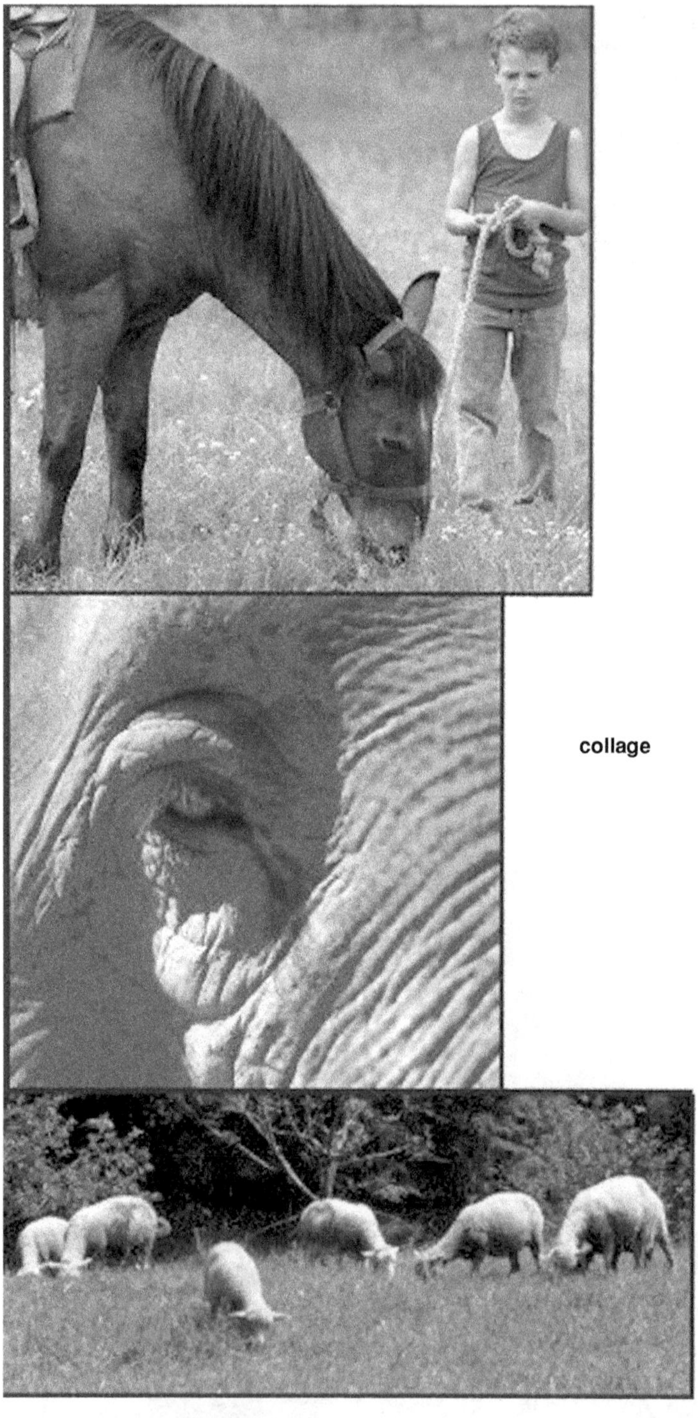

Figure 5.3d. All the photographs combined into a collage (photographs of horse, elephant, and sheep).

for some circumstances, since the word "animals" could really include many things besides the horse, elephant, and sheep?

Subject indeterminacy causes search failures within the realm of word-based documents, in which both the documents and the representations are words. How, then, are we to represent photographs with words and expect successful searches? Aboutness presents a challenge to which we have already alluded. If we have a difficult time avoiding indeterminacy in word representations of word documents, how can we possibly expand the number of conceptual tags with image-based documents? While images have been in use for millennia, it has only been recently that any large percentage of the population has had the ability to make and use images. This complicates our question because there is no strong background of accessible visual literacy on which to construct picture-based representations.

Initial Explorations

Two case studies of uses of photographs provide a different avenue of approach to the representation of documents. The first case involves a chance discovery of some antique lanternslide images, while the second is based on PhotoCD technology. The two cases span the use of photographs in educational environments, from the late nineteenth century to the present; and they both point toward an enriched mode of representation.

During the renovation of the administration building at a small university on the Great Plains, several small wooden boxes were discovered in the clutter. A few were salvaged because of their attractive appearance. One faculty member noticed that each box contained glass lanternslides and attempted to obtain as many boxes as possible. Approximately fifteen boxes were eventually located.

Each box contained one hundred slides. Each is a sandwich of:

- Two sheets of glass—0.0625 in. × 4 in. × 3.25 in.
- A piece of roll film, typically but not always, 2.25 in. × 3 in.
- Masking material of various sorts.
- Tape bindings.

Figure 5.4 presents the look and relative size of the antique lanternslide. The physical condition of the slides varies from excellent to poor. Many show no signs of wear or damage, while others have cracks in the glass or problems with mold growing. The subject matter of the necessarily haphazard sample of slides in hand ranges widely. A partial list of the topic areas includes:

- hand tinted copies of engravings of the Aeneid
- portraits of writers and artists—Renaissance to late nineteenth century
- locales mentioned in literary works

Figure 5.4. Antique Lanternslide.

- travelogue images of Scotland
- paintings of classical mythology images
- statues and other remains from antiquity
- American geography.

After these boxes of antique slides had been rescued from the brink of demolition, they sat unattended for several months, serving mostly as conversation pieces and paperweights. On occasion one faculty member or another would come across some of the slides and think of a way of using some of the images in teaching or research. Some of the images were unavailable from more standard sources. Since there are no projection facilities available on the campus for such slides, use was limited and interest did not turn to action.

By chance a few of the lantern slides were brought to the room where a digital analysis of video images project was underway. The addition of a home video camera to the computer imaging system enabled input of digitized images of approximately twenty of the lanternslide images.

On a casual, ad hoc basis various faculty members and graduate students called up the images on the computer and were uniformly pleased with the results. Several uses for the images in different courses and departments were conceived. Some of these included:

- source for stage settings and costuming
- lecture illustrations in history, classics, art history, English
- source for image fragments in video on collapse of Rome

- background images in desktop publishing
- comparison of artifacts with paintings of classical scenes
- hypermedia stacks for study of Shakespeare and antiquity.

As people from various disciplines made comments and suggestions they also began to realize the need for some access system. Several also pointed out that a list of descriptors suitable for people in widely differing fields would have to be long and multifaceted. The stage dresser seeking an image of Hawthorne's home would be seeking different aspects than would an English literature student, or a professor of architecture. The vocabulary of these differing users would also be quite different (O'Connor, 1992).

ABOUTNESS

The very different reactions of these casual users brought to mind the conversation with Maron regarding verbal description of user reactions. Aboutness is the term we will use to distinguish functional representation from mere description or application of a topic. We can say that aboutness is extra descriptive. It is likely to be generated, at least in part, by the subject of a work, though it may be that a secondary element to one user will be a primary element to another. Yet it goes beyond that to include, "what this means to me." Aboutness is the behavioral reaction of a person to a document. Each patron may have a different experience with the same document. All of the elements we have discussed earlier on will come to play in the personal reaction to the subject elements. We might say that aboutness has an adjectival component in addition to the noun.

We can imagine the patron looking for "something cheery for springtime," or "something depicting passionate commitment," or "some images showing harmony," or "something that makes me feel good." We may say, then, that aboutness is, indeed, descriptive. It describes the relationship that holds between a user's knowledge state and the physically present document.

Movie critics provide a good example of aboutness judgments. When some critics rave and others pan, it is not because they have seen different physical texts; rather, all the technical knowledge, topical knowledge, emotions, and beliefs of each critic are being engaged in the construction of a reaction to the physical text. Viewers may come to realize that their own complement of knowledge and belief and emotion structures more closely resemble one reviewer than others, so that the reviews of that critic will become surrogate aboutness judgments for the user.

Community Memory Interface

A word-based system for describing the aboutness of pictures can be constructed by changing our model of where the act of representation takes place. Typically, the rules for representation are established by some external agency—OCLC, technical services, Library of Congress, etc. What if we were to reestablish the point of representation activity as the patron group?

The digital environment enables keeping track of large amounts of data. The storage and manipulation capabilities of a computer could substitute gathering and ranking user-generated descriptors for the typical mere storage of agency generated descriptors. Such an approach offered potential for:

- accumulation of as many descriptors as users thought appropriate
- accommodation of multiple functional concepts
- accommodation of multiple levels of specificity
- multiple terms for same object or concept
- user determined descriptive terms
- multiple formats of descriptive terms.

There are, of course, also challenges:

- elicitation of adjectival, functional descriptors
- adaptation of users to a system that becomes more descriptive over time
- management of large descriptor lists for popular images

A community memory interface to a collection makes several assumptions. It assumes a new relationship between the interface and the users of the system. The users will be contributing to the system, in a sense customizing it, nurturing it, and teaching it. To illustrate this idea, imagine a recent graduate with a degree in library science beginning work at a reference desk. The new reference librarian, the interface to the collection, knows the documents, but is in a blank slate regarding patrons. However, after a time, as clients come into the collection and ask questions, make their likes and dislikes known, and discuss their areas of need, the librarian will develop profiles. These will include the idiosyncrasies of the more frequent clientele. The user profiles will enrich the librarian's ability to select documents not only by topic, but also by all those attributes that contribute to "what it means to mean—how it suits my purposes."

The interface is nurtured and enlarged and elaborated as illustrated in Figure 5.5. Few patrons would expect the new reference librarian to be as facile and knowledgeable of individual representation schemes, as a librarian on the job for a year or more. So too, we may imagine a digital system that gathers input from users and grows and becomes more elaborate in its representational capabilities.

Such an interface also assumes that at least some of the patrons will, upon occasion, be willing to take the time and effort to contribute to the system. The imagined community memory interface for the picture collection assumes only the most minimal representation of pictures at first. Patrons may have to do random searches. As a picture is found that is desirable for whatever reason,

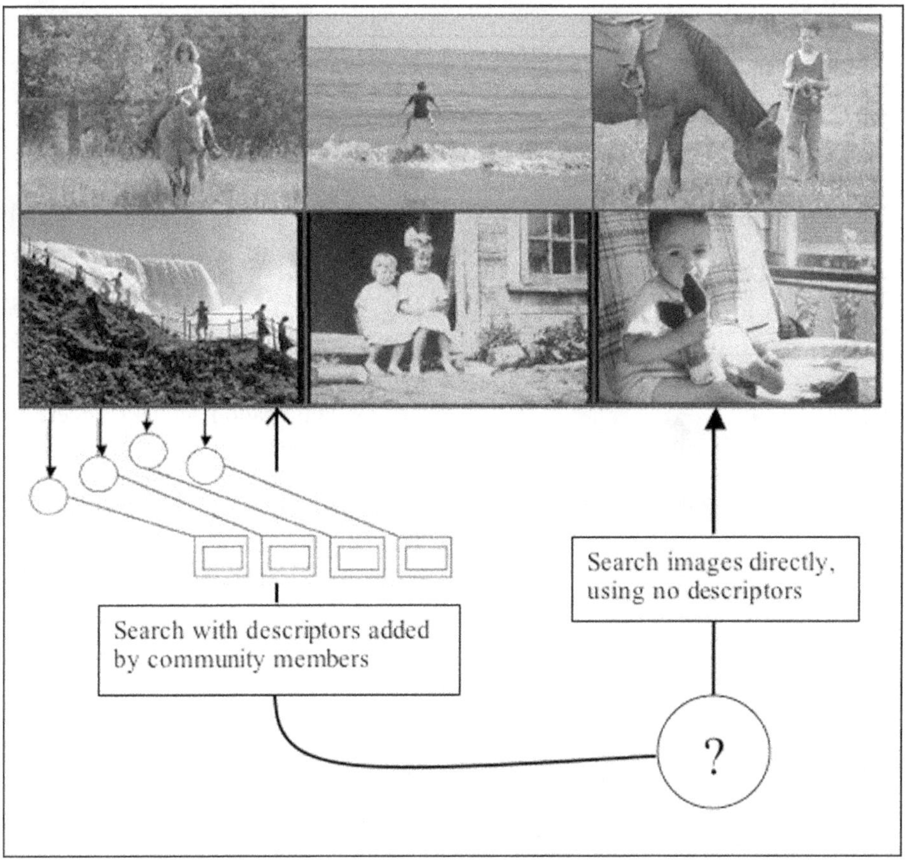

Figure 5.5. Diagram of the Basic Interface.

a request box will appear on the computer screen asking if the patron would care to add subject headings or comments about the picture to the access system.

As more and more use is made of the system, many images will begin to accumulate descriptors. Some images, though, may accumulate few or none. This will reflect the needs of the community using the documents. The patron who might be served by an image with few or no community tags will still have the option to browse through the images not yet labeled.

Table 5.1 presents the images and data for four of the pictures and demonstrates considerable variance. Indeed, some images elicited descriptors that are nearly opposites. Searching for opposites might provide to be a powerful tool in some circumstances. As Yoon (2006) suggests, since someone searching for a photograph to represent a concept may have one idea of what represents that concept, providing images that have been described by opposite terms might enlarge the pool of candidate photographs. Additionally, if someone has in mind a particular concept rather than a particular object it might be useful for the searcher to see other photographs that have been tagged with similar

Table 5.1. Variety of Responses from Different Community Members

	humorous, curiosity, cute, nice, relaxing, tender, enchantment, warmth, sweet, soft, lovable, surprise, delight, natural, joy
	tension, anticipation, anxiety, anger, ruggedness, determination, courage, disgust, calloused, tough and rugged, strong, unfeeling, resolute, determined, another era, Kansas, facing a challenge, needs a bath, disappointment
	dry and dusty, solitary, isolated, peaceful, lonely, peace, ownership, pride, independence, desolate, lovely, relaxing, barren and sad, boring, Arizona, vast, Indian reservation, beautiful, Colorado
	expansive, quiet, peaceful, desolate, rural road, view from the porch, prairie life, free of burden, cold pasture, winter morning, rugged, serene, bucolic, simple life, Texas, hot and dusty, suffering, dry, tired

terms. Note, for example, in Table 5.1 the term "rugged" is applied to both the cowboy and to the cattle and "relaxing" is applied to both the cat photograph and the ranch scene.

We would like to note that the community memory interface idea has significant overlap with photo tagging Web sites, but it also has significant points of difference. Among these is the idea that as described here, the collection of documents to be described exists, at least to some degree, in advance of users coming to it. It is the case that subsequent users can come to a collection such as that on Flickr.com and leave descriptions of images already in the system, but that is not the primary operative mode of such collections. Community members describing documents is a form of recording behavior resulting from engagement with the documents. In the community memory interface form of this activity individual behaviors are recorded purposely with the expectation that they might well be of use to another member of the community. Members of the Flickr.com community, on the whole, are tagging their own pictures for subsequent retrieval by themselves, while making the images and tags available should they happen to be of use. Within any one Flickr.com collection the photographer may have several, perhaps even several dozen, with a label such as "me." This is eminently reasonable, since the collection is tagged by and for the individual doing the tagging. This results in many millions of photographs tagged with "me" as irrelevant within the tagging for self- model.

MORE ON WORDS AND PHOTOGRAPHS

We have had the opportunity to conduct studies of user-constructed descriptors (O'Connor, O'Connor, and Abbas, 1999) Ordinarily in document collections categories are formed according to attributes of the documents themselves. The expectation, then, is that queries will be made in terms of document attributes. In those cases where users cannot articulate specific document attributes, perhaps we can, at least, make use of what they can say about what they want to accomplish. We can suggest areas of the collection not likely to be useful, we can suggest methods of navigation and evaluation and we can gather function descriptions made by previous users.

We, therefore, set about exploring users' functional descriptions of pictures. While our users would be seeing the pictures and making responses, we felt that eliciting descriptors beyond the topical might generate an access tool of some utility for those searchers who could express what they wanted to accomplish but could not be specific about what picture would work. For example, if a searcher wants an illustration for the concept of rugged determination, the rodeo cowboy photograph in Table 5.1 might be appropriate, because several previous users have used "rugged" and "determined" to describe that image. We were seeking a way of eliciting emotive, evocative, and associative descriptors for the pictures, as these would be the primary means of searching when specific assertions about the document could not be made.

First, we tried asking users simply to make up descriptions of each of a dozen images. Everybody who did this constructed a topical phrase resembling a Library of Congress Subject Heading. All the participants were librarians or library school students and seemed constrained to describe in the library way. Subsequently we had test users write captions, responses (how did this picture make you feel), and lists of items recorded in the picture (see Figure 5.6).

FIGURE 4
- ✖ Comments on the physically present photographic document
- ◆ Adjectives attributing states or emotions to the subject of the photograph. Note the anonymous nature of the adjectives: admiration, relaxed, angry, contemplative, resigned to fate, lonely, despondent, bored, isolated

Note also in the Caption column, the variety of assumptions about "place" – numerous locations in school setting, apartment and several metaphorical uses of the window for enlightenment or escape (e.g., open window to the world; Prince Charming, take me away!)

CAPTION	SUBJECT	RESPONSE
Escape from hot air	open window	◆ contemplative
A young Mary greets the. . .		◆ admiration
What can you tell	young girl	✖ She must be a student.
An open window to the world	young woman, open window	✖ Sharp contrast light and dark
Introspection	girl, city, window	◆ bleak
Mary in a quiet moment		◆ a relaxed Mary
oops!		
Anger waits.	woman	◆ looks angry
It's bright outside!	girl, window	◆ Reminds me of the early 70's.
Prince Charming, take me away!	woman, window	✖ nice shot!
What's next?		✖ attractive backlit scene
Someone by the window		Who is this person?
thoughtful afternoon	female at window	◆ contemplative
School days are back	teenage girl, windows, traffic	◆ She looks resigned to her fate.

Figure 5.6. Sample of Descriptors for One Image.

The first level of analysis consisted of gathering the adjectives and adjectival phrases that describe users' reactions to the images. These fall into categories making:

> some sort of direct statement about this picture: makes me feel happy some sort of nominal state attributed to the image: serenity, disgust, pride references to the physical characteristics of an image: this is a bright picture, "dark and moody."

Analysis of the Functional Descriptions

We then conducted a content analysis to see what categories would emerge. The categories that emerged from what actual users said about pictures are:

> Narrative & Emotive Descriptors—Introductory phrases (reminds me of . . . ; looks like)—Narrative paragraph (little stories)—Emotive terms (e.g., nostalgia, good memories)—Allusions to literature (Sleeping Beauty, Terminator)—Associative memories: Antonyms, Geography.

It was gratifying to see that we did, indeed, pick up descriptors that were other than topical. There was a wide range of narrative and emotive descriptors.

Figure 5.7. Lewis and Marguerite Clark in Maine.

In addition, there were two striking results—one we had anticipated, one we had not anticipated. We had anticipated antonyms would be present in some considerable number, and they were. One person would describe an image as lovely; another person would describe it as depressing. One person would describe an image as makes me happy; another would describe it as this makes me really homesick, I wish I hadn't looked at this picture.

Geographic attribution is a form of description we had not anticipated. Many people felt compelled to locate the image. Note that the rodeo cowboy image in Table 5.1 is attributed to Kansas, although there are no geographic cues other than the cowboy attire—the image was actually made in Davis, California. The ranch scene with a trailer in Table 5.1 is attributed to Colorado and to Arizona—it is in Idaho. This compulsion leads to an interesting representation issue we might term functionality and wrongness. Approximately 75 percent of the people who dealt with the image in Figure 5.7 wrote something about location. Half of those said that it was in the Oklahoma Panhandle or some Dust Bowl area. It was actually made on a farm on the Canadian border in Maine in 1913. We must then ask if an image that has none of the defining attributes of having been made in a particular place or time might still be an appropriate response to some sorts of queries for images related to a specific place or period.

SUBSEQUENT CONSIDERATIONS

The above suggests that pictures are not words, but words can be used as representation tools, especially if the construction of those tools is put into the hands of the users. The rules for highlighting and the methods of coding are made manifest to the users because they made them. Of course, this assumes either a certain homogeneity of users or means for a patron to select search terms applied by users with some particular profile. Now, it may turn out that if there are enough users of the system, no matter how heterogeneous they may be, several small clusters of very different types of description may develop for some pictures. Many patrons, then, would have available representations constructed by members of the microcommunity to which they belong.

In subsequent research we conducted in which we asked participants to sort thirty photographs into categories of their own choosing demonstrated that there was very little overlap in the contents of the sorted piles. That is, even with a reasonably heterogeneous group of participants, the levels of generality and definitions were highly variable. Where one participant might have put together all images containing vehicles, another distinguished between private vehicles and public transportation, and in an as yet unpublished piece, a photo of a truck and a photo of a train car and a photo of a brick wall were combined because they were all red (Greisdorf and O'Connor, 2002 (a)).

In other research we have conducted, we confirmed that viewers append descriptors for attributes or contents that are not in the image at all. When shown gray-scale images of scenes of beaches, for example, many viewers appended "blue." When asked about this after the experiment, viewers noted that the picture was of a beach and ocean water is blue. In a similar vein, viewers seeing gray-scale images of a beach with trees or a clearing in the woods, frequently appended terms such as "boat" or "camping" even though there was no image of a boat or a tent or any human-made object (Greisdorf and O'Connor, 2002 (b)).

Aboutness, in the functional sense we have used, is a powerful representation because it directly includes the user's knowledge state in the representation process. Evidence so far suggests that a community memory interface is one method of integrating aboutness into the retrieval process. It may just take some time to engineer the dynamic, learning system required for the implementation requests based on aboutness.

CHAPTER SIX

RESPONSES TO INDETERMINACY

LEARNING FROM FAILURES

CUTTER SUGGESTED and library science adopted representation at the level of the whole book (Wilson, 1983). There might be some theoretical arguments to be made in favor of this level of generality, but such an approach to representation for use is limiting. There is a practical argument for such representation of documents; that is the expenditure of resources to maintain a paper catalog. If one were designing a representation scheme for a large research library using a paper catalog one would be faced with an extensive set of logistical problems. If we assume just 500,000 documents, or what would be only a modest university research library, and a system with one card for author, one card for title, and three cards for general level subject headings, we would still have 2.5 million pieces of paper to file and maintain. Even adding two or three additional subject heading cards would greatly magnify the space and maintenance requirements. Knowing that users of the document collection may well want to find information deep within a document or set of documents means that we would have to provide a great many additional pieces of paper for each document. Attempting to provide deeper access is made simpler in the digital environment.

Resolving search failures resulting from incompatibilities between user representations and document collection representation systems is generally accomplished in one of two ways, commonly termed reference and browsing. If the patron can give voice to a topic or set of topics that would fill the information gap, then adjustment of patron and system representation conventions can be made with the intervention of a reference librarian or other system intermediary. Search failures in those instances when the information need can be articulated suggest:

- different terminologies are being used for the same concept
- patron is unsure of the level of specificity required
- patron is unsure of knowledge structures in areas that might be helpful

In such cases, the system can provide assistance in translating and refining the search terms. The assumption is that the patron and the system have represented the appropriate parts of the object/event space in similar ways. All that is required is adjustment of the conventions for coding and decoding. System assistance may be in the form of a:

- reference librarian
- database search intermediary
- on-line help screens
- transparent systems of adjustment (e.g., system searches for "Twain" and for "Clemens" even if the patron only types in "Twain")
- some form of user-inclusive (e.g., weighted query) interface
- combinations and expansions of these approaches.

More difficult and less amenable to simple translation efforts are those searches that are "functional" (Wilson, 1977). Such searches do not have an articulated target concept or topic. They are based on finding any information that fulfills a functional need. That is, the searcher is looking for whatever she/he needs to know in order to accomplish some task or resolve some issue, even when they cannot express their problem or discomfort in tidy terminology. Since there is no expressed topic, there is no issue of adjusting representations of the topic. A powerful response to failures of this sort is to ignore the system's representation conventions entirely. A patron assumes that any part of the collection is just as likely as any other part to yield useful results. Idiosyncratic methods of sampling and evaluating are substituted for topic representation.

Reference librarians and browsing will be the focal points for our considerations of responses to subject indeterminacy. Reference work will here be considered in terms of translation and adjustment. Browsing by scholars will be our focus for personal approaches to sampling document collections. Browsing will occupy considerable space in our explorations because it is so important, yet is seldom articulated as a search strategy.

"PARTNERS" AND "INTERMEDIARIES" IN THE "SEARCH PROCESS"

If a patron had "all the time in the world" and the ability to conduct a search, there would be little need for intermediaries such as reference librarians or database searchers. Since this is rarely the case, such intermediaries are often useful partners in the search process. Representation abilities account, in large part, for the utility of intermediaries. Intermediaries function, in general, to reconcile patron representation abilities with the collection. Translation and ad hoc use of "chunking" are the primary representation capabilities of intermediaries.

The intermediary, through observation and conversation, establishes an attribute palette of the patron. At the same time, the patron establishes an attribute palette of the intermediary's abilities. Conversation, in its broadest sense, establishes:

- common ground or joint attribute palette
- nature of patron question state
- jointly constructed request attribute palette.

The request attribute palette is used to establish some subset of candidate documents. This may be accomplished by inserting the request into the formal retrieval apparatus; or it may be accomplished by the intermediary making use of personal knowledge that represents document contents in a different manner. We might say that the intermediary uses the jointly constructed request to find and interrogate documents with some overlap with the patron's information need. The patron (perhaps with assistance) determines the sufficiency and significance of the overlap. The degree of sufficiency and overlap help determine whether additional searching is required and, if so, where it should be done. Representation of the patron's question state is enhanced by intermediary's:

- knowledge of representation conventions within the collection
- elicitation of potentially relevant concepts from patron
- iterative evaluation with patron of sample documents
- ability to refine request attribute palette according to evaluations.

Representation of the documents is enhanced by the intermediary's:

- subtle understanding of formal representation conventions
- ability to translate user terms to system terms
- understanding of what may exist at different levels of specificity
- knowledge of document structures
- knowledge of content clusters across documents
- critical evaluation abilities.

In its simplest implementation, this model requires little understanding of user attributes by the intermediary or intermediary attributes by the user. Only the words used by the patron to express an information requirement are considered. A topic that would satisfy the patron has been expressed, but it is in terms different from those used for representations of the collection. The intermediary merely finds a synonym, or the proper level of specificity, or the proper form of expression. Its true virtue lies in its ability to use the formal representation system as a framework to support translation, linkages across levels of specificity, and linkages between segments of formal clusters of documents. All this is accomplished as intermediary representation in the service of aligning a patron's coding with that of the system and bringing need and document together.

BROWSING

Browsing is fundamentally a shift in the locus of representation (O'Connor, 1993; Rice, McCreadie & Chang, 2001). The a priori representation by someone else according to some set of rules is traded for individual sampling and representing by the individual for the individual. In a manner similar to the switch from precoordinate indexing to postcoordinate indexing particularly with the introduction of the digital environment for searching, the seeker takes on some of the burden of representation but has control over the nature of the representation. In pre-coordinate indexing a cataloger strings together several words into complex phrases describing an item—they precoordinate terms. Library of Congress Subject Headings are perhaps the most prominent example of precoordinate representation of documents. In postcoordinate indexing the searcher decides which single terms to string together—postcoordinate. Using a group of single words in a Google search would be a good example of postcoordinate representation of the searcher's concept. So, in precoordinate indexing, the work is done by an agency not the searcher, while in postcoordinate indexing the work is done by the searcher. This is a tradeoff that is often acceptable.

Creative scholarly work requires functional access (Farrow, 1991). There is a perception by researchers in a variety of fields that "serendipity," "luck," "browsing," or some such process standing outside the formal bibliographical apparatus has made a significant contribution to their work. Profiles of scholars in the sciences, social sciences, and humanities indicate that researchers make little use of the established access mechanisms for finding documents. The standard formal systems for representing documents often do not present to the researcher adequate means for discovering catalytic works. Browsing is a means for accomplishing such discovery.

Browsing leaves the decision of just what is to be represented up to the patron. It leaves depth of penetration into the collection and into each individual document up to the patron. The tradeoff in this method is the requirement for more patron resources of time and effort. Clearly, for many patrons browsing is not an option. Yet for those engaged in the creation of new knowledge, as well as those who have been frustrated in any form of search, browsing may be the best method of searching. We can see browsing as a form of indexing and abstracting. Representation of the collection and of individual documents is still accomplished—except the patron is now the agent of representation. Pointing to parts of the collection is accomplished in some random fashion. Selection of attributes takes place ad hoc rather than a priori. Whereas in the standard bibliographic apparatus the agency sets the rules for representation of documents, representation of questions, and the method of comparing the two; in browsing, the patron:

- is in control of location and depth of engagement with the collection
- formulates the rules for highlighting

- constructs the coding system
- determines the acceptability of tradeoffs
- assumes responsibility.

In a very real sense, the browser has chosen our earlier proposition that one could examine the whole collection until what was sought was found. The constraints of time are approached by sampling methods rather than by dependence on the pointing and summarizing abilities of others.

Browsing as Searching without a Topic

Browsing consists of a wide spectrum of idiosyncratic processes for searching, sampling, and evaluating documents when significant attributes of a target or goal are not fully articulated or evident. Serendipity is, here, not "dumb luck" but rather the willingness of the scholar to "search in a literature not obviously relevant," to acknowledge the possible value of an unlikely item, to make many connections, and to make evaluations. We need to be aware of a critical distinction that has roots in the agricultural etymology of browsing. The *Oxford English Dictionary* (Simpson & Weiner, 1989) notes that browse means: . . . to feed on the leaves and shoots of trees and shrubs; to crop the shoots or tender parts . . . (sometimes carelessly used for 'graze', but properly implying the cropping of scanty vegetation).

The entry on grazing adds:

> To feed on growing grass and other herbage. . . . To put (cattle) to feed on pasture; also to tend while feeding. (Simpson & Weiner, 1989).

When an animal is browsing, it is hunting for sustenance; it must find and evaluate the food. When an animal is grazing, it is simply eating in an area where supply and evaluation are not issues. Browsing is deliberate searching. So, too, for the scholar browsing is serious work; it is a deliberate search for new connections or support for those new connections. Browsing is not idle, purposeless, or undirected; though, it may not have a clearly defined target topic. We might do better to use "grazing" for many of the activities in a library or database that are often termed browsing. When librarians put "related" works nearby on the shelves, they are typically said to be supporting browsing. Yet, by determining which connections establish relatedness, they are supplying the pasture and tending to the user; they are supporting grazing.

When somebody is searching, they must be searching for something. However, that something need not be well conceptualized or clearly articulated. Something can be the function of filling in a knowledge gap, without the scholar being able to specify a topic that would fill the gap. A scholar may well set out, rather like a detective, knowing a problem area but having little or no

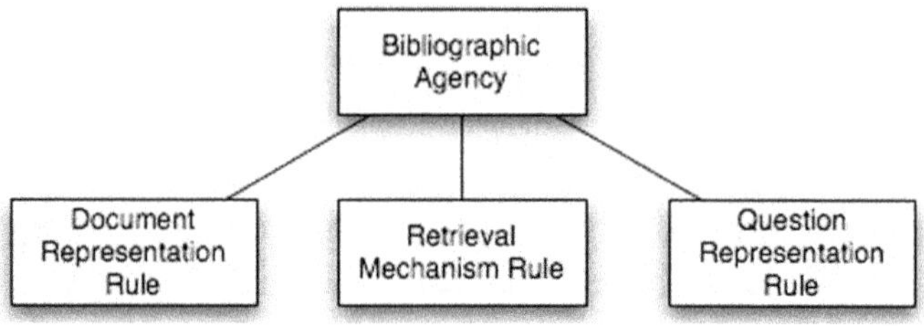

Figure 6.1. The System Determines Document Attributes and Searcher Attributes That Are to be Considered for Retrieval.

preconceived topical description. For a scholar's query to be well conceptualized, it may, indeed, be necessary that it not be tagged, precisely so that it not be hampered by the inappropriate satisfaction derived from an "illusion of knowledge" (Weisburd, 1987).

We noted earlier that one still cannot walk up to a reference librarian and ask to be shown the new knowledge documents. If it can be given a subject heading and pointed to, it is already known so it is not available to be made new. Similarly, we ought not to expect a scholar to be able to give a topical description to a knowledge gap. This in no way implies a lack of deliberateness.

As we discussed earlier, the bibliographical apparatus determines which subset of the attributes of each document is to be made available (see Figure 6.1). Likewise, it establishes just which subset of attributes of the searcher is useable in a search. The attributes of the document that are typically represented include descriptive tags such as author, title, date, and publisher; as well as subject descriptors for topics determined by the system to be addressed by the work. The attributes of the scholar that are typically allowed are descriptive rather than functional, for example, simple topic descriptions of the question, languages of acceptable documents, dates, and publishers. It may be that there is a fundamental disjunction between the purposes of the formal bibliographical apparatus and the requirements of the scholar. Reduction of ambiguity is a compelling reason for much of the descriptive cataloging and the subject analysis that are provided as access mechanisms. Yet, thriving on ambiguity is recognized as a primary quality of creative activity.

Browsing Activities

Browsing provides the scholar with the means to rectify the situation of no overlap between the query concept, whether articulated or vague or not posited at all, and the terms applied by the bibliographical agency. Different sampling strategies are engaged depending on the reason for the lack of overlap. The various strategies for browsing can each be identified with one of the sorts of internal functional representation of an anomalous state of knowledge that a scholar might bring to a collection. Each of these is distinct from the topical retrieval for which the typical bibliographical apparatus is designed. The type of anomalous state of knowledge any scholar brings to a collection will determine which sampling and evaluation strategies will be put into play; yet there are significant commonalties. Browsing approaches the difficulties posed by subject indeterminacy by removing constraints on the content and size of attribute lists for both the searcher and the document. The scholar may engage any attribute or set of attributes, no matter how unrelated it might seem to any particular topic. Hobby interests, title of an undergraduate course, cognitive style, political leanings, color preferences, and numerous other self-descriptors ranging from the seemingly trivial to the seemingly substantial may be engaged in an ad hoc way as a search goes on. The functional requirements stimulating the search will guide the choice of starting point, sampling point, and evaluation criteria. Similarly, the studiousness of the searcher will determine the sampling size, search evaluation, and number of iterations of the process. The physical nature of the collection, that is whether it is a collection of hard copy documents, a full text database, or database of representations, will likely affect the manner in which glimpses are made and the locations in which they are made. Each of four sorts of browsing activity is described in terms of:

- point in the collection at which browsing starts
- sampling size
- which attributes of the document are considered
- which attributes of the scholar are engaged
- sort of comparison between document and scholar attributes.

The four sorts of activity that we will call browsing are regions on a spectrum of activity, rather than distinct activities. They share the attributes listed above and they all assume that the searcher does the representation and the evaluation of documents. The four sorts of activity are:

1. expansion
2. segmenting and ranking (vague awareness)
3. monitoring the information environment
4. catalyzing new knowledge (shaking up the knowledge store).

Expansion

Expansion can be termed a "near known topic" search. In a sense, it is the boundary case between grazing and browsing. The arrangement of documents on a shelf or in a file by closeness of topics is similar to putting an animal to pasture. If a suitable document is found, documents with a similarity to some of the attributes will be nearby. So long as the attribute on which shelf position was determined is the attribute sought by the scholar, expansion to either side may yield useful results. Such a browsing activity begins as a targeted search. However, to the degree that nearby topics were not originally considered or articulated, their subsequent engagement yields a functional search. The boundary between the topical and the functional, between grazing and browsing, is porous. The sampling location(s) is specified by the location of a known item or known class. The size of the sample is limited only by studiousness. There exists a high overlap between the query attribute list and the document attribute list. Moving away from the original target document may present data or attributes or ways of characterizing attributes that had previously been overlooked; thus, it is not necessarily the case that movement from the known item will result in less overlap of document and query, so much as it may result in a modification of the query.

Vague Awareness

Vague awareness searches are conducted when the searcher is aware of a problem or a lack but is not able to state concisely and exactly what it is, though a useful document would be recognized if glimpsed. The searcher makes use of the formal bibliographic apparatus to make a first order partitioning of the collection by ranked probabilities of utility. The primary concept is to maximize the amount of useful data one takes in for analysis. Suppose you notice frequent use of similar metaphors in news reports about some illness and you begin to wonder about:

- something like the mythology of illness
- or social consequences of representation of disease
- or the feminine virtue of consumption and how that relates to AIDS funding
- or "something like that" dealing with representation and illness.

That is, you have a curiosity about all the ways in which disease is seen as something beyond a mere assault of some infectious agent or a biological process gone awry. You might look to the Library of Congress Subject Headings list for something like Representation of Disease but find that there is no such heading. You might try a key word search using "disease" and "representation," which would yield a work such as *Disease and Representation: Images of Illness from Madness to AIDS*. References in this work might prove interesting; though the Library of Congress Subject Headings applied to the work probably would not. The Library of Congress Subject Headings used to represent this book are:

- Mental illness—History
- Diseases in Art
- Disease—Psychology
- Medicine in Art
- Sick role

The two that mention art might prove useful, though there would likely be many works listed under these headings with little relevance to your search.

You might recall that Susan Sontag had written something about illness and metaphor. An author search would turn up AIDS and Its Metaphors. This too might have some interesting references. If you were to happen upon work by Lakeoff, you might find insights about individual and social representation. However, again there is no obvious connection between societal representation of disease and the subject headings such as Categorization (Psychology), Cognition, and Thought and Thinking by which much of Lakoff's work is labeled. Therefore, it is unlikely that you would come across his works just by means of a subject search. You might not immediately think of looking under Women in Art or in the N (Fine Arts) section of the collection, yet here you would come across a work with a title not obviously relevant (*Idols of Perversity*) but having a chapter entitled "The Cult of Invalidism." This chapter examines the role of painting in: . . . exploit[ing] and romanticiz[ing] the notion of woman as a permanent, a necessary, even a "natural" invalid. It was an image that in the second half of the nineteenth century came to control and not infrequently destroy the lives of countless European and American women.

This and the associated references might be of considerable interest to you. Again, while it might be possible to characterize your knowledge gap by giving examples of possible areas or items of interest, there is no single or small set of topical descriptors. In such a search there is no specific sampling location, other than the broad segmenting of the collection into zones likely and less likely to prove fruitful (ranking). Also, there is no particular sample size, though the size is likely to be small, so as to maximize the number of glimpses per time unit. There is a relaxed specification of the threshold of overlap of query attributes and document attributes.

Monitoring the Information Environment

Monitoring the information environment rests on an assumption by the individual scholar that he/she does not know everything, even within an individual discipline. No clearly articulated query can be made; rather sampling methods that keep the scholar aware of new developments are put into place. This may mean skimming of tables of contents, scanning of shelves in particular portions of a collection for new titles, or even chatting with colleagues. Location and size of sample are preset based on the satisfactory level of overlap of attribute lists in previous experience. That is, a region with high variability in attribute values. This might be the new acquisitions section or new nonfiction display. It may also be a sampling mechanism (or set of mechanisms) with a constrained set of attributes (appropriate language, reading ability, fields cognate with interests of searcher). One simple implementation of this approach is in common use now: the recent acquisitions collection or new book section. Herein a small number of documents, each of which is likely to be of a recent date, is present, sometimes in a classified order and sometimes in a random order. Such a subset collection usually contains documents from fields across the breadth of the whole collection. Any document that seems interesting will likely contain references and descriptors leading back into the whole collection. Time is condensed and novelty is likely to be high.

So, we might say that almost any sort of document searching activity that is not primarily based on use of author, title, or subject heading is a form of browsing. Browsing is almost any sort of searching activity in which the searcher takes on the responsibility for sampling and determining the rightness or fitness of a document for the task at hand, even when that task is essentially unstated.

Catalyzing New Knowledge

Catalyzing new knowledge or creativity may be seen as the ability to make combinations of dichotomous or previously unrelated concepts, then evaluate the combination for a possible fit or for a more accommodating model. Browsing enables the combining of user-selected characteristics of the searcher with a user-selected set of characteristics of a document and evaluating the utility of the combination. Since the intent is to generate a new combination, there is no way to segment the collection. Short of engaging each and every document, a random sampling is made on the assumption that any location is just as likely as another to yield fruitful results. This approach to browsing assumes an extremely relaxed threshold of congruence between scholar attributes and document attributes. There is no prespecification (prediction) of useful class or individual entity attributes that are likely to be useful (except, perhaps, for the negative specification = NOT the documents or class(es) with which I am already familiar). Also, there is no specification of search query attributes, except for the limiting case of "I know I don't know what I need to know, so I will entertain any combination of attributes." That is, neither the sampling location nor the sampling size nor the degree of congruence of attribute lists is specified. Willful violation of the concept of least effort is at the heart of such searching. A searcher gives up the reduction of search time and search space provided by the formal apparatus in turn for freedom to represent as required. Informal discussions with faculty members working in two large research libraries yielded several variations of one strategy, which suggests both the idiosyncratic nature of browsing and the expectation of greater effort:

1. park your car
2. write down the license number of a nearby car
3. enter collection where the call numbers contain the license plate number

4. do some sampling.
5. expect that most of the time your search will yield little or nothing
6. hope the search just might yield the spark to ignite a new idea.

Components of Browsing Activity

Having looked at four sorts of browsing activity, we can now examine the primary components of each of those activities. In a sense, these are the subgoals that were achieved by the steps or attributes discussed above. We may give the subgoals or components useful labels:

1. make glimpses
2. connect attributes
3. evaluate connection
4. evaluate search.

Make Glimpses

The first phase in the process of discovering a "difference that makes a difference" is the examination of document attributes. In order to evaluate a document's potential for resolving an anomalous state of knowledge, a searcher must read (engage may be a better term for documents in various media) all the coding, some subset of the coding, or some comprehensible representation of that coding. Morse has proposed that maximizing the likelihood of discovery depends on maximizing the number of glimpses per time unit (Morse, 1973). Each glimpse is the inputting of one document attribute to the searcher's connection making system.

Selection of a starting point within a collection or identification of a sector to be searched amounts to a global glimpse of the megadocument comprised by the collection. The likely importance of the selection and the manner in which the selection is made are both dependent on the type of question initiating the response. If the searcher has a vague idea of what would be a useful document it may be useful to select portions of the collection that have some connection to the concept. If the searcher is seeking "to shake up the knowledge store" (Overhage & Harman, 1965) in an effort to generate or sustain creative activity, a random starting point will likely be engaged (though not entirely random, as it is probable that the portion of the collection with which the searcher is familiar would be left out of the search).

Examination of attributes of individual documents is glimpsing at the local level. A searcher seeks to minimize the time between useful glimpses without inhibiting the ability to evaluate the attribute made evident by any individual glimpse. The individual glimpse is the instrument that enables the searcher to create the appropriate representation system. If representation is taken to be the set of rules by which certain elements of a document are selected or highlighted, then the browsing searcher can be seen as the rule maker. As such, the searcher can vary the rules as input (or lack of input) warrants. The useful value of an attribute and even the sort of attribute are determined ad hoc by the scholar interacting with the collection.

Control over "depth of penetration" into a collection was identified in the Intrex study as a primary attribute of browsing. The collection of documents is, in effect, a stream of data only incidentally segmented into books, videos, or database records. A searcher may start at any point on the virtual stream of documents and move at will to other points, making glimpses of large physical and conceptual chunks of the data within the collection; for example, classification segments, series, or individual whole documents. At any point along the stream a user may penetrate the collection to greater and greater depth: chapter, verse, sentence, phrase, for example. Any datum at a particular depth can be related to any other datum at any other depth at the same point on the stream or any depth at any other point on the stream.

Such control enables the searcher to represent the document at any useful level of specificity and at any point within the document. Since the glimpses input data directly from the document, there is no issue of translation or differing terms for the same concept as happens when an external representation of the document is made. There is still no certainty that the searcher will discover a useful concept even if a particular work in hand addresses it. The sample size or number of document data items considered at each glimpse may be the wrong size to catch or to emphasize the contents which address the issue; the searcher may not have the vocabulary or expertise to decode the text appropriately; or, if new knowledge is being sought, a relevant concept may just not be recognizable.

Connect Attributes

Central to creative activity is gullibility (Guilford, 1985), which may be taken as a "willingness to catch similarities" or the holding of two or more seemingly antithetical propositions. This requires that the searcher "know thyself"; that is, have available the full array of appropriate attributes (and their current values) of his/her internal representation. The type of search will determine which attributes are likely to be of value. If there is a vague awareness of the knowledge gap driving the search, then titles and subtitles within a limited set of subject areas might be appropriate. If the search is driven by a desire to generate new knowledge, then it may be impossible to predict what attribute or attribute value would likely be meaningful. A searcher may look to document attributes of any sort and any size at any level of specificity. Single words, entire chapters (or analogs in other media), style, level of presumed expertise, type of graphics, authorial stance, color of binding, and location in a collection are but a few of the physical attributes and conceptual attributes that might be considered by a searcher. A document or set of documents likely to comprise an answer would share some significant set of attributes with the description of the searcher. Search query attributes (which in browsing may range from a limited set of one or a few qualities to an unspecified and volatile set—in the sense that those that are brought into play at any particular point may vary) and document attributes are compared through some sampling mechanism.

Three sorts of connections between document attributes and searcher attributes are possible:

1. A particular document attribute may be paired with a particular searcher attribute for evaluation as a valid proposition.
2. Document attribute may link or act as a catalyst for linking two attributes of the searcher's internal representation of the problem.
3. An internal representation attribute may link or serve as a catalyst for linking two document attributes.

Achieving some threshold degree of overlap between document attributes and searcher attributes yields a candidate document for filling the knowledge gap. Of course, determination of what constitutes significant overlap remains with the searcher. One attribute might be sufficient or some threshold percentage might be required. Then, either the general characteristics of the class or the document attributes that are not congruent with the query attributes can be used to fill in the scholar's knowledge gap or to refine the search process.

Evaluate Connection

Just as browsing transfers the representation of both documents and queries to the searcher, so too, it transfers the responsibilities for evaluation of documents. For the bibliographical apparatus evaluation is typically a statement of whether or not there is a match or a significant overlap of topic descriptors for questions and topic descriptors for documents. This reduces the burden of analysis for the searcher, yet presents the difficulties and failures of subject indeterminacy. Conversation between the hemispheres or the human information processing paradigms brings together the pattern recognition capabilities of the "right" and the logico-symbolic capabilities of the "left." In the idiosyncratic search the combinations of attributes generated from glimpsed data are subjected to the testing and scrutiny of the searcher's evaluative abilities, as illustrated in Figure 6.2. To paraphrase Pauling: "The way to come up with good ideas is to generate a lot of connections and simply throw out the bad ones"(Weisburd, 1987). Of course, the means for simply throwing out the bad are not entirely self-evident and they may well bear little resemblance to the formal methodologies of any relevant discipline (though it is not likely that the evaluations will be made with total disregard for such methods). The momentary validity of a linkage or proposition will rest on a pattern ("right" hemisphere evaluation)

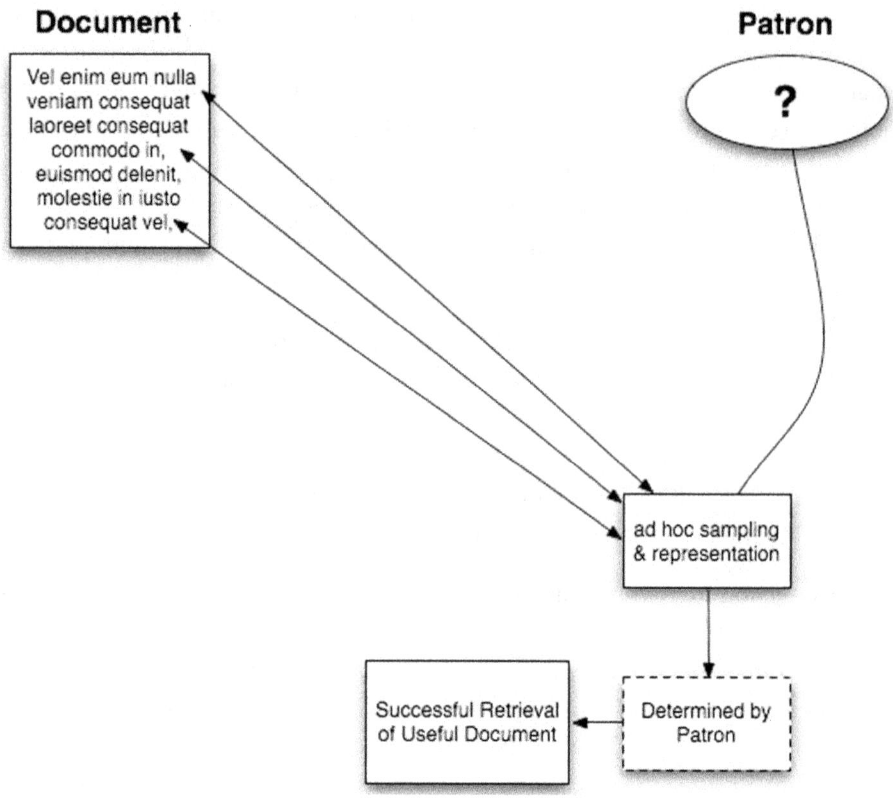

Figure 6.2. Successful search without use of formal system, but at greater cost.

rather than logical analysis. A linkage may not in itself prove valid yet show the way to another that might. The evaluative conversation, like gullibility, presupposes considerable studiousness in at least two senses. First, there has been time allocated to immersion in a topic or set of topics. Such immersion undergirds the recognition of patterns and the facility with methodology normally associated with expertise. Second, the time and ability applied within the individual search are likely to be considerable, though, of course, the possibility of a useful item early in a search exists.

Evaluate Search

Linked closely to the connection evaluation is evaluation of the search as a whole. The outcome of the connection evaluation is likely to be one of these:

- This is a satisfactory connection.
- This is not a satisfactory connection.
- No decision can be made.

If the connection is judged to be satisfactory (which need not mean that it will hold up to further scrutiny but only that it seems worth pursuing), then the search may be considered complete. It may be that browsing will continue but this might be considered a second search if the scholar is looking for yet other new connections; or it may be that the nature of the search will change as the scholar looks for supportive materials. If a connection is judged unsatisfactory, then a decision must be made about the search as a whole. Are there sufficient resources (time, enthusiasm, money) to continue searching at this time? If the search is to be continued, a decision has to be made at the local level: should sampling continue at the same level or with the same attribute, or should the sample location change? The absence of a clearly articulated target suggests that there may be no means of determining when a search is "finished." Discovery of a useful document may suggest the end of the search, or it may suggest a line of continued search. Exhaustion of resources may bring a halt to the current search process, but need not be considered a "failed" search. At the least, the portions of the collection examined this time need not be considered the next time (unless, of course, a discovery in a subsequent search triggers a connection with a previously examined document).

DISCUSSION

The personal nature of searching in the "literature not obviously relevant" (Overhage & Harman, 1965), does not necessarily render the bibliographical apparatus useless. Even if the searcher is the primary agent of representation, system resources can be devoted to enabling more rapid presentation of attributes, as well as more rapid and more informed evaluation of connections. Key word searching, rapid scanning of long lists of "hits," and "Internet surfing" from one library to another within seconds already speak to the capability system resources to shrink the time required to examine document attributes. Mechanisms of abstract construction also enable a system to facilitate idiosyncratic browsing activity. An abstract enables a searcher to make a decision while expending less effort than would be required to engage the whole document. The document collection can be taken as one large document; so far as the scholar is concerned, the boundaries imposed by book covers or database files are of little consequence, so long as useful information is found. There will likely be varying degrees of articulation of the knowledge gap. Optimal searching for some levels of articulation will require segmenting the collection and assigning probabilities of likely utility. Our question in this circumstance will be: How does the scholar "crop the scanty vegetation" in order to bring to light "undiscovered public knowledge"? (Swanson, 1986).

We then have to decide if we can construct tools to facilitate scanning, penetrating, and evaluating. Are there times when simply stepping aside entirely is the best method of facilitating representation? Can we make evident to scholars the fact that searching depends on representation and that there are concrete elements to the activity that could be optimized?

RESPONSES TO INDETERMINACY

Intermediaries and browsing activities serve the searcher by overcoming differences in representation systems. Intermediaries help to translate between coding systems and, at times, help to clarify patron concepts. They may also have "chunking" abilities that make connections that are not evident in the primary apparatus (White, Bates, & Wilson, 1992). This may enable them to respond to questions that require information from deep portions of a document. They might be able to say:

- I remember a physics book with a little bit on Homer and the wine dark sea.
- I was just reading a novel that discusses film lighting and politics.
- There was just a little article in last week's paper about El nino and the weather.
- There was a documentary on PBS just last night that had two minutes on this topic.

Browsing steps outside the system, thus it avoids the system's deficiencies. On the other hand, it requires considerably more effort on the part of the searcher. It is, therefore, not an activity to be taken lightly. Intermediaries and browsing is a powerful tool for the "discovery of the valuable in the mass of mostly worthless and uninteresting" documents (Wilson, 1968). Browsing activity offers us a probe. It is valued by scholars precisely because it operates outside the bounds of the formal access system. Therefore, it provides us a window through which to view expanded concepts of representation.

A NOTE ON STRUCTURE

Use of an intermediary and browsing are workarounds when the formal bibliographic apparatus does not work. Each makes more use of the structure of documents: turning to the table of contents for a summary of the message, flipping through pages to sample types of data; checking author credentials on the dust jacket. Finding that one document has three entire chapters on a topic of interest, together with well-designed illustrations in a textbook presentation, while another on the same topic is a self-published essay with no illustrations may be useful in determining the utility and cognitive authority for any individual patron.

We might ask: "What is wrong with engaging message structure using an intermediary or diving in oneself?" The immediate answer, of course, is: "Nothing." That is if all one is doing is seeking some particular piece of information. Even then, there is a considerable expenditure of ad hoc resources, particularly time. What if a patron is searching for something that does not depend simply on finding preexisting data? What if comparison is required? Why is the first Blues Brothers movie so much funnier than the second (or is it?). How is the use of the word "love" distributed throughout "Romeo and Juliet"? Almost any form of analysis of a single document or multiple documents will depend on structure. So, too, may selection among documents—if one wishes to read Moby Dick, one might want to know that the words are all the words put down by Melville in the order he intended; so, a comic book version might not do, a shooting script of either of the two feature films might not do, even an illustrated version might not do, since there were no illustrations in the first edition.

DUST JACKETS AND THEIR DIGITAL KIN

Dust jackets or book jackets and their digital kin provide a form of representation that addresses some of our concerns with the failures of the standard bibliographic apparatus (O'Connor & O'Connor, 1998). When we browse in a bookstore we make use of an access tool not usually available in library catalogs or even with direct browsing of the library stack shelves—the book jacket. The richness of the book jacket as a representation was essentially ignored in most libraries but was retrieved by Web based retailers such as amazon.com.

Book jackets present representations that are not ordinarily available in library systems, including statements about the assumed reader, the qualifications of the author, and evaluative comments from named authorities. Such attributes have been posited as helpful or even necessary in making relevance judgments but had not been easily available within brick and mortar libraries.

Let us turn to a small example of book jackets and representation as a thought piece on access.

Wilson notes that even documents physically in hand may be inaccessible linguistically, conceptually, or critically (Wilson, 1977). So if one is in a large library that requires many steps between the catalog and a document, one would like a sufficiently robust representation so that there won't be an unpleasant surprise when the document is at hand, Nowadays, similarly, one does not want to order a book on-line only to have it show up in the mail and be something very different from the catalog description.

Background

Of course, the book jacket serves two utilitarian purposes that are not directly user-centered. It provides some degree of protection for the document and it serves as a sales tool—even academic presses have to be concerned with sales figures. However, a good deal of expense and effort go into the construction of the academic book jacket to benefit the work's subject and audience (AAUP, 1996).

> No, you can't always judge a book by its cover, but . . . it's damn near impossible to sort through and evaluate thousands of books without them. . . . I would observe that the help-to-hype ratio for most book jackets is pretty high . . . (Dwyer, 1993).

Figure 6.3. Free Book Covers—Help Yourself.

During a description of the book jacket design process given by the sales manager for a successful academic press, the word "representation" popped up over and over. The words of the title were designed to "represent" the content to the primary audience; the graphics on the book jacket were chosen to "represent" in some way the stance of the author or to grab the attention of the most likely readers (even academic presses have to be concerned with the bottom line); blurbs were written to "represent" the assumed intellectual level of the reader—general lay audience, specialized graduate students—review blurbs were chosen not only because they made positive comments but also because the cognitive authority of the reviewers would "represent" how the field positioned the work in the book.

At the time, this particular press spent approximately $1,250 designing a book jacket to represent each book. So we had the almost comedic situation of the provider of the book spending a large amount of time and money and employing the talents of several people to provide a representation; then when the book arrived at its library destination, most of that representation was discarded! See Figure 6.3. The words of the title stayed without the graphic component; the author name stayed without the photograph and biographic blurb; the publisher name and publication date stayed. The subject headings provided by the cataloging in publication on the back of the title page stayed; but so much was gone.

Problem Reiterated

Many searches in document collections are conducted with no clearly defined target. That is, the exact title or author or call number is not known.

Even when the searcher has a reasonably well-articulated information requirement, just which documents will satisfy that requirement are not self-evident. Reducing the number of documents to be examined and reducing the time to examine each document are fundamental reasons for the construction of access mechanisms—some manner of representation of the documents.

Representation here will be taken to be a system for highlighting salient characteristics of a document and, necessarily, leaving some characteristics behind (Marr, 1982). Some aspects of the document will be used to stand in place of the whole document for some purpose. The purpose assumed at the time of representation will determine just which characteristics will serve as surrogates for the whole. The representation available at the time of the search will determine what can be accomplished with the representation. It is important to note information is lost in the representation. The surrogate has only some of the characteristics of the original; it performs only some of the functions of the original; both its utility and its faults lie in its smaller size. Yet, it makes some sense that a richer representation will provide more access routes and more evaluative power to the searcher.

Probability of satisfaction has been proposed as the operative concept for information retrieval (Maron, 1977). Assuming that the representation process has adequately and accurately identified all the salient characteristics, the system could predict the likelihood that a particular requirement could be satisfied by any particular document. Obviously, even defining what "all the salient characteristics" might be would be a major task. We can point out, though, that most retrieval systems before the advent of the World Wide Web presented very few of the salient characteristics.

That is, they represent primary topics within a work and they have generally set an arbitrary, operational number of representation elements (for example, the three Library of Congress subject headings typically applied to books). Typical library retrieval systems have also neglected to include representations of a set of factors closely linked to relevance. In the 1970s, M.E. Maron identified as important attributes in relevance judgments: comprehensibility, credibility, importance, timeliness, and style.

This set of factors echoes Wilson's assertion that the physical availability of every document in the world does not necessarily equate with accessibility. Recall that a work may be linguistically inaccessible, conceptually inaccessible, or critically inaccessible (Wilson, 1977). We might, then, suggest a scholar searching through any significant number of works would benefit from representations of these factors. There are generally a large number of informational elements on an academic book jacket; could we say that these provide useful representation of both the aboutness of a document and the additional factors influencing likelihood of satisfaction?

Figure 6.4. Front of Sample Dust Jacket.

Closer Examination of Book Jackets

As a small exercise we examined the representation practices on a few book jackets from the University Press of Kansas, of which *Rodeo in America: Wranglers, Roughstock, and Paydirt* (Wooden & Ehringer, 1996), presented in Figure 6.4 (gray scale version of front cover) and Figure 6.5 (interior blurb), is one example.

Figure 6.5 presents a piece of descriptive material from the interior of the book jacket. This is, in effect, an extended subject descriptor. The reader is told that the work is about: rodeo as a national pastime, the essential character of rodeo, current rodeo culture, and rodeo's hold on the American imagination. The reader is also given the first hint of the authorial approach of the work with the phrases "celebrates" and "behind the chutes." A second portion of the book jacket presents the reader with another set of style attributes: "anecdotes and observations." In addition, the reader learns that work is also "clarifying its many dimensions. . . ." A second and deeper (in the sense of relating to portions

Rodeo in America celebrates a great national pastime and tradition. Taking the reader "behind the chutes," Wayne Wooden and Gavin Ehringer reveal the essential character of rodeo culture today and show why it retains such a

Figure 6.5. Extended Description of Sample Book on Book Jacket.

of the work rather than the work as a whole) list of subjects is presented here.

Emergent Categories

After examining a dozen book jackets we sketched a general set of representational categories: credentials of the author, credentials of reviewers, evaluative comments, for whom the book is intended, graphics, subjects (at differing depths, that is, not just the most general), style, and summary. Not all are evident on each and every dust jacket. As is typical with content analysis categories, precise boundaries and membership characteristics were difficult to establish. Examples from *Rodeo in America* indicate the type of material associated with each of the categories.

Credentials of Authors

> Wooden is professor of Sociology and coordinator of the Criminal Justice and Corrections Program at California State Polytechnic University, Pomona. He is author of . . .
>
> Ehringer is a freelance journalist and former media assistant at the Professional Rodeo Cowboys Association. He has published more than 500 articles in journals such as . . .

Credentials of Reviewers

> White, publisher of Western Horseman Slatta, author of *Cowboys of the Americas Hoy*, author of *Cowboys and Kansas*.

Evaluative Comments

> The definitive book on rodeo . . . most comprehensive, probing look to date . . .

> A book like this . . . provides . . . a sense of what rodeo is really like. . . . entertaining and highly readable.

Intended Audience

> . . . guide for aficionados and novices alike . . .
> . . . provides the uninitiated with . . .

Subjects

> Character of rodeo culture today . . . why it retains such a strong hold on the American imagination.
>
> Glamour and glory, hazards and hardships, . . . many dimensions as a sport, business, community event, family tradition, and pop culture icon.
>
> Bareback and bull riders, calf ropers and steer wrestlers . . . clowns [etc.].
>
> Allure and demands of rodeo life.

Style

> Taking the reader behind the chutes.
> Filled with telling anecdotes and insightful observations.
> Based on research and interviews conducted at the National Finals
> . . . highlights rodeo's . . . , while clarifying its . . .

Graphics

Repeated image of a bronc rider (see Figure 6.4) with mixed Western fonts.

Note: Shotts (1997) detailed the process of selecting the particular image for the cover, the color scheme, and the fonts. A full color mock up was presented to colleagues at other presses. The critique resulted in reversing the photograph in order to work with the cover text (even though this reverses the handedness of the rider).

Summary

Three paragraphs summarizing the material in the book

Content Analysis of a Larger Sample

Using the categories sketched in our preliminary examination, we set about looking at a larger sample. For this study we did not collect the contents of each category on each book jacket, we simply noted whether the category was present or absent. Graphics were not noted because every book jacket, by definition, had some form of graphical design even if only color selection and font.

Book Jacket Attribute	Number of Jackets with Attribute	Percentage of Total
Subject indicator	219	96.1
Evaluative statement	183	80.3
Summary	227	99.6
Author credentials	223	97.8
User description	107	46.9
Reviews	157	68.9
Reviewer credentials	144	63.2

Figure 6.6. Percentage of Document Sample with Each Attribute.

Each week for eight weeks, we made a random selection of 50 book jackets from the box of jackets discarded at the circulation desk. Jackets from novels and duplicates were eliminated from the sample group, as were those that had been damaged to the point where we could not read all material. The final set for examination consisted of 228 items. Figure 6.6 presents the results of the analysis. It is clear that the representation categories, which map well to Maron's suggested criteria, do appear in significant number on dust jackets.

As we have said earlier, representation implies loss of some information. When we highlight certain aspects or choose certain attributes over others, something is left behind. Loss of information is the strength of the surrogate as a search tool. Less information means less to sort through while searching. Problems arise when only a few attributes are left, especially if they are of only limited types. When a 250-page book is represented by three phrases at the level of the book as whole, critical, and evaluative representation are gone, as is access to smaller portions of the book.

If we look at the representation of *Rodeo in America* that is found in an academic library catalog, we see only a small amount of information in comparison with that on a book jacket, which is in turn still very small compared to the book as a whole. See Figure 6.7 for the online catalog record. Note that for a Subject Search, one must input exactly the subject residing in the system. Thus, American Rodeos and Rodeo Cowboys would not work. Similarly, Cowboys would not work for a Keyword Search because Cowboys is not in the title. While it is the case that Web search engines typically use more sophisticated counts of words as well as thesauri, the initial presentations of results are still essentially lists of unevaluated documents.

CONVERSATION REPRESENTATION

Book jackets present several types of salient characteristics of the documents they represent. We might say that they present "conversational representations" because those engaged in representing the document have a vested interest in presenting characteristics of value to searchers and in presenting those

Author Wooden, Wayne S.
Title Rodeo in America : **wranglers, roughstock, & paydirt / Wayne S. Wooden & Gavin Ehringer.**
Publisher Lawrence, Kan. : University Press of Kansas, c1996.

Copy Status | More Details | Find Similar Items | Full Record | Print Version

Descript. xi, 297 p. : ill. ; 25 cm.
Notes Includes bibliographical references (p. [265]-271) and index.
ISBN/ISSN 0700608133 (alk. paper)

Author Wooden, Wayne S.
Subject Rodeos -- United States -- History.
Cowboys -- United States -- Biography.
Author/Ed. Ehringer, Gavin.

LOCATION	CALL #	STATUS
Deck 5	791.8 W854r	DUE 09-20-07

Figure 6.7. Online Catalog Record for Our Sample Book.

characteristics in a manner useful to the searchers. The categories that emerge from examining book jackets demonstrate a concern with the functionality of the representation; they present responses to the anticipated questions:

> "What can I do with this book?"
> "Do I have reason to trust in its cognitive authority?"

Reviewers represent a portion of the likely readership.

Figure 6.8 presents the construction of the "representation palette." Each of several people engaged in the representation process holds in mind an image of the prospective user(s) profile(s). Subject indicators and summaries appear on the vast majority of the book jackets examined. These provide the form of topical representation customary in access systems, with two significant differences. On the whole, they leave less behind in the representation tradeoff and they are in the vocabulary of the assumed user group.

Topical representations and descriptive representations such as title, publisher, and number of pages remain stable over time; they may be termed diachronic. Evaluative statements, author credentials, user description, reviews, and reviewer credentials all speak to a different sort of representation. These are of the sort suggested by Maron and Wilson and may be termed synchronic. Timeliness, readability, and credibility are among the synchronic characteristics often presented on book jackets.

Author credentials and reviews speak to the cognitive authority of the work in hand. Of course, reviews are highly likely to be positive; however, Shotts notes that most academic publishers look for reviews that will also represent the content and style of the work and speak to the targeted audience. If a reader is familiar with the reviewer's work or understands the value of reviewer credentials, these can be used to assess credibility. That is, a reader might say either "I don't know the author, but I like the reviewer's previous work so well

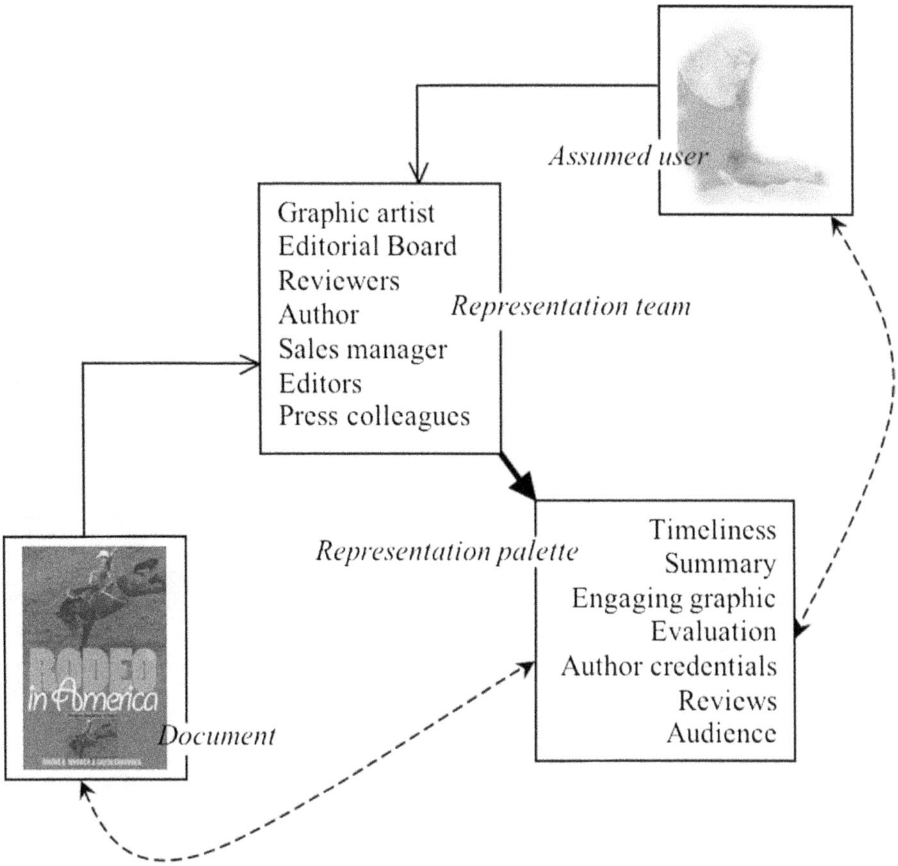

Figure 6.8. Representation Palette.

I'll give this a try," or "I so dislike this reviewer's own work I can't imagine that I would find value in the book in hand." Book jackets, thus, provide both an enriched form of the representation seen in traditional access systems and a form of representation not often found in access systems yet important to evaluation and selection.

The simple and immediate consequence of such an assertion is to ask why book jackets are so often discarded. Of course, the immediate response can be the expenditure of resources required to make such relatively fragile materials available in the environment of a large paper document collection.

What we see in the digital document environment is that the logistics of providing both topical and functional or evaluative representation prove less troublesome. The legacy of the book jacket as an enhanced representation palette provides a substantial foundation for robust digital representations.

CHAPTER SEVEN

DOING THINGS WITH WORD-BASED DOCUMENTS

STRUCTURAL ANALYSIS

HERE WE BEGIN to address providing structural analysis as a tool or suite of tools for users to engage more directly with the topography of documents. In this chapter we will address just document structure. In the following chapter we will address structure and behavior; and then we will address the use of behavior to describe structure.

In many reviews of *Explorations in Indexing and Abstracting*, the chapter on computer-based extraction of words was the primary cause for concern, even among those who otherwise liked the book. There seemed to be an assumption that the very idea of using computers meant that there was an "us vs. them" situation and that the book favored "them—the computers." The use of a "straw man" that could easily be knocked down by the computer program was brought up, as was a supposed self-congratulatory tone about the computer program doing so well. Several reviews noted that humans are capable of more subtlety than that displayed by the computer program.

The discussion of use of computers and what could be accomplished with a very simplistic keyword extraction program was presented as a thought exercise. Surely, if the discussion had been meant as state-of-the-art computational analysis of documents and document collections, there would have been rather more sophistication and subtlety, not to mention something more than a few lines of code written in C#. On the one hand, the simple program extracted representations much like those of a human indexer, even though it lacked subtlety and the speed that would have been available even at the time of the writing of that earlier book in the mid-1990s.. On the other hand, the program also served as a test bench against which to think about what goes on in human indexing.

In the subsequent years, use of computers for access tasks has become quite routine. We will construct a similar, updated thought exercise in the course of this chapter.

THOUGHTS ON INDEXING AND ABSTRACTING SYSTEMS

One might well ask if there is any value to having indexing and abstracting systems. We have just spent considerable time discussing significant shortcomings of formal document representation systems. We have discussed reference intermediaries and browsing as responses to the problems posed by typical retrieval tools. User-appropriate chunking of the collection, user control over depth of penetration, and user determined vocabulary are some of the elements that make reference and browsing powerful tools. The absence of these elements in typical retrieval systems is, in large part, the reason for their failure. Is there any value, then, to having document representation systems? The answer, of course, is yes. Indeed, there are several parts to an affirmative response. These include:

- even older systems work for those who know them (e.g., librarians)
- many searchers have questions that easily fit system constraints
- digital environments provide for very sophisticated formal systems
- collection size and time still constrain browsing and reference.

Before we explore means for involving the searcher in the representation of questions and documents, we must elaborate upon a distinction and consider some caveats. We must make a distinction between representation that takes place before the searcher comes to the document collection and that which takes place, at least in part, after the searcher has engaged the collection. Descriptive terms for these two sorts of representation have been developed in the realm of indexing. We can broaden the usage to include both the pointing and the summarizing functions—indexing and abstracting.

Precoordinate representation rests upon the indexer/abstractor constructing precise descriptions of document concepts. Essentially, the entire burden for description is on the indexer/abstractor/cataloger at this point. This means that there is no burden on the searcher other than identifying the sanctioned description that suits the request. If the representation of documents is in close accord with user requirements and conventions, then rapid access to appropriate documents is possible. Library of Congress Subject Headings are one well-known precoordinate system.

Postcoordinate representation is accomplished, in part, by the user. Elements that are generally simpler in construction than those in precoordinate systems are refined and combined by the searcher. The user need not guess a precise string of words. Sets of terms with combinations using Boolean logical operators—AND, OR, NOT—are powerful search tools. In earlier postcoordinate searching on systems such as DIALOG, the logical operators were explicitly stated. Indeed, since connect time was expensive, the ordinary method was to construct the logical string of terms on a piece of paper, check the validity of the logic, then connect to a mainframe computer. Since most searches are AND searches, such as "Red Sox" AND "World Series" or "Democritus" AND "atoms" AND "void" many systems now simply allow typing in the terms. In fact, if one types the "and" into a Google search, a polite note appears telling the searcher that the "and" is supplied automatically. This does not mean that OR and NOT are not very useful. If one is looking for recipes with chickpeas and wants to be sure not to miss those that use garbanzo beans, then OR is a handy logical operator. If one is searching for music from the 1960s but really does not want to hear the Top 40s overcommercialized music, then NOT can be very useful—music AND 1960s NOT "Strawberry Alarm Clock."

Comparison of Requests

Suppose I wanted to find some works on the "disputes and the ideas for cooperative resource management" for rivers in the West, particularly the Missouri River. Perhaps I could restate my interests in terms such as: "western water law and management" or "law and politics of interstate water allocation." What might a request to the retrieval system look like in Library of Congress Subject Heading terms, in Boolean terms, and in a weighted request system?

Remember that in a precoordinate system, I must come up with a word or string of words just like that constructed by the indexer. I might try terms constructed from the primary words in my self-description of my need. Terms such as "cooperative resource management" and "interstate water allocation" would seem natural. However, they would not retrieve a test document on this topic, *River of Promise, River of Peril: The Politics of Managing the Missouri River* by Thorson.

If I were to think in terms of the Missouri River, I would be successful. The river's name, with a qualifier describing my area of interest, is one of the headings applied to this book in the Library of Congress Cataloging-in-Publication (found on the reverse of the title page in many books). It is also possible that if I had generalized my search to "water" and had skimmed through all the entries, I would have come across a heading on "water supply" that would have been satisfactory. The three Library of Congress Subject Headings applied to this work are:

- Water-supply—political aspects—Missouri River Watershed
- Missouri River Watershed—water rights
- Federal-state controversies—United States.

The searcher with adequate time and the knowledge that the system operates with very specific descriptors might try variations on original word combinations or might try generalizing (e.g., from "interstate water allocation" to "water"). However, several pieces of research over the past few decades

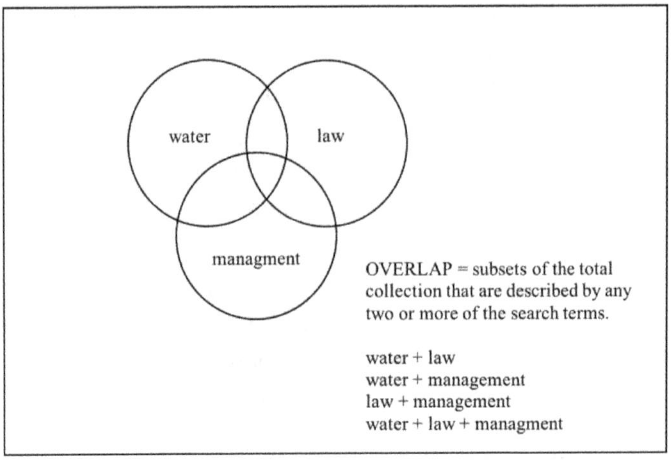

Figure 7.1. Overlap of Collection Subsets in a Boolean Search.

indicate that most searchers will not go to significant lengths to change a query once it is composed (for example: Blair, 1990). Of course, it is now common to make use of a computer to search for titles with a specific word or set of words and avoid the subject heading search as an initial motive. Yet, this assumes that a title will actually contain the word the searcher assumes would be in a title. In a Boolean postcoordinate system I would be able to say to the system "find me all the works in the collection that have been described by all of the following terms." The system would then seek each and every work with each of the terms and then determine the overlap as in Figure 7.1. Again, the terms are likely to be simpler. I might say: "Find works described by 'water' AND 'law' AND 'management'—these terms could be presented in any order."

I might wish to try "river" in place of "water"; or I might say: "I would like anything you have that would be described by either "river" or "water," so long as it is also described by my other terms also. This would yield a query: water OR river AND law AND management. It might also be desirable to limit the search, saying: "Only show me things printed more recently than five years ago"; or "in the United States, but NOT in the East."We must still remember that such a system relies on the documents having been described previously. However, the simple terminology enables the use of computers, thus enabling rapid description by numerous terms.

In most weighted descriptor systems I would be presented with the option to list the terms I thought would be applicable to my search, then say to what degree each of them was important. For example, I might say that I am very interested in rivers, so I would give it a weight (on a scale of 1 to 10) a 9 or 10. It is also very important to me that politics and management issues are included, so I would weight these with 8 or 9. If the rivers are located in the West, that would be good, but I will look at almost anything, so I might weight

"West" with a 6. I might also be able to say that if photographs are included, that would be helpful but it is not particularly important, so perhaps a weight of 4 would be appropriate.

Before I have come to the collection an indexing system has weighted all the terms that apply to every document in the collection. Most of the documents may well have absolutely nothing to do with rivers or the West or the law. They will have weights of zero for these terms. Other works may be travelogues and speak of beautiful rivers in New Hampshire or resource management in national forests. These will have some small overlap with my request. So too will works on politics and ecology, but many of these will be too broad and talk about resources globally or the history of Congressional action on national parks.

Then there will be a group of works that has to do with rivers and resource management and law. Some of these will be directly on my topic and others will have considerable overlap but will also have a broader scope or a narrower scope. The weighting of terms should accomplish two important goals:

- Locate all the works described in much the same way as my request.
- Generate a ranking of how close each of the works in the collection is to my query.

The ranking will essentially tell me the likelihood that I will be satisfied by each and every one of the documents in the collection. I would probably want to check any documents of 90 percent or greater likelihood first, but I would be free to continue down the ranking if the "best" works were not available or proved too narrow. Weighted systems eliminate the binary retrieval problem. There is no longer a necessity for a perfect match between a request and a document description. The system does not say: "There was no perfect match to your query, so there are no works to put into your hands. Try a different approach."

While it is not necessary that postcoordinate systems be built within digital environments (indeed, they were invented in the paper environment), they are certainly enhanced in computer-based systems. A wide variety of approaches to computer assisted description and retrieval is in various stages of research and implementation. Hybrid combinations of systems are becoming common, sometimes just by ad hoc usage. Many search engines for the Internet present weighted lists of retrieved documents.

In the mid-1980s, as keyword searching became available on automated academic library catalogs, searchers moved away from subject searches as their initial approach, in favor of keyword searches, they discovered that it can be ...ful to go back to the subject search with the heading from a work ...say to the system: "Find me more like this one."

The system can then look for the subject heading and retrieve documents that do not have the keyword in their title but are, nonetheless, on the topic.

Machine Augmented Representation

Machine representation of documents provides an opportunity to examine in detail the theory and mechanics of rule-based indexing and abstracting. The manner in which human indexers or catalogers represent documents is less subject to careful scrutiny because of the individual and interior nature of the processes involved. Also, human indexers or catalogers are often under system constraints that do not allow for consistent application of a set of rules. That is, they may be required to represent a set number of books each day and, so, not be able to read the entire work with deep scrutiny. Still, a close examination of a simple example of computer generation of a representation will provide a touchstone for consideration of the conceptual mechanics of representation.

The Use of Discontinuities

When we read a book or an article, we are constantly making distinctions between the background and the squiggles of ink. We are also grouping squiggles into letters, distinguishing one letter from the next, and distinguishing one word from the next. All of these activities may be described as observing discontinuities in the data stream.

Bateson suggests that information is a "difference that makes a difference" (Bateson, 1979). First we have to detect a discontinuity—the difference between the medium of the message and the squiggles, then between each of the squiggles, then between clusters of squiggles. Then we must make some determination of how much of a difference is significant. Figure 7.2 models the general concept of detecting points of difference in the data that is input to the patron.

If we encounter the cluster of squiggles "the," we know that this is an individual cluster, generally because there is a blank space on either side of it. The cluster "the" is handy as a little pointer, but has little meaningful content on its own. Once that item to which "the" points is encountered, it generally is the meaningful term and "the" is put aside. It is a difference that makes little, if any, difference.

If the cluster following "the" is "buffalo," we have a cluster that does not appear so frequently in most texts as "the" and which, therefore, presents a candidate for making a difference. Once we decode the cluster, the actual determination of difference takes place. If the cluster "buffalo" appears fairly frequently in a text, it will probably represent a meaningful concept. If it is seen too frequently, it may actually lose some of its difference-making ability. One could imagine a book of uses of buffalo on the Great

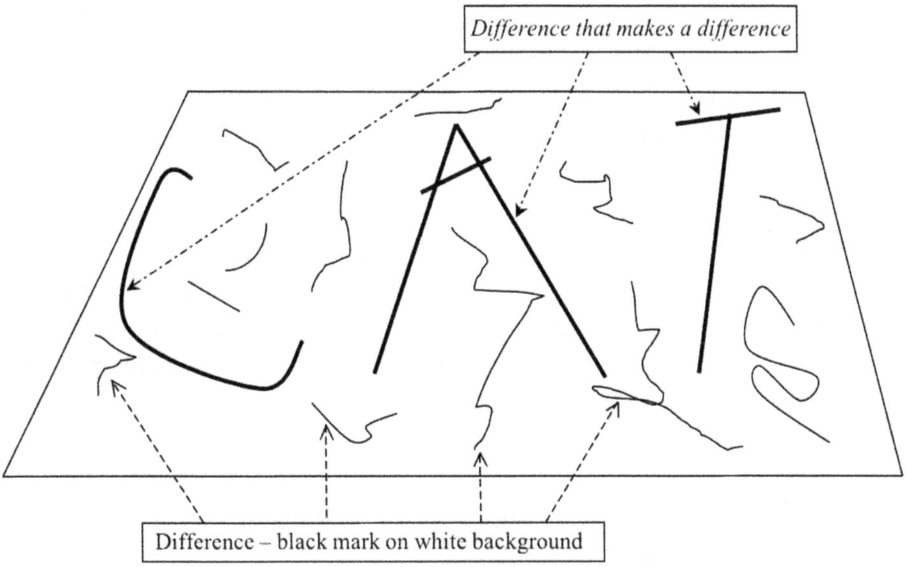

Figure 7.2. Seeking Differences That Make a Difference.

buffalo bones, buffalo blood, buffalo tail, buffalo horns, buffalo heart, buffalo hide, buffalo hair, and so on. Once the book had been found, "buffalo" would be too broad a term to distinguish aspects of use of the animal.

Clearly, different circumstances will determine just how much difference is made by any set of squiggles. Just as clearly, the squiggles remain fixed—they are the major diachronic attributes. We can usually assume that a person indexing or abstracting a document is presented with the same stream of data from the page (or the analog in other media) as would any other reader. It must be said here that dynamic documents on the World Wide Web do offer a counter example to the fixed data stream model. The person making an index or abstract must determine some level of difference that will be significant. Then when differences at or above that level are detected that person must decode them and then give them a conceptual tag—the index term or abstract.

The problems of indeterminacy, those times when the system's representation of a document is not appropriate for a patron who would have been pleased with the document, are founded largely in the detecting and tagging of differences. If so much depends on detecting discontinuities in the data stream, can we simply:

- Detect the points of difference?
- Say how big they are?
- Say where they are?
- Let the patron determine the significance?

In fact, this is the basis for machine indexing and abstracting. Most work in machine representation of documents has been conducted on word-based documents, though the burgeoning interest in multimedia documents has begun to yield models for machine-based representation of image and sound documents.

Computers store text files by having a string of "1"s and "0"s stand for each letter and each punctuation mark in the text. Each "1" or "0" represents an electrical state of "on" or "off" and is termed a bit. The ASCII (American Standard Code for Information Interchange) seven-bit code is a standard representation for letters, using a seven-place string for each letter. A computer program can use this code to examine each and every character in a text. By looking for the code that represents the blank space between words, the program can cluster letters into words. By counting how frequently the words appear in the text, the program can produce a measure of the size of the difference that cluster has compared to the text as a whole.

In practice, we know from studies of frequencies of word occurrences that there are many words that are unlikely to be meaningful to most system users. Such words are often included in the program so that when the computer detects them, they are simply left out of consideration. Stop list (sometimes termed a "kill list") is the general term for this part of a program. Appendix A lists the terms in a typical stop list. Notice that the major portion of these words is comprised of pronouns, articles, prepositions, forms of the verb "to be," and adjectives. In many instances, though certainly not all, these words do little to represent topics.

Extraction is the most common form of machine representation of documents. The representation or highlighting rule is simply "present all words that are not on the stop list." It is common to make additions, such as:

- alphabetize the words
- tell how many times each word appears
- arrange the words by frequency
- give the address of each word
- show the words on either side of the selected word

It is also possible to extract words not by frequency, butby:

- where they appear in the document (title, opening or closing sentence, etc.)
- type of word (noun, verb, adjective)
- emphasis by bolding or italics

Extraction can be augmented by use of a thesaurus to bring words for the same concept together and including them all in the frequency count. It is also possible to use a thesaurus to translate terms to a sanctioned list of terms. Such approaches require careful consideration of the patrons, since they reintroduce the issues of conceptual tagging and translation.

Abstracts can be produced with an extension of the extraction method of representation. Simply extract whole sentences by finding punctuation marks. The rule for finding those sentences could be either "select sentences by where they appear" or "select sentences that contain the most frequently appearing words on the list of extracted terms." Especially in technical literature, where editorial policies tend to enforce format, extraction by location is not as haphazard as it might seem at first. If, for example, the first paragraph must contain the hypothesis of the research and the next to the last paragraph must contain summary results, then location is not difficult.

Systems based on extraction remove the barrier of an intermediary constructing concepts and their tags from the document data stream. They filter out the elements least likely to be of significance and allow the patron to determine depth of penetration. However, they do not directly include the patron's information requirement in the making of the rule for highlighting. Such systems also cannot account for synchronic changes. Future searchers might not understand the terminology, or references, of the author.

Sophisticated versions of machine representation are constantly being developed and tested. It is beyond the scope of this chapter to consider these. We will return to additional methods for word documents and for multimedia documents as we consider more sophisticated representation rules.

AN ELEMENTARY WORD EXTRACTION PROGRAM

Examining an elementary extraction program will enhance understanding of both the binary representation of words and the application of rule-based representation to word-based text. Our sample text is displayed in Figure 7.3. We will follow the steps of a program designed to:

- extract the words from the document that are not on our stop list;
- alphabetize the words on the list of extracted terms;
- calculate the frequency that the words appear in the document; and
- provide an address within the document for each word.

Note that in the display of the flow of our program, as shown in Table 7.1, in the second column we have the term "Stop Word?" followed by "True" or "False." This does not mean that the stop word is true or false, but rather it means that the word is on the stop word list (True) or it is not (False). True and False might just as well have been Yes and No, but are the more common convention in representing the flow of a program.

Table 7.1 presents the general flow of the extraction portion of the program. It presents segments of the ASCII seven-bit binary code, with the numbers translated into decimal form for ease of reading.

PhD in Library and Information Management

theory core

Information Engineering
Informational Psychology
Sociology of Information
Information Organization Management

Each doctoral student will construct a program of advanced coursework and substantial research on a foundation of theory drawn from these fields. A faculty dedicated to both research and instruction, a curriculum both rigorous and congenial, and a nurturing academic community will foster student abilities to contribute to society's understanding of the creation, diffusion, and utilization of information.

Each students will first acquire the theoretical concepts and research abilities associated with a master's degree program.

In close cunsultation with appropriate faculty members, each student will be challenged to investigate and develop theory within these aspects of the Library and Information Management discipline.

Aesthetics; Contexts of Use; Dynamics of Human Systems; Culture; Engineering; Management Policy; Visualization; Organizational Design; Economics; Values and Ethics.

Substantial course and laboratory work will be devoted to developing expertise in the selection of research topics, and methodologies, implementation, data analysis, and reporting.

Cognate coursework in related fields will strengthen the theory base and research capabilities of each doctoral student.

An advanced seminar in graduate level teaching or in managerial issues will enhance each graduate's ability to make a substantial contribution to the discipline and to society.

Each doctoral candidate will contribute new knowledge to the field through the writing and public defense of a dissertation.

Figure 7.3. Sample Document for Computerized Extraction Example.

Extraction depends on comparison of each character to the ASCII code to determine if it is a letter—a significant difference for our purposes. When this first level of difference determination is accomplished, letter clusters (words) are then compared to the stop list to ensure that we extract only clusters of sufficiently significant difference. In outline form the flow is:

1. open the text file
2. execute steps 3–10 as long as there are characters in the text file
3. input one character
4. check to see if that character is either a blank or a letter
5. if it is a letter, add it to the string which will become a word
6. if it is a blank space, pick up the word string
7. compare the word string with each word in the stop list

Table 7.1. Flow of Extraction Program

Term	Stop Word?	Frequency	Index
Organization	**False**	**1**	**143**
Character	M	77	156
Character	a	97	157
Character	n	110	158
Character	a	97	159
Character	g	103	160
Character	e	101	161
Character	m	109	162
Character	e	101	163
Character	n	110	164
Character	t	116	165
Token	[10]	10	166
Management	**False**	**2**	**156**
Character	E	69	168
Character	a	97	169
Character	c	99	170
Character	h	104	171
Token	[32]	32	172
Each	**True**	**1**	**168**
Character	d	100	173
Character	o	111	174
Character	c	99	175
Character	t	116	176
Character	o	111	177
Character	r	114	178
Character	a	97	179
Character	l	108	180
Token	[32]	32	181
doctoral	**False**	**1**	**173**
Character	s	115	182
Character	t	116	183
Character	u	117	184
Character	d	100	185
Character	e	101	186
Character	n	110	187
Character	t	116	188
Token	[32]	32	189
student	**False**	**1**	**182**
Character	w	119	190
Character	i	105	191
Character	l	108	192
Character	l	108	193
Token	[32]	32	194
will	**True**	**1**	**190**
Character	c	99	195
Character	o	111	196
Character	n	110	197
Character	s	115	198
Character	t	116	199
Character	r	114	200
Character	u	117	201
Character	c	99	202
Character	t	116	203
Token	[32]	32	204

(Continued)

Table 7.1. (Continued)

Term	Stop Word?	Frequency	Index
construct	**False**	**1**	**195**
Character	a	97	205
Token	[32]	32	206
a	**True**	**1**	**205**
Character	p	112	207
Character	r	114	208
Character	o	111	209
Character	g	103	210
Character	r	114	211
Character	a	97	212
Character	m	109	213
Token	[32]	32	214
program	**False**	**1**	**207**
Character	o	111	215
Character	f	102	216
Token	[32]	32	217
of	**True**	**2**	**215**
Character	a	97	218
Character	d	100	219
Character	v	118	220
Character	a	97	221
Character	n	110	222
Character	c	99	223
Character	e	101	224
Character	d	100	225
Token	[32]	32	226
advanced	**False**	**1**	**218**
Character	c	99	227
Character	o	111	228
Character	u	117	229
Character	r	114	230
Character	s	115	231
Character	e	101	232
Character	w	119	233
Character	o	111	234
Character	r	114	235
Character	k	107	236
Token	[32]	32	237
course work	**False**	**1**	**227**
Character	a	97	238
Character	n	110	239
Character	d	100	240
Token	[10]	10	241
and	**True**	**2**	**238**
Character	s	115	242
Character	u	117	243
Character	b	98	244
Character	s	115	245
Character	t	116	246
Character	a	97	247
Character	n	110	248
Character	t	116	249
Character	i	105	250
Character	a	97	251
Character	l	108	252
Token	[32]	32	253

(Continued)

Table 7.1. (Continued)

Term	Stop Word?	Frequency	Index
substantial	**False**	**1**	**242**
Character	r	114	254
Character	e	101	255
Character	s	115	256
Character	e	101	257
Character	a	97	258
Character	r	114	259
Character	c	99	260
Character	h	104	261
Token	[32]	32	262
research	**False**	**1**	**254**
Character	o	111	263
Character	n	110	264
Token	[32]	32	265
on	**True**	**1**	**263**
Character	a	97	266
Token	[32]	32	267
a	**True**	**2**	**266**
Character	f	102	268
Character	o	111	269
Character	u	117	270
Character	n	110	271
Character	d	100	272

8. if there is a match, empty the word string and return to input
9. if there is not a match, store the word for later use
10. empty the word string and return to input.

This basic framework could be extended to count the frequency of words to create a text cloud to provide an abstract of sorts for the document, build a concordance of terms in context for the document, record the addresses of each term and alphabetize them to create an index of the document, or produce other novel forms of representation to facilitate interaction between the user and the document. For those interested in pursuing the program further, Appendix A lists the primary pieces of code for the program in C#.

All of these steps yield a list of terms that do not appear on the stop list. A similar set of steps will alphabetize the words and count how many times each one is found in the text. The sort routine could also be set to order terms by frequency of occurrence, though that has not been done for this example. The alphabetic sort of our sample text is presented in Table 7.2. The frequency of each word is given in parentheses following the word.

One striking attribute of this list is its size (105 words), even with a stop list of over 500 terms and a one-page document as the text. Even with the removal of prepositions, many adjectives, and many verb forms, there is a substantial set of significantly different clusters of squiggles. Upon reflection, we might consider adding some of the terms to the stop list. Terms such as "acquire," "associated," and "drawn" would seem to be of little significance.

Table 7.2. Keywords Alphabetized with Frequency of Occurrence

Aesthetics (1)	Cognate (1)	Contexts (1)	Culture (1)
Design (1)	Dynamics (1)	Economics (1)	Engineering (2)
Ethics (1)	Human (1)	Information (5)	Informational (1)
Library (2)	Management (4)	Organization (1)	Organizational (1)
PhD (1)	Policy (1)	Psychology (1)	Sociology (1)
Substantial (1)	Systems (1)	Use (1)	Values (1)
Visualization (1)	abilities (2)	ability (1)	academic (1)
acquire (1)	advanced (2)	analysis (1)	appropriate (1)
aspects (1)	associated (1)	base (1)	candidate (1)
capabilities (1)	challenged (1)	close (1)	community (1)
concepts (1)	congenial (1)	construct (1)	consultation (1)
contribute (2)	contribution (1)	core (1)	course (1)
coursework (2)	creation (1)	curriculum (1)	data (1)
dedicated (1)	defense (1)	degree (1)	develop (1)
developing (1)	devoted (1)	diffusion (1)	discipline (2)
dissertation (1)	doctoral (3)	drawn (1)	enhance (1)
expertise (1)	faculty (2)	field (1)	fields (2)
foster (1)	foundation (1)	graduate (1)	graduate's (1)
implementation (1)	information (1)	instruction (1)	investigate (1)
issues (1)	knowledge (1)	laboratory (1)	level (1)
make (1)	managerial (1)	master's (1)	members (1)
methodologies (1)	new (1)	nurturing (1)	program (2)
public (1)	related (1)	reporting (1)	research (5)
rigorous (1)	selection (1)	seminar (1)	society (1)
society's (1)	strengthen (1)	student (5)	substantial (2)
teaching (1)	theoretical (1)	theory (4)	topics (1)
understanding (1)	utilization (1)	work (1)	writing (1)

More vexing is the separation of terms that would normally be more meaningful if taken together, such as: "Information" + "Management"; "Information" + "Engineering"; "Academic" + "Community"; and "Faculty" + "Member." It would be possible to write subroutines to take care of some of these problem cases. It is also quite realistic to think of the computer serving as the tool to make the first pass, enabling the information professional to make adjustments and enhancements based on a working knowledge of the clientele. Such issues point up the fact that even a machine environment does not make problems disappear. However, it does make certain problems evident and offer possible solutions.

Table 7.3 presents only those terms that appear two or more times. In addition to the frequency of appearance, the table lists the address of the words.

Clearly, this is a much shorter list (seventeen words, or about 16 percent of the whole list) and the terms are what one would expect in a document about a new doctoral program in "information," " management," with a "substantial" focus on "students" and their acquiring a rigorous grounding in "theory" and "research." Filtering out the terms appearing more than two times yields a list that could be a standard set of descriptive terms.

Table 7.3. Extracted Words from Figure 7.3 with Frequencies of At Least Two

Engineering(2)	76, 1014
Library(2)	9, 892
Management(4)	33, 173, 916, 1028
Information(5)	21, 64, 130, 144, 904
abilities(2)	494, 682
advanced(2)	238, 1442
contribute(2)	507, 1652
coursework(2)	247, 1321
discipline(2)	928, 1593
faculty(2)	341, 777
fields(2)	330, 1343
program(2)	227, 726
substantial(2)	264, 1559
doctoral(3)	193, 1418, 1628
theory(4)	48, 304, 855, 1370
research(5)	276, 367, 671, 1225, 1388
student(5)	202, 486, 615, 799, 1427

- Information (5)
- Management (4)
- Doctoral (3)
- Research (5)
- Student (5)
- Theory (4)

Making the other terms available to those with further interest enables deeper levels of representation of the details of the document.

A one-page document is not a realistic test of a system; however, it does present the potential, as well as some of the challenges offered by the digital environment. It should be noted that the extraction of the terms sorting, and counting frequencies likewise takes only a fraction of a second.

The reason for attending to this exercise in machine representation is not simply to compare human and machine indexing. Rather it is to demonstrate the potential utility of representing the structural attributes of the physically present text, the discontinuities in the data stream. The machine environment enables precise attention to detail and the rapid multiple application of simple rules. This yields an ability to present complex constructs.

Precise measurement and manipulation allow the computer to provide contour maps of documents. The rules of representation can be specified and made known, just as are the rules for contour maps. Different users can make different uses of different levels of detail in the maps. The rules can even be modified according to patron needs.

Most importantly, the making of conceptual tags is eliminated or significantly reduced. This results in lifting the responsibility of constructing a conceptual tag from the indexer or abstractor and barriers from the patron.

Depth of Representation

The level of specificity at which documents are represented largely determines the patron's depth of penetration into the document collection, as well as the individual documents. Unless the patron actually obtains each document and determines depth of penetration, the system's representation is the only window available. We have made the case through exercises and models that representing at the level of the document may well leave a wealth of material hidden from users. We have also examined a very simple model of computer representation of a tiny document as a possible approach to returning some control over depth of representation to the patron. Browsing has been posited as a response to some of the difficulties posed by having an external agency set a single level of specificity, among other things. Machine-assisted representation is one approach to imbuing a system's representation of documents with some of the dynamic rules for highlighting found in browsing, such as varying the level of specificity, searching for particular combinations of words, and producing a topographic map of the frequencies of all the words in a document. The possibilities and problems of machine representation bear further consideration. Issues of scale are particularly important.

What happens when we use our simple word extraction program on a text of more typical size? We need a framework for elaborating our considerations of machine-augmented representation. The letter in Figure 7.4 highlights that operation offers one method of evaluation of the computational approach to indexing. The indexer timed a single, close reading for comparison with the time it would require the machine to read through the text and extract terms. In round figures, that comparison is just over three minutes for the computer and a little over an hour for the indexer. It must be noted that current versions of word frequency programs run considerably faster, ordinarily in small fractions of a second. It should also be noted that some reviews of *Explorations in Indexing and Abstracting* took exception to details of this process, such as asserting that applying a small number of keywords was not the same as making a back-of-the-book index. We respond that all these representational practices are intended to provide access by pointing to a document or portions of a document.

Similarly, there were several reviews claiming that the first edition argued for doing away with human indexing and replacing it with machine-based indexing. We respond to that in two ways. The earlier book did not advocate eliminating humans from the loop; rather it used the simple extraction program as a way to demonstrate the indexing process and to suggest that it could be a very useful tool in a time when there are so many documents and so few people to index them by hand. Also, we would like to point out that the programs for accomplishing machine-based indexing (and the more complex representations such as cosine similarity measures and ranking by number of links) are actually

I have read the article only once, although I am familiar with some of the related readings you cited. I did not use any particular thesaurus of terms [for this stage]. . . . It took me a little more than one hour to read the article, but I was reading closely, rather than skimming. . . .

Index Terms Selected (Note - these are in no particular order . . . I could weight them if you think that would be helpful. Those which I consider to be most important are asterisked.)

- * Browsing
- Topical description
- * Document representation
- * Document retrieval
- Indexing
- * Search process
- Access methods
- Computer-assisted searching
- Anomalous state of knowledge

One topic [for which] I couldn't come up with an appropriate term … is:

"incongruence between searcher's terms and document representations in the bibliographical system"

I also debated … whether the types and stages of browsing should be included. (expansion, vague awareness, monitoring, knowledge creation make glimpses, connect attributes, evaluate connections; evaluate search) . . . . It seems that these headings and stages could also be transmuted into index terms which may be useful to someone. However, the terms by themselves are so ambiguous that I wonder whether they would only contribute to false hits rather than add anything meaningful to the document representation.

Figure 7.4. Letter from Indexer about Article on Which Our Browsing Discussion Is Based.

written by humans. Additionally, the programs are subject to review and to tweaking.

At the end of the computer's run all the words not on the stop list had been extracted. At the end of the indexer's reading, the final decisions of what to highlight had yet to be made. It did take the computer another half-minute to sort all the extracted terms into alphabetical order and tabulate frequencies of occurrence for each term.

It is critical to note the phrase "I finally decided upon." The rules for extraction, generally, are not explicit in the process of most human indexing. There is, in saying this, no value judgment of the quality of the representation made by the indexer. It is simply important to note that it may be difficult or impossible for a human indexer to specify the exact mechanism for highlighting. It may well be that a personal knowledge of the types of users of the system will enable very good representations. However, we are left without any method of addressing issues of consistency across time and across settings.

We must be careful to remember that inter-indexer consistency is not necessarily a desirable system characteristic. Indexing that is consistent but not useful to patrons does not constitute a good representation system. Also, it is possible to imagine a situation in which one of several indexers is consistently different from all the others, but in so being, is consistently representing documents in a manner hospitable to a particular type of user.

When we speak here of consistency, as offered by a computer environment, we are speaking of a system whose rules of extraction are known (or can be made known) to the patron and whose approach to extraction will be consistent. The approach to extraction may well be (ought to be) tunable to each use. A representation of a document could be based on the information needs and the decoding abilities of the patron, as we have suggested. This would likely mean that there would be significant inconsistency in the system across uses by different patrons or even the same patron at different times. However, there would be consistency in presenting to each patron the palette of attributes most appropriate to that patron.

A good reference librarian or on-line search intermediary will often take the time to elicit the bounds of the question state and the decoding capabilities of the patron. It is even likely that a selection of potentially useful works will be presented to the patron for evaluation. This form of representation of documents approaches the customized constructions implied by the definitions of representation that we have used.

Two difficulties arise, however. There is the possibility that external constraints will mean a different level of service for different patrons. Different reference librarians or searchers may have more or less skill in eliciting representation requirements and in translating those into effective searches. Even the same intermediary at different times may well perform differently (Cooper, 1969). Also, so long as representation tools are constructed before they are used, the human librarian or search intermediary is constrained to use those a priori representations or to operate on personal knowledge of documents. While they may have a better working knowledge of the subtleties of representation practices than a patron, they are still operating at whatever level of penetration and with whatever tagging of concepts have been provided by somebody else.

Of course, talented humans will be capable of making rich and subtle representations tailored to individuals. However, it may be that much of that effort could be accomplished with greater facility by incorporation of machine augmentation of the extracting and sorting processes. Rapid accomplishment of almost unimaginably large numbers of small steps is the forte of the machine system. Humans involved in representation are likely to be constrained by time. Thus, general level representation often results not from a lack of ability or because of theoretical necessity, but from too little time to carry out the number of iterations of steps necessary for greater depth.

The list of terms provided by the indexer of the browsing article (see Figure 7.1) is nine items long. There were no suggestions made to the indexer about depth or breadth. On the list provided, we note that the items marked with asterisks are full document descriptors. Those not so marked are at levels of generality above and below that of the whole document. The terms "indexing" and "access methods" include much more than is covered in the article or Chapter Six. Belkin's term "anomalous state of knowledge" is important, but it is, clearly, only one way of describing the psychological state that might stimulate browsing activity. The other two terms, "topical description" and "computer-assisted searching" are similarly specific.

The "incongruence between a searcher's terms and document representations in the bibliographic system" is central to the article/chapter that was indexed. This is the primary reason for browsing and it is the framework for constructing alternative models of the search process. The difficulty expressed in the indexer's note reflects the difficulty in tagging concepts. Identifying the concept has been accomplished, but coding it in a manner that is both expressive and manipulable has proved to be difficult. Using "incongruity" by itself leaves open the possibility of many "false drops"—users coming to the document on the promise of the representation, only to be disappointed that the concept is not used in an expected or useful manner. Making evident the relationship between the user and the bibliographic system brings one back to the long expression. The indexer notes with insight that the same situation holds for the terms describing types and stages of browsing activity.

Again, we must point out that this is good indexing in the traditional sense. The representations are sufficient to many uses. The indexer did not attempt to do a mediocre representation, nor should we find any fault with the effort. Yet the indexer's own insights and frustrations with system inadequacies are evident in the notes accompanying the list of terms. This frustration reflects the lack of subtlety available to indexers in the attempt to provide powerful tools to patrons.

MACHINE REPRESENTATION RESULTS

The extraction and sorting program used in this chapter is based on the program fragments presented earlier. It is a very simple program and does not incorporate many of the sophisticated methods of textual analysis that have been developed over the last several years. It is, however, instructive in both its speed of operation and the results it produces.

These results point to the promise of machine augmentation of representation, while also pointing to some of the problems that have had to be resolved in order for computers to construct useful tools. Table 7.1 is a printout of the extracted terms in the order of their extraction. Table 7.2 is a listing of the words after they have been alphabetized and counted. It should be noted that Table 7.2 contains words that are truncated for memory management purposes. It also contains some typographic errors made by the author in the original text, such as "bserved" instead of "observed" filed in with other "b" words.

The most immediately striking difference between the indexer's list of terms and the computer's list of terms is sheer size. If we count only those terms on the indexer's primary list, there are nine; on the computer's list, 2,657. The indexer's list is less just over three-tenths of 1 percent of the size of the machine's list, even though there is a stop list of over five hundred words, which are excluded from consideration.

In and of itself this difference in size does not necessarily mean that the computer generated list is better. In fact, the indexer's comment about "false hits" and manageability are severely magnified. The first step we want to take in considering the machine results is to examine the entries closely. The first pass of the text through the program made use of the existing stop list. Yet, there is nothing magical about the stop list in place. It was developed from looking at words commonly found in stop lists and adding others as various texts were run through it. The current text is likely to point out necessary additions.

A close look at this first pass is instructive. As we noted earlier, words beginning with upper case letters are alphabetized as a group, followed by all words beginning with lower case letters. This has immediate impact of two sorts. Any words that occur in both the upper and lower case groups are not here grouped together. If this were to be deemed important (and it likely would be in most systems), we would want to remove case sensitivity from the counting routine. Also, any words that are on the stop list in a lower case form will not stop an upper case form of that word from showing up on the extraction list. Thus, "for" might be on the stop list, but "For" would be extracted because the ASCII numeric representation of "F"(70) is different from that of "f" (102).

Having said these things about the list of extracted and sorted words, let us go through the list to find words that should be put onto the stop list because they are of little value to our current text, and likely to other texts. The stop list is available for examination by users, so that any word on the list could be removed for particular searches. We went through the entire list and made these changes. Candidate terms for inclusion on the stop list are:

- Nouns and adjectival or noun forms of verbs that are too general to offer discrimination capabilities to a patron include: Achieving, Activity,

Adding, Figure, Using, act, affiliation, containing, getting, giving, holding, implying, importance, initiating, intent, leading, leanings, license, looking, making, nothing, parts, possibility, proposition, putting, ranging, removing, requirement, standing, start, starting, stepping, striking, taking, task, tending, throwing, troubling, varying, way, ways.

- Proper names offer an interesting challenge. For many patrons they will simply add to the clutter; yet, for others, the presence of a familiar name can be an important clue to the contents and, perhaps, the line of thinking behind the contents. Since the names on our list appear only infrequently, we might want to leave them in and consider means to make them evident when necessary.
- There are more than sixty articles, particles, prepositions (except "of"—see Meadow, 1988), adverbs, and general adjectives that were, for some reason, not on the original stop list: Any, Clearly, Different, Earlier, First, Fine, Herein, However, Just, NOT ("Not" and "not" are on the stop list, but this emphatic spelling had not been anticipated), Short, Similarly, Single, Subsequent, Therefore, Three, above, active, adequate, aside, available, awry, best, beyond, chosen, clearly, closely, common, concisely, considerable, countless, current, either, entire, entirely, equally, exactly, extremely, fairly, fill, four, frequent, fruitful, full, fully, further, general, half, hard, high, immediately, important, incidentally, individual, indiviual (typographic errors are just character strings to the machine), interesting, less, likewise, long, maybe, mostly, nearby, normally, precisely, properly, subsequent, tantamount, why.

In general, verbs and adverbs are excluded from the stop list because they are not directly linked to concepts. Some verbs, such as "catalyze," "create," and "describe," which are in fact directly linked to concepts are left on our list. In addition to the general classes of terms listed above, which could be included on the stop list for the next run through the program, there are some interesting special cases.

- "Catalyzing" appears only once, but is tied to an important concept;
- "Congress" is actually a part of the phrase "Library of Congress." Thus, we would want to build a subroutine to keep the elements of proper names together;
- "Idols" is part of a title "Idols of Perversity." It too should be kept with its kin;
- "Serendipity" appears only once, but is often used as a synonym for "browsing." Thus, we would want to make it evident, despite its low frequency. Also, we might want to consider whether it should be counted together with "browsing" when determining frequencies;

- "abilities" and "ability" comprise the first of several clusters in our list which are made up of words with the same stem. We would want to consider clustering these terms;
- "century" presents the same sort of problem as the compound proper names and the titles above, yet with an added difficulty. There are no clues such as "several words each beginning with upper case letters" or "upper case letters not at the beginning of a sentence." With "century," we would have to know beforehand that it sometimes occurs together with a number to denote a particular century, in this case the "nineteenth" (a term that appears later in the list);
- "dumb" (from the phrase "dumb luck") is similar to "century," except that there is the rule "since an adjective is generally connected to a noun, scan for a nearby noun";
- "everything" presents the possibility of a very interesting index entry. This would be a term at a very high level of generality!
- "gullibility" is another word standing for a concept fundamental to browsing, yet since it appears only once in the list, it runs the risk of being excluded from searches by all but the most motivated of patrons;
- "library" and "librarian" appear fewer times than might be expected in an article on browsing. This is because the setting for browsing is generalized to any collection of documents and the subsequent use of more general terms such as "bibliographic agency";
- "queries" and "questions" happen to fall together within this list, so they can be seen as synonyms and counted together. What, then, are we to do about those synonymous words that are in the list, but are not immediately self-evident. Should there be a thesaurus to link the terms? Should the linked terms appear together or have "see also" notes? What if one term is really a subset of another, rather than a synonym at the same level of specificity?
- "stream" appears five times, a relatively high frequency. Yet it is used only metaphorically for a three-dimensional and time-varying model in the source document. Would a patron looking for material on bodies of water be happy to find this document?

Depth Gauge

Having discussed the list and the shortcomings that we might want to address, we should now look at the possibilities presented by the frequency counts that the program tabulated during the sorting routine. The frequencies give us a means of setting the depth of penetration into the collection. If we wished, we could say that only terms that appear with a particular frequency or greater will be used as descriptors. However, we have seen earlier, in our

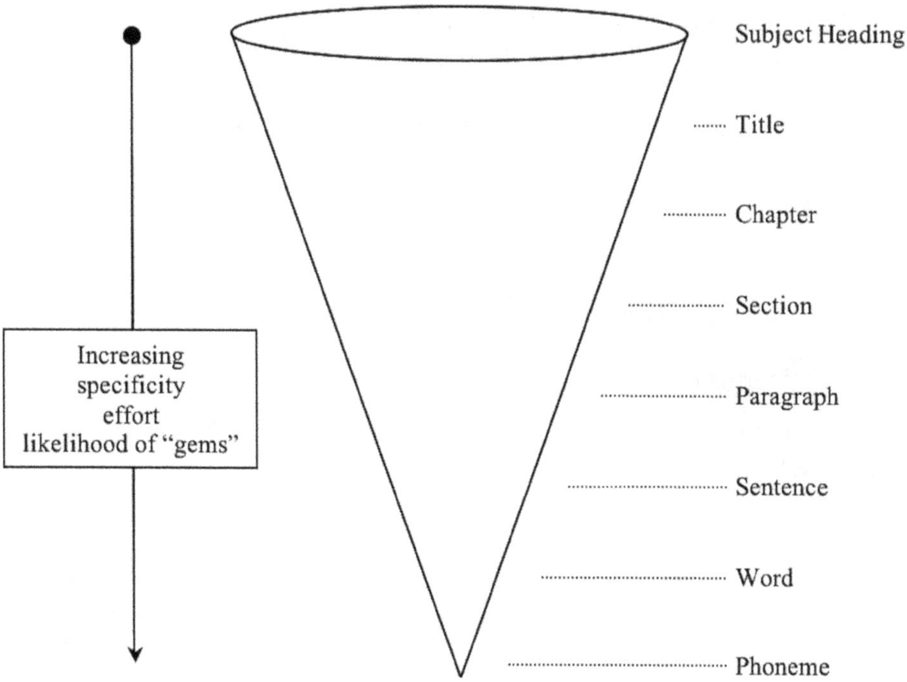

Figure 7.5. Document Depth Gauge.

discussion of optimal depth that there is no way for a system to set a depth that will be satisfactory to all different users. Instead, we can make available all of the extracted terms, with the frequencies used as a depth gauge, as in Figure 7.5.

Setting the depth gauge at different levels yields compelling results. We see at the highest level of generality, a set of terms very much like what we would expect of a human indexer with a system constraint to apply a handful of terms at the level of the document. As we set the depth gauge at lower thresholds, we see elements from deeper within the document begin to appear.

In our list of terms extracted from the source document the most frequent terms occur forty-three, forty-seven, and forty-nine times. If we were to cluster terms beginning with both upper and lower case versions of the same letter, or if we were to cluster "search" and "searcher" we would get figures somewhat higher. If we take forty as our fist depth reading, we are saying, "show us only the terms which appeared very frequently, and, therefore, ought to be associated in some strong way with the major concepts of the document." High frequency is indicative of broad concepts rather than details. The output presented in Figure 7.6 is the subset of terms derived by setting the depth at its most shallow level of penetration.

Begin sort of 2657 terms at: 01:22:13
End sort of 2657 terms at: 01:22:39

Alphabetical sort of file "brzchp" showing words appearing > 40

attributes	(49)
document	(47)
search	(43)

Total terms in list 3

Figure 7.6. Output of Sort and Tabulate Routine with Depth Set at "Shallow."

The article and chapter are about browsing as a search method, which optimizes connection of user attributes and document attributes. So Figure 7.6 presents a fair representation. The only elements conspicuously absent are "browsing" and "user." If we combine the upper and lower case forms of "browsing", as in Figure 7.7, then the total number of appearances of the word is more than forty and it would appear on this list. Similarly, if we were to combine the totals for "search" and "searcher" and put both words on the list, we would bring a synonym for "user" into the broad output.

Alternatively, we could set the depth gauge to its next level and pick up "searcher"(38), as well as "collection"(36) and the plural form "documents"(38). In the shallow range there are so few terms that we increment the depth, the threshold, in steps of five. In fact, there is no change in list membership when

Begin sort of 2657 terms at: 01:22:13
End sort of 2657 terms at: 01:22:39

Alphabetical sort of file "brzchp" showing words appearing > 40

attribute[s]	(71)
[B]browsing	(42)
document[s]	(85)
search	(43)

Total terms in list 4

Figure 7.7. Output As in 7.6, But Two Forms of "Browsing" Combined, Yielding a Total Large Enough for Inclusion at This Level.

we move from a threshold of 35 to a setting of 30. Both lists have the same six terms.

As we move the depth indicator to 25, we pick up the lower case "browsing." We are still at a relatively shallow depth, so that even without combining forms of the word it would show up as a descriptor in many searches. Moving down to what might be termed the bottom of the shallow zone, we begin to see changes.

By setting the depth at 20, we pick up another four terms: the singular "attribute"(22), "knowledge"(21), "representation"(24), and "scholar"(25). Note that "scholar" appears only on this list rather than the "greater than 25" list because our threshold statement is "any word occurring more than the threshold number," which in this case is 20.

Setting the level at 15, as in Figure 7.8, brings us to a point where the nature of the list begins to change. The total number of items on the list is now more than four times the size of the first list with its depth of 40. We begin to see more subordinate concepts, such as "connection," "set," "sampling." We also begin to see adjectives, such as "new," and "useful." Since these appear with some considerable frequency, a patron might find them useful.

As we increment the depth indicator from level 15 to level 1 in increments of 1, we pick up more and more subordinate concepts and adjectives. The total

```
Begin sort of  2657 terms at: 01:22:13
End sort of    2657 terms at: 01:22:39

Alphabetical sort of file "brzchp" showing words appearing > 15

               attribute      (22)
               attributes     (49)
               [B]browsing    (42)
               collection     (36)
               connection     (20)
               document       (47)
               documents      (38)
               knowledge      (21)
               new            (18)
               representation (24)
               sampling       (16)
               scholar        (25)
               search         (43)
               searcher       (38)
               set            (17)
               useful         (20)

Total terms in list            17
```

Figure 7.8. Nature of Output List Begins to Change.

number of terms on the list increases, of course; slowly at first, but increasing as we approach level 1. At a level of 10, there are 25 terms; at level 7, 46 terms; at level 5, 71 terms; at level 3, 134 terms; and at level 2, 237 terms. Even with the great increase, though, we see that there is a very significant difference between the open list (depth 1), which had 2,657 terms, and depth 2 with less than one-tenth that number.

Such a demonstration suggests that the simple method of counting word frequencies can represent a document in the typical manner of a few terms at the most general level, as well as a manner in which the user can choose the amount of detail (and the consequent amount of effort), which seems appropriate for any particular use. The numbers provide the patron with a contour map of the document terrain; the use and determination of meaning are left to the user.

Frequency figures for each term serve as depth indicators in two ways. If a patron chooses to see all terms extracted from a document, then the number of appearances can give an indication of the breadth of the term. If the number is large, the word is used significantly in the document; if it is small, the term probably represents a detail or a subordinate concept. We must be careful to point out that the correlation is not always exact. The user and the system must account for:

- synonyms
- variant forms of the same word stem
- the possibility of an infrequent word still referring to a significant concept
- user looking for concepts not necessarily intended by the author.

The patron can also determine the level of observation and just examine the descriptor lists at that level. If all works in which a term appears are desired, the threshold will be set very shallow, to cast the broadest net. If works that discuss a concept in some depth are desired, then the threshold will be set with a higher number. This means the term appears frequently and is likely to represent a significant aspect of the text.

Tag Cloud As Term Frequency Display

The very same frequency data described above can be used to generate a tag cloud, a form of display that has found considerable popularity recently. Here we simply associate the word frequency with font size. So we might say any word that occurs two to four times print at 10 point; any word that occurs five to seven times print at 12 point; twenty times print at 50 point, and so on.

Of course, there are systems with much more sophisticated analysis capabilities. It is now possible to take a document that a patron likes, analyze the word frequencies and statistical structure of the document, and then have the computer search all documents in the collection for similar profiles. If the seed document was of use to the patron, then similar documents (presented in a list of ranked degrees of similarity) should also be of use to the patron.

Figure 7.9. Tag Cloud of Terms in Browsing Article.

Statistical analyses can also lead to concept clusters, rather than just single terms or groups of synonyms. Yet, even the systems with considerably more sophistication than our small example are based on the machine extraction of characters and addresses and frequencies.

Even our small example was able to extract well over two thousand terms in a matter of minutes and then sort the terms and tabulate frequencies in thirteen seconds. Even if the system were to be used only by the human indexer, and not directly by the patron, the speed, algorithmic consistency, and the possible insights about elements at varying depths, make the machine a powerful tool for representation.

APPENDIX A

a
about
above
across
after
afterwards
again
against
all
almost
alone
along
already
also
although
always
am
among
amongst
amoungst
amount
an
and
another
any
anyhow
anyone
anything
anyway
anywhere
are
around
as
at
back
be
became
because
become
becomes
becoming
been
before
beforehand
behind
being
below
beside
besides
between
beyond
bill
both
bottom
but
by
call
can
cannot
cant
co
computer
con
could
couldnt
cry
de
describe
detail
do
done
down
due
during
each
eg
eight
either
eleven
else
elsewhere
empty
enough
etc
even
ever
every
everyone
everything
everywhere
except
few
fifteen
fify
fill
find
fire
first
five
for
former
formerly
forty
found
four
from
front
full
further
get
give
go
had
has
hasnt
have
he
hence
her
here

hereafter
hereby
herein
hereupon
hers
herself
him
himself
his
how
however
hundred
i
ie
if
in
inc
indeed
interest
into
is
it
its
itself
keep
last
latter
latterly
least
less
ltd
made
many
may
me
meanwhile
might
mill
mine
more
moreover
most
mostly
move
much
must
my
myself
name
namely
neither
never
nevertheless
next
nine
no
nobody
none
noone
nor
not
nothing
now
nowhere
of
off
often
on
once
one
only
onto
or
other
others
otherwise
our
ours
ourselves
out
over
own
part
per
perhaps
please
put
rather
re
same
see
seem
seemed
seeming
seems
serious
several
she
should
show
side
since
sincere
six
sixty
so
some
somehow
someone
something
sometime
sometimes
somewhere
still
such
system
take
ten
than
that
the
their
them
themselves
then
thence
there
thereafter
thereby
therefore
therein
thereupon
these
they
thick
thin
third
this
those
though
three
through
throughout
thru
thus
to
together
too
top
toward
towards
twelve
twenty
two
un
under
until
up
upon
us
very
via
was
we
well
were
what
whatever

when
whence
whenever
where
whereafter
whereas
whereby
wherein
whereupon
wherever
whether
which
while
whither
who
whoever
whole
whom
whose
why
will
with
within
without
would
yet
you
your
yours
yourself
yourselves

APPENDIX B

```
using System;
using System.Collections.Generic;
using System.Text;
using System.IO;

namespace WordExtractor
{
    class Program
    {
        static void Main(string[] args)
        {
            string text;

            StringBuilder s = new StringBuilder();
            int address = 0;
            int position = 0;
            bool resetAddress = true;

            List<string> stopWords = new List<string>();
            StreamReader stopWordsReader = new StreamReader("C:/Projects/WordExtractor/stopwords.txt");
            string line;

            while((line = stopWordsReader.ReadLine()) != null)
            {
                stopWords.Add(line.ToLower());
            }

            foreach (string word in stopWords)
            {
                Console.WriteLine(word);
            }

            stopWordsReader.Close();

            SortedDictionary<string,int> frequencies = new SortedDictionary<string, int> ();

            StreamReader sr = new StreamReader("C:/Projects/WordExtractor/sample.txt");
            StreamWriter sw = new StreamWriter("C:/Projects/WordExtractor/output.txt");

            text = sr.ReadToEnd();
            text += " ";

            sw.WriteLine("<table border=1>");
            sw.WriteLine("<tr align=\"center\"><td><b>State</b><td><b>Character</b></td><td><b>ASCII</b></td><td><b>Index</b></td></tr>");

            foreach (char c in text)
            {
                position++;

                if (char.IsLetterOrDigit(c))
                {
                    sw.WriteLine("<tr align=\"center\"><td>{0}</td><td>{1}</td><td>{2}</td><td>{3}</td></tr>", "Character", c, (int)c, position);

                    s.Append(c);
                    if (resetAddress)
                    {
                        address = position;
                    }
                    resetAddress = false;
                }
```

```

                if (char.IsPunctuation(c))
                {
                    sw.WriteLine("<tr align=\"center\"><td>{0}</td><td>{1}</td><td>{2}</td><td>{3}</td></tr>", "Punctuation", c, (int)c, position);
                }

                if (char.IsWhiteSpace(c))
                {
                    if (s.Length > 0)
                    {
                        sw.WriteLine("<tr align=\"center\"><td>{0}</td><td>[{1}]</td><td>{2}</td><td>{3}</td></tr>", "Token", (int)c, (int)c, position);

                        string key = s.ToString().ToLower();
                        bool isStopWord = stopWords.Contains(key);

                        if (! frequencies.ContainsKey(key))
                        {
                            frequencies.Add(key, 1);
                        }
                        else
                        {
                            frequencies[key]++;
                        }

                        sw.WriteLine("<tr align=\"center\"><td><b>Term</b></td><td><b>Stop Word?</b></td><td><b>Frequency</b></td><td><b>Index</b></td></tr>");
                        sw.WriteLine("<tr align=\"center\"><td><b>{0}</b></td><td><b>{1}</b></td><td><b>{2}</b></td><td><b>{3}</b></td></tr>", s, isStopWord, frequencies[key], address);
                    }
                    s.Length = 0;
                    resetAddress = true;
                }
            }

            sw.WriteLine("</table>");
            sw.Close();
            sr.Close();

            StreamWriter freqTable = new StreamWriter("C:/Projects/WordExtractor/frequencies.txt");

            foreach (string key in frequencies.Keys)
            {
                if(! stopWords.Contains(key))
                {
                    freqTable.WriteLine("{0} ({1})", key, frequencies[key]);
                    Console.WriteLine("{0} ({1})", key, frequencies[key]);
                }
            }

            freqTable.Close();

        }
    }
}
```

CHAPTER EIGHT

FUNCTIONAL APPLICATIONS OF INFORMATION MEASUREMENT

THOUGHTS ON MEASUREMENT OF INFORMATION

THESE EXAMPLES of measurement of information take the same process used in the keyword extraction program and apply them to other sorts of documents. Recall that in the keyword program we used numeric descriptions of the elements of word-based documents and looked for particular sorts of changes, such as blank spaces, punctuation marks, and comparison with stop list words. There were lots of numbers, but the computer was able to manipulate them rapidly. In describing video and PowerPoint documents, we again turn to large amounts of numeric descriptions. Again, a computer is quite capable of operating on these numbers to find useful discontinuities.

It is not immediately obvious or even sensible to think that information is a measurement of uncertainty and that contrary to common usage of the term more information is more uncertainty. Before we speak of our examples of representing different sorts of messages, we should step back and think about measuring information in terms of measuring uncertainty. Let us do a thought experiment measurement of uncertainty in a collection of photographs.

Here we have photograph of a monarch butterfly caterpillar (Figure 8.1). The original shows a green plant, red aphids, and a caterpillar with bands of yellow, black, and white. The realities of the publication process for academic books mean we must content ourselves with a monochrome rendition of the original photograph. If we are to measure, one of the first things we must do is select a unit of measurement. Fortunately, digital images are constructed from small measurable components that will serve our purposes—pixels. These small units (picture elements = pixels) are the cells of a grid, with each cell carrying data for brightness and how much red, green, and blue are mixed at each point to render the particular color at that point. In the original caterpillar photograph there are 697,344 pixels; these are distributed in a grid of 1,024 × 681 pixels. The next photograph is an enlargement of the caterpillar showing the individual pixels (Figure 8.2).

Figure 8.1. Photograph of a Caterpillar.

If we imagine the grid as a set of columns and rows then we can address each cell. The upper left-hand cell would be row one, column one (1,1); the next cell in the top row would be row one, column two (1,2); the first cell in the second row would be (2,1); the 127th cell in 585th row would be (585, 127). So, we have addressable uniform units of measure. Let us now apply this grid notion to a photograph of the blue sky (Figure 8.3).

This photograph of a cloudless sky on a summer afternoon in Texas presents a nearly uniform field of data. If we were to apply our grid to this image and measure what values are at location (1,1) we would have the numeric value for sky blue. If we were then to make our measurement at (1,2) we

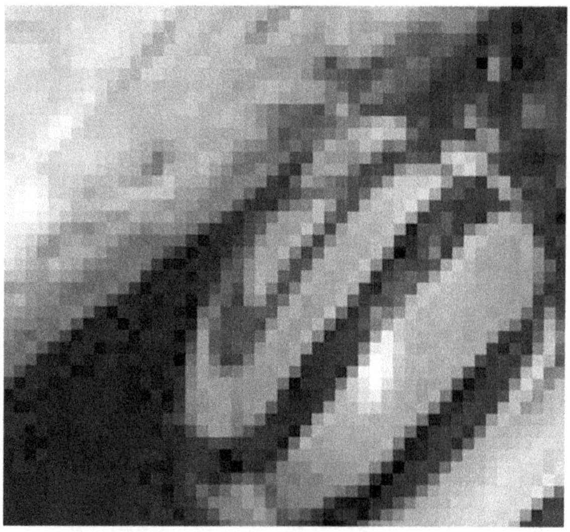

Figure 8.2. Closeup of Pixels Making Up Caterpillar Image.

Figure 8.3. Photograph of the Blue Sky.

would have the same numeric value for sky blue. If we were then to ask what value might be at the next cell (1,3), we would not be foolish to guess that the same value would be there. For each subsequent cell in which we found the same value, the more certain (or less uncertain) we would be about the value in the next cell. In this photograph of the blue sky with essentially no variation there is very little uncertainty from pixel to pixel. The uniformity (perhaps even boredom) bespeaks the lack of uncertainty, the small amount of information. That is, the message is the whole picture, so the amount of data remains the same across all the pictures in our example; but the amount of uncertainty varies. In the picture of the sky the uncertainty is low, so the information is low.

Of course, the small amount of information does not necessarily mean a small amount of meaning. Nor does the particular message even dictate a particular meaning. To a sailor, a photograph of the blue sky might mean: "Finally, we can set sail." Yet to a farmer in the midst of a drought it might mean: "One more day of desperation."

What if we now apply our grid to a photograph of bamboo? It may help to know that the original shows stalks in green, some leaves in green, some leaves in yellow, and some in brown (Figure 8.4).

Figure 8.4. Bamboo.

Figure 8.5. Boys in a Tree.

If we go through our cell-by-cell measurement again, we will see that we have a quite a few cells with green, then a few in yellow, then a lot in green, then a few in brown. After a while we would know that the predominant color is green. Thus we could make a reasonable guess that any next cell would be green; however, unlike the blue sky photograph, we would not be so certain. Now, it is also the case that if the next cell was not green, we would be fairly safe in saying it will be yellow or brown. So, we do not have as much certainty, but we are not faced with chaos. We have less certainty and, thus, more information. There is more variety to be seen in the bamboo photograph than there was in the blue sky photograph.

What if we turn to a family snapshot of two little boys in a tree? (see Figure 8.5).

Even without knowing the colors of the shirts and rubber boots and leaves, we can see that there is more here. If we apply our grid thought exercise here, we can see that there will be more uncertainty. Because branches appear in front of pants and the background is sky here, fence there, and fallen leaves across the bottom, there is little predictability from cell to cell. There is less certainty in predicting the color value of the next cell. There is less certainty in this photograph than there was in either the bamboo or the sky photo. In that technical sense, there is more information. This goes along with what we see in the photographs: uniformity in the blue sky, small number of repeating patterns in the bamboo, and very little uniformity or repetition in the photograph of the boys.

It is in this sense of the predictability of the data stream that we speak of uncertainty as information. The examples we present here take advantage of our ability within the digital environment to make fine-grained and rapid measurements of the message signal.

INFORMATION ANATOMY AND PHYSIOLOGY

Measurement of document structures, or of "native elements" (O'Connor & Wyatt, 2004) of documents, is meaningful only to the degree of functionality of the measurements. Representing the structures that support the most traditional—or superficial—aboutnesses of documents can only increase representation robustness. Traditionally, one might use author, title, media, number of pages, keywords, and so on to represent an item. The addition of measurements of inherent attributes adds a new depth to representation, such that the possible user of the document might more completely find meaning at the representational level. This process for understanding documents is not a new one, nor is it specific to information science. Long before we began measuring structure and function of information, scientists exercised the process: first we observe anatomy (structure), and then we determine physiology (function). There is a mere baby-step from information science to biology in this regard, especially when one recognizes the document as organism (Anderson, 2006), which is to say, a "whole with interdependent parts" (Simpson & Weiner, 1989).

A Shannon Revival

Through the 1970s, some researchers in the field of communications accomplished a series of studies showing measurements of form attributes of television programming for the purpose of being able to say something about impacts of TV show structures of various shows on television-viewing audiences (see Watt, 1979; Watt & Krull, 1974). Their measurements were derived from Claude Shannon's original formula for measuring syntactical predictability in communicated messages via telephony. Watt and Krull were among the first to revive this representative equation and apply it to additional communication media.

A study of two documentary films with similar content but with very different structures (O'Connor, 1991) brought Shannon's ideas of the "binary relationship" (Anderson, 2006) of communication documents to light, suggesting possibilities for functional uses for studying filmic structures and other media. This study demonstrates that two films that might be traditionally indexed with the same keywords for representing content (marathon, film, running) are actually very different structurally, and that these structural differences can be perceived by viewers who describe one film as "dynamic," "exciting," and "engaging," and the other film as "dull," "boring," and "snoozer." Viewer reactions to film structures should well serve to also represent films (Anderson, O'Connor, & Kearns, 2007).

Three of our consequential studies provide more detailed accounts of functional applications of the measurement of information. When you read these studies, you will notice that they contain a lot of numbers. These numbers are the results of information measurement, that is, using Shannon's equation to quantify information. Once the formula is set, the calculations are effortless with the entry of the sorted variables associated with each specific entropy measurement.

DANCING WITH ENTROPY: FORM ATTRIBUTES, CHILDREN, AND REPRESENTATION

(The work in this section was first published in a different form in the *Journal of Documentation* [2004], by Kearns & O'Connor.)

There were two major representation issues addressed in the generation of this study: representations for children are generally insufficient and rarely, if ever, reflect children's own perceptions and opinions of the documents and library records, indexes, and other surrogates almost never include considerations for noncontextual information.

The title "Dancing with Entropy" suggests that "appropriate and functional representation depends on knowledgeable partners." Marr (1982) asserts representation is a system for highlighting certain characteristics of an entity together with an explanation of the code for doing this. The user of the representation has to know the code. Thus, designing representation of children's materials ought to speak to the elements that are important to children in ways that make sense to them (or those who might make selections on their behalf). Creating surrogates is like dancing with entropy: the creator assumes to know something about the user and the user about the creator. Without the assumed knowledge of the other, information retrieval cannot be a channel of communication (Blair, 1990; Kearns & O'Connor, 2004, 146).

This work helps enable the dance by comparing children's perceptions of Video document structures (perceived entropy measurements, PEM) with calculated structural measurements of the same video documents (calculated entropy measurements, CEM).

Groups of children were shown one of two sets of video documents. Each set consisted of two videos that were represented by TVGuide.com with the same categorical keywords, though one video was listed specifically for child audiences. Video 1a (Wild Discovery's "Creatures of the Magic Water") and video 1b (Zoboomafoo's "Hail to Tails") are both described by TVguide.com as providing information about unusual animals. Video 1a is categorized as a documentary (assumed for an adult audience) and video 1b is categorized as an educational children's program. Video 2a ("Best of the Joy of Painting") and Video 2b ("Out of the Box") both present information about arts and crafts. Video 2a is categorized as arts and literature (assumed for an adult audience) and Video 2b is categorized as an educational children's program.

The form attributes, or structures, of each video were measured with Shannon's information theory formula in the style of Watt (1979) and Watt and Krull (1974) in the following permutations of Shannon's original formula.

Once these formulae were applied to the structural attributes of the four Video documents in the test set, the following calculated entropy measurements resulted (see Table 8.2).

After viewing both videos in one set, each of the 10 girls was asked a series of questions to evoke her perceptions of the structure of the videos, apart from the content, with an instrument for measuring comparative judgments with line graphs for responses to questions. The questions asked for each line graph include adjectival representations of entropy sifted from existing literature, including Weaver (1949) who used "confusing" (p. 117); Augst and O'Connor (1999) who used "dull" (p. 357) and "dynamic" (p. 355); Watt (1979) who used "exciting" (p. 56), "interest," and "boring" (p. 68); and Campbell (1982) who used "dull" and "exciting" (p. 67). Specifically, they were asked, "Would you want to see the 1st video again?" "Would you want to see the 2nd video again?"; "How exciting was the 1st video?" "How exciting was the 2nd video?"; "How much do you like the 1st video?" "How much do you like the 2nd video?"; "How funny was the 1st video?" "How funny was the 2nd video?"; "How boring was the 1st video?" "How boring was the 2nd video?"; and "How surprising was the 1st video?" "How surprising was the 2nd video?" In response to each question, the child placed his/her sticker on the number line, and that location was later translated into a corresponding number between 0 and 1, such that it might be compared on the same scale to the calculated entropy measurements. This method was used to quantify viewers' perceptions. The results are called perceived entropy measurements.

Table 8.1. Video Form Attributes

Set Time Entropy (HST, where H is Entropy)	The degree of randomness of the time of visual duration of discrete physical locations in a program	$-\sum_{i=1}^{k} \frac{t_{set\,i}}{t_{show}} * \log_2 \frac{t_{set\,i}}{t_{show}}$	Where $t_{set\,i}$ = total time the *i*th set appears t_{show} = total time of the show k = number of sets
Set Incidence Entropy (HSI)	The degree of randomness of the appearance of discrete physical locations in a program	$-\sum_{i=1}^{k} \frac{n_{set\,i}}{n_{set\,show}} * \log_2 \frac{n_{set\,i}}{n_{set\,show}}$	Where $n_{set\,i}$ = number of times the *i*th set appears $n_{set\,show}$ = number of times all sets appear in the show k = number of sets
Verbal Time Entropy (HVT)	The degree of randomness of the time of audible behavior on the part of characters in a program	$-\sum_{i=1}^{k} \frac{t_{char\,i}}{t_{verbal}} * \log_2 \frac{t_{char\,i}}{t_{verbal}}$	Where $t_{char\,i}$ = total time the *i*th character produces sound t_{verbal} = total verbal time k = number of characters
Verbal Incidence Entropy (HVI)	the degree of randomness of the performance of audible behavior on the part of characters in a program	$-\sum_{i=1}^{k} \frac{t_{char\,i}}{t_{char\,show}} * \log_2 \frac{t_{char\,i}}{t_{char\,show}}$	Where $n_{char\,i}$ = number of times *i*th character verbalizes $n_{char\,show}$ = total verbalizations in show k = number of characters
Set Constraint Entropy (HSC)	The degree of randomness of the constraints of the discrete physical locations in a program	$\frac{t_{inside}}{t_{show}} * \log_2 \frac{t_{inside}}{t_{show}}$	Where t_{inside} = total time spent with indoor locations t_{show} = total time of the show
Nonverbal Dependence Entropy (HNV)	The degree of randomness of the use of only visuals to carry the narrative	$\frac{-t_{show} - t_{verbal}}{t_{show}} * \log_2 \frac{t_{show} - t_{verbal}}{t_{show}}$	Where t_{verbal} = total verbal time for all characters t_{show} = total time of the show
Character Appearance Entropy (HCA)	The degree of randomness of the appearance of characters in the program	$\frac{-t_{appearance}}{t_{show}} * \log_2 \frac{t_{appearance}}{t_{show}}$	Where $t_{appearance}$ = total number of times characters enter and exit the set t_{show} = total time of the show

Table 8.2. Calculated Entropy Values for the Test Videos

	Video 1a	**Video 1b**	**Video 2a**	**Video 2b**
HST	0.333	0.285	0.000	0.136
HSI	0.519	0.491	0.000	0.500
HVT	0.000	0.484	0.000	0.400
HVI	0.000	0.461	0.000	0.407
HSC	0.000	0.214	0.000	0.092
HNV	0.498	0.411	0.134	0.527
HCA	0.168	0.393	0.000	0.506
$\bar{x}$H	0.217	0.391	0.019	0.367

Table 8.3. Numerical Representations of Comparative Judgments

	Again	Exciting	Like	Funny	Not boring	Surprising	
VIDEO1A							
a	0.600	0.600	0.900	0.450	1.000	1.000	0.758
b	0.900	0.450	0.750	0.900	1.000	0.650	0.775
c	0.200	0.300	0.600	0.100	0.100	0.250	0.258
d	0.600	0.350	0.45	0.050	0.550	0.500	0.417
e	0.500	1.000	0.95	0.900	0.700	0.000	0.675
f	0.350	0.550	0.5	0.050	0.600	0.650	0.450
	0.525	0.5417	0.692	0.408	0.658	0.508	0.556
VIDEO1B							
a	0.850	0.650	0.950	1.000	1.000	0.950	0.900
b	1.000	0.950	1.000	0.500	1.000	0.850	0.883
c	0.600	0.500	0.750	0.750	0.850	0.300	0.625
d	0.150	0.150	0.250	0.150	0.200	0.300	0.200
e	1.000	1.000	1.000	1.000	0.950	0.100	0.842
f	0.650	0.700	0.750	0.800	0.650	0.500	0.675
	0.708	0.658	0.783	0.700	0.775	0.500	0.688
VIDEO2A							
g	0.975	0.025	0.975	0.025	0.975	0.025	0.500
h	0.000	0.000	0.400	0.000	0.100	0.200	0.117
i	0.700	0.950	1.000	0.150	1.000	0.500	0.717
j	0.600	0.700	0.750	0.000	0.750	0.650	0.575
k	0.000	0.550	0.550	0.000	0.550	0.500	0.358
l	0.600	0.150	0.550	0.000	0.400	0.050	0.292
	0.479	0.396	0.704	0.029	0.629	0.321	0.426
VIDEO2B							
g	0.875	0.875	0.725	0.475	0.725	0.125	0.633
h	1.000	1.000	1.000	0.450	1.000	1.000	0.908
i	0.925	0.950	1.000	0.100	1.000	0.500	0.745
j	0.600	0.850	0.800	0.200	0.750	0.650	0.642
k	1.000	1.000	1.000	1.000	1.000	1.000	1.000
l	1.000	0.650	1.000	0.300	1.000	0.350	0.717
	0.900	0.888	0.921	0.421	0.913	0.604	0.774

The numerical representations, between 0 (zero) and 1 (one), of these comparative judgments are shown in Table 8.3. (Results are shown both as averages for each child and group averages for each question.) The children thought Video2b was both significantly more exciting ($P = 0.026$) and significantly more funny ($P = 0.041$) than Video2a.

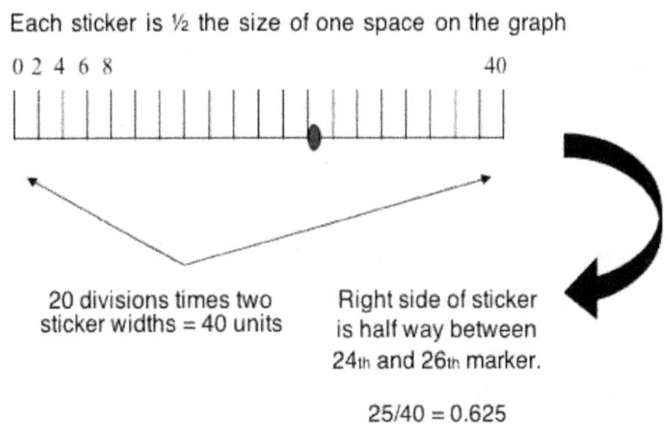

Figure 8.6. Sample of Sticker on Line.

When the perceived entropy measurements are compared side by side with the calculated entropy measurements, the measurements show similar trends in the two representations of video document structures. Though the numerical representations of the relationships vary, the relationships themselves remain the same throughout the two methods of representation.

With due consideration given to the limitations of a small study sample of convenience and to the influence of document content, we can say that there is a demonstrable correlation between the calculated and perceived entropies. Therefore, we can accept the hypothesis that mechanically calculated entropy will be sufficiently similar to perceived entropy made by children so that they can be used as useful and predictive elements of representations of children's videos, thus offering one simple solution for addressing both of our original concerns for issues in representation. That is to say that children's own perceptions of video document structures can be represented by the more easily obtained surrogate of mechanical structural calculations. Both children's perceptions and document structures are relevant to the functional representation.

CLOWNPANTS IN THE CLASSROOM: MEASUREMENT OF STRUCTURAL DISTRACTION IN POWERPOINT DOCUMENTS

Defining "Clownpants"

"Clownpants" in multimedia presentation design is the predictability of unpredictable elements; that is to say that by confusing the structure of a message and engaging entropy with hyperbolic structural change or form over structure. That is, by using frequent structural changes such as seemingly random combinations of mixing font types, numerous font colors, inserting different transition effects between each pair of slides, animating content, combing clipart with photographs, and so on, and by doing this with regularity causes the viewer to expect entropic elements, thus robbing them of their novelty. "No pants" in multimedia presentations indicates that, to some degree, the presentation of information is underdressed, or bare, and is predictable as such. Using single font, no illustrations, no audio clips, and having the presenter simply read the text on the screen presents little novelty to the viewer, little of the surprise that maintains engagement with the information processing task (Watt, 1979).

Clownpants is not meant to be yet another set of guidelines to follow for effective PowerPoint presentation construction, for many such sets already exist that express functional tips (see Mahin, 2004; Vik, 2004; DuFrene & Lehman, 2004; Bartsch & Cobern, 2003; Bird 2001; Brown, 2001); rather, measurements of PowerPoint document structure offer one possibility for quantifying commonly accepted (see Parker, 2001; Schwom & Keller, 2003; Byrne, 2003;

Norvig, 2003a, 2003b; Livraghi (2005); Worley & Dyrud, 2004; Ellwood, 2005) structural distractions, misuses, and malengineering. Exploring this clownpants continuum seems to be an infinite feat: can one information seeker's perception of clownpants be quantified? Or scaled to fit this spectrum? Viewers' perceptions of information of moving image documents have been calibrated to mechanically calculated numerical representations of the same documents using the Mathematical Theory of Communication (Kearns & O'Connor, 2004). That is to say that some viewers' perceptions can be represented as numbers on a 0 to 1 scale by applying Claude Shannon's formula for determining the rate of exchange of information in any communicated message: entropy.

A PowerPoint presentation, like any other document, is a binary system in which structure and meaning have a complementary relationship (Anderson, 2006). Information must not be confused with meaning—no more than syntax equals semantics in a communicated message—nor can information and meaning be used interchangeably (Shannon & Weaver, 1949). Moles complies, asserting that "information differs essentially from meaning: information is only a measure of complexity" (Moles, 1966, p. 196). Information, in this synthesis, is the physical presentation of a communication; it is a separate attribute of the message, distinct from the message content. When the information transfer itself confuses a receptor, the actual content or meaning of the communicated message is compromised. Information is separate from meaning, however, when the purpose of a multimedia presentation is to deliver content, message structure can be its own noise. When the structure is more complex than the decoding ability, we might call this "clownpants." When the structure is not sufficiently complex, we might call this "no pants." That is, very high complexity, clownpants, may result in low engagement because the predictability of unpredictable elements is high. Similarly, when the structure never changes, is boring, and uniform, and meaning is conveyed through bare syntax, the presentation wears "no-pants," and engagement is low: boredom by baredom. Much like the anticipation or expectation one feels when watching a clown because creating surprises is central to the clown's job; and much like, if one sees a naked man walking on the street, the unexpected becomes expected: he has bared his barest, like the empty PowerPoint (PPT) presentation, and has left nothing to the proverbial imaginations of viewers. The viewer stops paying attention to what the person is saying, in both the clownpants and no pants presentation because the information (NOT the meaning) is overwhelmingly distracting. At the very least, "presentation format should do no harm to content" (Tufte, 2004, p. 24) (see Figure 8.7) and the goal—seemingly—should be to use high entropy components in multimedia design to create emphasis and to draw-in and hold viewer attention. A teacher wearing clownpants and a teacher wearing no pants are media whose formats will distract from the message.

Figure 8.7. Clownpants as Distraction from Lecture Content.

The desired communication (content, semantics) seems less important than the method of content delivery.

Entropy measures based on the original formula of Claude Shannon (1949) and the interpretations of this formula by James Watt (1979) and Kearns (2001) demonstrate a means of measuring form attributes of PowerPoint presentation. Numerical representations of form attributes of PPT presentations indicate some degree of clownpantsiness in the communicated message. Following, we derive a set of form attributes and present a variation of the approach of Watt and Krull (1974) for making entropy measures of those attributes. We then calibrate the system of entropy measurements against an actual set of PowerPoint presentations. These presentations were made by preservice teachers as instructional tools. We also make use of their peer evaluations to augment our calibration and to have evidence of their reactions.

If you were entering a biology classroom to attend a lecture on the physiological aspects of endurance training you would be surprised if the professor

Figure 8.8. The "Norm" as Potential Distraction.

walked in wearing clownpants, as in Figure 8.7. The surprise might be diminished if the professor explained that the clownpants were a metaphor to explain some aspect of the lecture. The pants would still be strange but they would likely not stand in the way of the content of the lecture. If no explanation of the pants is made, the message is overshadowed by the signal set of the size and color of the pants along with the nagging question: "Why is he wearing those?" It would make no difference that the lecturer holds a Ph.D. in the field and is a well-respected researcher—he is still wearing clownpants and that is just weird.

For many students these days, seeing a professor in jeans or casual slacks, as in Figure 8.8, is quite ordinary, though it was not long ago that a suit or sport coat would have been the expected attire for a professor, so that in the mid-twentieth century as young male faculty members began to wear jeans and casual slacks with T-shirts, some students and other faculty members saw the jeans as a distraction. All this to say that any particular attribute may interfere with content at some time, but not necessarily under all circumstances.

Wattian Entropy for Multimedia Presentations

Kearns and O'Connor (2004) demonstrated how Shannon's original entropy equation could be applied to the communication of moving image documents, so long as one understands that information is measurable (Moles, 1966; Shannon & Weaver, 1949) and that these entropy measurements can represent user perceptions of the communications. Watt and Krull (1974) and Watt (1979) modified Shannon's statistical model to measure the information of several "form attributes" of moving image documents. Kearns (2001) extrapolates the measurability of information in media other than moving image documents and suggests that these entropy calculations can also represent reader or viewer perceptions of books and photographs. Some of the form attribute entropies were developed from this articulation of measurable attributes of books for children and of photographs and were applied to form attributes of PPT presentations. For this study, information of form attributes is measured in multimedia presentations, for the purpose of quantifying the clownpants-no-pants continuum. Ten form attributes of PPT presentations were selected for this articulation; their definitions, formulae, and descriptions are shown in Table 8.4, and Table 8.5 shows the entropy calculations of these form attributes applied to 24 PPT presentations by pre-service teachers.

Entropy measures of PPT form attributes were selected to specifically address elements of multimedia presentations that make them different from traditional presentations (overhead transparencies, mimeographed handouts, grayscale photocopies), assuming that each of these form attributes is a measurable form of communication. The communicated information of color attributes is measurable with Color Incidence Entropy (HCO) and Color Range Entropy (HCR); of animation attributes with Animation Distribution Entropy (HAD) and Animation Incidence Entropy (HAI); of slide transition attributes with Transition Variance Entropy (HVT) and Transition Incidence Entropy (HTI); of sound attributes with Sound Effects Entropy (HSE); of text attributes with Word Incidence Entropy (HWI) and Weighted Text Entropy (HWT); and of image and graphics attributes with Weighted Picture Entropy (HWP).

For calculating Color Incidence Entropy (HCO) (from Kearns (2001)) and Color Range Entropy (HCR), each slide of each of the 24 PPT presentations was converted into a JPEG image at the default size of 960 × 720 pixels. Then, using PaintShopTM Pro colors were counted. For Animation Distribution Entropy (HAD) and Animation Incidence Entropy (HAI), one animation event was defined in terms of the custom animation window within PPT, since the application lists animation events chronologically and in terms of their relation to other animation events. If the purpose of the animation was, for example, to quickly insert ten squares, one after the other, all automated to enter sequentially, PPT calls it one animation event. Transition attributes are

Table 8.4. Calculating Entropy of 10 PPT Form Attributes

Entropy Type	Formula Interpretations for PPT Presentation Attributes	Description
HCO Color Incidence Entropy	$HCO = -\frac{\sum_{i=1}^{k} \frac{n_{colorpage}}{n_{pixels}} * \log_2 \frac{n_{colorpage}}{n_{pixels}}}{n_{slides}}$	Where $n_{colorpage}$ is the total number of colors appearing on each page n_{pixels} is the total number of pixels per slide n_{slides} is the total number of slides in the presentation
HCR Color Range Entropy	$HCR = -\frac{r_{color}}{n_{pixels}} * \log_2 \frac{r_{color}}{n_{pixels}}$	Where r_{color} is the color range of the total presentation n_{pixels} is the number of pixels per slide
HTI Transition Incidence Entropy	$HTI = -\frac{n_{transitiontypes}}{n_{slides}} * \log_2 \frac{n_{transitiontypes}}{n_{slides}}$	Where $n_{transitiontypess}$ is the number of different slide transition effects used in the presentation n_{slides} is the total number of slides in the presentation
HSE Sound Effects Entropy	$HSE = -\frac{n_{sounds}}{n_{slides}} * \log_2 \frac{n_{sounds}}{n_{slides}}$	Where n_{sounds} is the number of sounds and sound effects in the presentation n_{slides} is the total number of slides in the presentation
HAD Animation Distribution Entropy	$HAD = -\frac{\sum_{i=1}^{k} \frac{n_{slideanimationevents}}{n_{totalanimations}} * \log_2 \frac{n_{slideanimationevents}}{n_{totalanimations}}}{n_{slides}}$	Where $n_{slideanimationevents}$ is the number of animation events per slide $n_{totalanimations}$ is the total number of animation events in the presentation n_{slides} is the total number of slides in the presentation
HWI Word Incidence Entropy	$HWI = -\frac{\sum_{i=1}^{k} \frac{n_{wordsperslide}}{n_{slides}} * \log_2 \frac{n_{wordsperslide}}{n_{slides}}}{n_{slides}}$	Where $n_{wordsperslide}$ is the number of words appearing on individual slides n_{slides} is the total number of slides in the presentation
HWP Weighted Picture Entropy	$HWP = -\frac{t_{anticipated}}{n_{pictures}} * \log_2 \frac{t_{anticipated}}{n_{pictures}}$	Where $t_{anticipated}$ is the total amount of time anticipated as the goal for the presentation $n_{pictures}$ is the total number of pictures, images, and graphics in the presentation
HVT Transition Variance Entropy	$HVT = -\frac{t_{transitiontypes}}{n_{transitions}} * \log_2 \frac{t_{transitiontypes}}{n_{transitions}}$	Where $n_{transitiontypes}$ is the number of different slide transition effects used in the presentation $n_{transitions}$ is the number of transitions used in the presentation
HWT Weighted Text Entropy	$HWT = -\frac{t_{anticipated}}{n_{words}} * \log_2 \frac{t_{anticipated}}{n_{words}}$	Where $t_{anticipated}$ is the total amount of time anticipated as the goal for the presentation n_{words} is the total number of words in the presentation
HAI Animation Incidence Entropy	$HAI = -\frac{\sum_{i=1}^{k} \frac{n_{slideanimationevents}}{n_{totalanimations}} * \log_2 \frac{n_{slideanimationevents}}{n_{totalanimations}}}{n_{animatedslides}}$	Where $n_{slideanimationevents}$ is the number of animation events per slide $n_{totalanimations}$ is the total number of animation events in the presentation $n_{animatedslides}$ is the number of slides containing animation effects

Table 8.5. Entropy Calculations of 10 PPT Form Attributes of Presentations Designed by 24 Pre-Service Teachers

	HCO	HCR	HTI	HSE	HAD	HWI	HWP	HVT	HWT	HAI
Subject 01	0.212040	0.278344	0.136803	0.464386	0.287803	0.301378	0.127721	0.352214	0.294357	0.313543
Subject 02	0.124237	0.407826	0.136803	0.464386	0.102033	0.288973	0.471466	0.000000	0.141349	0.459148
Subject 03	0.113362	0.100435	0.125003	0.000000	0.158496	0.215401	0.406696	0.332193	0.196096	0.528321
Subject 04	0.257731	0.440185	0.257542	0.464386	0.222204	0.269334	0.526264	0.375000	0.228350	0.381891
Subject 05	0.176343	0.181259	0.136803	0.360201	0.273162	0.282642	0.379933	0.352214	0.528321	0.351208
Subject 06	0.137513	0.152921	0.115070	0.000000	0.301993	0.326368	0.398284	0.314494	0.102062	0.332193
Subject 07	0.260740	0.337757	–	0.442179	0.325755	0.269488	0.530197	–	0.162417	0.326089
Subject 08	0.202271	0.202089	0.115070	0.430827	0.000000	0.303270	0.509709	0.447169	0.207830	–
Subject 09	0.181788	0.178987	0.464386	0.464386	0.293512	0.291733	0.524397	0.000000	0.186785	0.377372
Subject 10	0.080849	0.081689	0.125003	–	0.200000	0.299320	0.389975	0.332193	0.101928	0.500000
Subject 11	0.331380	0.405602	0.136803	0.000000	0.324255	0.316827	0.358737	0.352214	0.285992	0.324255
Subject 12	0.130634	0.144083	0.136803	–	0.332193	0.320398	0.460882	0.352214	0.194947	0.332193
Subject 13	0.234687	0.368842	0.360201	0.442179	0.295296	0.268548	0.398284	0.461346	0.153525	0.331692
Subject 14	0.094310	0.105634	0.115070	0.430827	0.083481	0.322787	0.430827	0.517047	0.102331	0.459148
Subject 15	0.139485	0.177751	0.136803	0.464386	0.100729	0.323142	0.450548	0.352214	0.129748	0.456984
Subject 16	0.189033	0.176744	0.257542	0.442179	0.324327	0.294758	0.450548	0.311278	0.276878	0.326083
Subject 17	0.160468	0.220355	0.125003	0.530702	0.105664	0.320082	0.510142	0.528771	0.169159	0.528321
Subject 18	0.125465	0.260769	–	0.464386	0.331190	0.285091	0.450315	–	0.133048	0.331190
Subject 19	0.137047	0.253482	0.125003	0.447169	0.290311	0.276898	0.379933	0.500000	0.153860	0.290311
Subject 20	0.287712	0.368373	0.136803	0.332193	0.333058	0.293076	0.506842	0.151044	0.482206	0.322110
Subject 21	0.223025	0.412018	0.115070	0.526264	0.276181	0.304774	0.345939	0.000000	0.177482	0.312640
Subject 22	0.179282	0.237741	0.125003	0.511219	0.167674	0.275158	0.510142	0.332193	0.159448	0.419184
Subject 23	0.157680	0.173561	0.115070	0.528321	0.273299	0.305678	0.367845	0.000000	0.261560	0.320899
Subject 24	0.148267	0.417103	–	0.332193	0.250181	0.000000	0.521959	–	0.306397	0.450326

measurable with Transition Incidence Entropy (HTI) and Transition Variance Entropy (HVT), and in presentations that contained no transition effects, the number of transition effects equals 0. Measuring sound attributes is possible with Sound Effects Entropy (HSE). The number of sounds used in each presentation reflects both sound effects added to animations and inserted sound clips from the sound clips gallery. It was counted as one sound effect even when a sound effect was set to repeat until the next click of the mouse, or, similarly, to repeat x number of times. Text attributes were calculated with Word Incidence Entropy (HWI) (from Kearns (2001)) and Weighted Text Entropy (HWT). Text is visual information and though it is difficult to separate from the meaning the text gives to the presentation, this study does not attempt to measure content attributes. Also, students were asked to include specific textual information on a title slide. In order not to eliminate the title slide from the HWI, and yet not to give it more undo influence, a simple average was used to normalize the HWI. Weighted Text Entropy (HWT) and Weighted Picture Entropy (HWP) are the only two attributes that measure entropy against a time constraint. These preservice teachers were expected to design ten-minute presentations. These entropies measure their choices to include text or pictures/graphics weighted against the expected length of the presentation. The cells in Table 8.5. shown with a "–" had values that produced errors when inserted into the formula.

HCO, HCR, HTI, HAD, and HWT measures for Subject 10, for example, are all very low, and yet HAI is 0.5, which is the highest entropy measurement. This student used one single animation effect to emphasize the most important semantic point in the presentation. The effectiveness of this strategy is shown in HAI = 0.5 for this presentation. Similarly, other students opted to employ fewer sound effects (HSE01, HSE02, HSE23, HSE21, for example), which result in high entropy values for this form attribute, and in emphasis drawn to that particular sound effect event, and the content attached to the event, in the presentation. Whereas HSE06 and HSE11 have values of 0 because they each engineered their PPT presentations to include the same sound effect to occur with each slide transition, causing the sound effect to be more of a distracting than an attractive feature.

Formulating Clownpants Index (CPI) with Distraction Factor (DF)

The entropic burst defines the moment when information becomes reactive. Entropic burst is the moment at which cognitive structure strays from the anticipatory response (Hayes, 1993); or that instant that all else is forgotten (Patrick Wilson, personal communication, 1999) and the viewer accepts that it is okay to react to the surprise; or where the PPT presentation has been engineered to alter cognitive state (Shannon, 1949).

Designing multimedia presentations with entropic bursts means finding a functional balance between format and content, syntax and semantics, and clownpants and no-pants. This balance occurs when entropy measurements are in mid-range (Watt & Krull, 1974; Watt, 1979, Kearns, 2001; Kearns & O'Connor, 2004). The elements that are moderately high entropy (unpredictable, surprising, exciting) measure around 0.5 on this scale. Low-entropy elements (predictable, boring, unexciting) measure closer to 0 and elements whose entropy is so high that their unpredictability becomes predictable measure close to 1 on this same scale. The mid-range identified by Watt and Krull is in reference to television programming, but the concept of mid-range entropy balancing between novelty and familiarity applies to any message form. The degree of entropy in a communicated message can be represented as a normal curve. The closer an entropy measurement of a PPT form attribute rests to either extreme, the more that element distracts from the semantic absorption of the desired communication, similar to Shannon's notion of noise distracting a communicated message (1949). The distraction factor, then, is measurable in the degree of clownpants and no pants and can be represented as a bi-modal curve. Distraction from the semantic message is high because the syntactic message is louder.

$$DF = (| 0.5 - H |) * 20$$

when

$$H = -\Sigma \, pi * \log_2 (pi)$$

Figure 8.9. Calculating the Distraction Factor of Syntactic Attributes in Multimedia Presentations.

This Distraction Factor (Figure 8.9), then, in multimedia presentations can be represented numerically with a formula and expressed as a number (Table 8.6) on the familiar scale of 1 and 10, where 10 is a high distraction factor.

The distribution of distraction factors on the Clownpants Index fluctuates for each form attribute just as calculated entropy measurements for each form attribute vary. For Subject 16, for example, Weighted Picture Entropy is high (HWP = 0.450548, see Table 8.5) so the Distraction Factor of this form attribute is low (DFWP = 0.98904 in Table 8.6), when other Distraction Factors are higher. The visual representation of the Distraction Factors of the form attributes of Subjects 1, 9, 16, and 23 are shown in Table 8.7. Both Subjects 9 and 23 had a Distraction Factor for the form attribute Transition Variance (DFVT) equal to 10, demonstrating that the variance of their selections for transition effects between slides was distracting by a DF of 10 from the content. When distraction factors are greater, information has become greater, louder, and stronger than content. When DF is high, we call this clownpants, whether the distraction is results from too much or too little physical information, since no-pants can be as distracting as clownpants. Recall those Sound Effect Entropy measurements for Subjects 6 and 11 as 0: the resulting distraction factors from this low-entropy component are perfect tens (DFSE = 10) on the CPI.

Table 8.6. Distraction Factors Calculated for 10 Form Attributes of 24 PPT Presentations

	DF_{CO}	DF_{CR}	DF_{TI}	DF_{SE}	DF_{AD}	DF_{WI}	DF_{WP}	DF_{VT}	DF_{WT}	DF_{AI}
Subject 01	5.75920	4.43312	7.26394	0.71228	4.24394	3.97244	7.44558	2.95572	4.11286	3.72914
Subject 02	7.51526	1.84348	7.26394	0.71228	7.95934	4.22054	0.57068	10	7.17302	0.81704
Subject 03	7.73276	7.99130	7.49994	10	6.83008	5.69198	1.86608	3.35614	6.07808	0.56642
Subject 04	4.84538	1.19630	4.84916	0.71228	5.55592	4.61332	0.52528	2.5	5.43300	2.36218
Subject 05	6.47314	6.37482	7.26394	2.79598	4.53676	4.34716	2.40134	2.95572	0.56642	2.97584
Subject 06	7.24974	6.94158	7.69860	10	3.96014	3.47264	2.03432	3.71012	7.95876	3.35614
Subject 07	4.78520	3.24486	–	1.15642	3.48490	4.61024	0.60394	–	6.75166	3.47822
Subject 08	5.95458	5.95822	7.69860	1.38346	10	3.9346	0.19418	1.05662	5.84340	–
Subject 09	6.36424	6.42026	0.71228	0.71228	4.12976	4.16534	0.48794	10	6.26430	2.45256
Subject 10	8.38302	8.36622	7.49994	–	6	4.01360	2.20050	3.35614	7.96144	0
Subject 11	3.37240	1.88796	7.26394	10	3.51490	3.66346	2.82526	2.95572	4.28016	3.51490
Subject 12	7.38732	7.11834	7.26394	–	3.35614	3.59204	0.78236	2.95572	6.10106	3.35614
Subject 13	5.30626	2.62316	2.79598	1.15642	4.09408	4.62904	2.03432	0.77308	6.92950	3.36616
Subject 14	8.11380	7.88732	7.69860	1.38346	8.33038	3.54426	1.38346	0.34094	7.95338	0.81704
Subject 15	7.21030	6.44498	7.26394	0.71228	7.98542	3.53716	0.98904	2.95572	7.40504	0.86032
Subject 16	6.21934	6.46512	4.84916	1.15642	3.51346	4.10484	0.98904	3.77444	4.46244	3.47834
Subject 17	6.79064	5.59290	7.49994	0.61404	7.88672	3.59836	0.20284	0.57542	6.61682	0.56642
Subject 18	7.49070	4.78462	–	0.71228	3.3762	4.29818	0.99370	–	7.33904	3.37620
Subject 19	7.25906	4.93036	7.49994	1.05662	4.19378	4.46204	2.40134	0	6.92280	4.19378
Subject 20	4.24576	2.63254	7.26394	3.35614	3.33884	4.13848	0.13684	6.97912	0.35588	3.55780
Subject 21	5.53950	1.75964	7.69860	0.52528	4.47638	3.90452	3.08122	10	6.45036	3.74720
Subject 22	6.41436	5.24518	7.49994	0.22438	6.64652	4.49684	0.20284	3.35614	6.81104	1.61632
Subject 23	6.84640	6.52878	7.69860	0.56642	4.53402	3.88644	2.64310	10	4.76880	3.58202
Subject 24	7.03466	1.65794	–	3.35614	4.99638	10	0.43918	–	3.87206	0.99348

Table 8.7. Visual Representations of Distraction Factors for Subjects 1, 9, 16, and 23

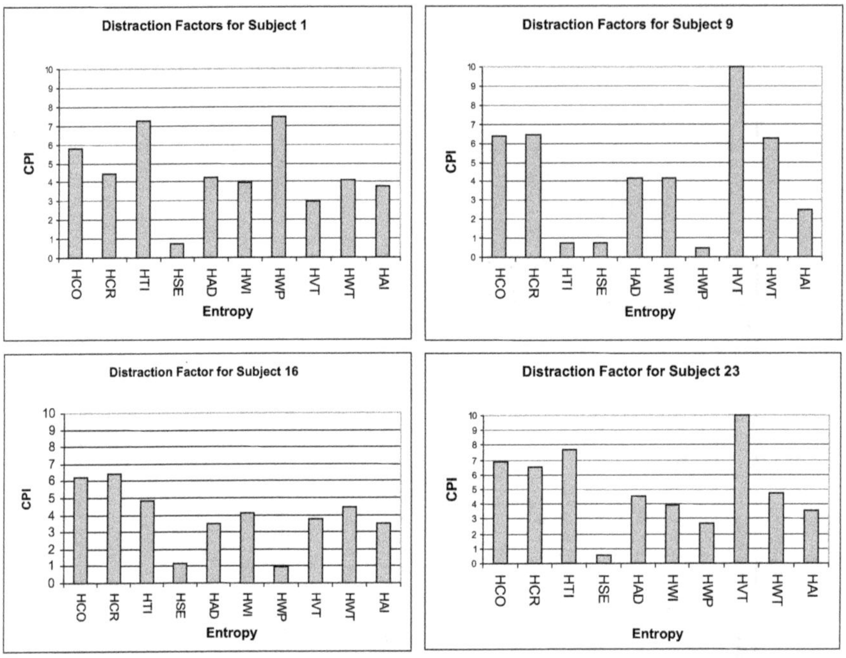

If distraction factors of all physical attributes are all high, or all are low, no emphasis has been made. The PPT designer has merely delivered content flatly, and likely as effectively as reading that content from the text with no vocal inflections. Some distraction is good because it creates emphasis. Building "distractions" or surprises onto every slide, makes your information predictable, but noticing discontinuities (Augst & O'Connor, 1999) or change in visual fields (Watt, 1979) generates higher viewer attention.

Thoughts

> *"There are more than one hundred elements [to comedy], but the most important is the element of surprise. Boo!"*
>
> (Idle, 1999, p. 122)

For perception, surprise, as in Figure 8.10, is associated with the peak of the curve (Kearns & O'Connor, 2004). Ordinarily, entropy is a measure of structure that rises from 0 (zero) to near complete chaos as it approaches 1 (one). However, another way of expressing the notion of entropy is to say that it is inversely proportional to the likelihood of occurrence. With letters and words, we have some sense of the likelihood of occurrence (we know "e" will appear much more frequently than "w" and that "the" will appear more frequently than "kayak" in general use, though in a book on boating, "kayak" would be expected.)

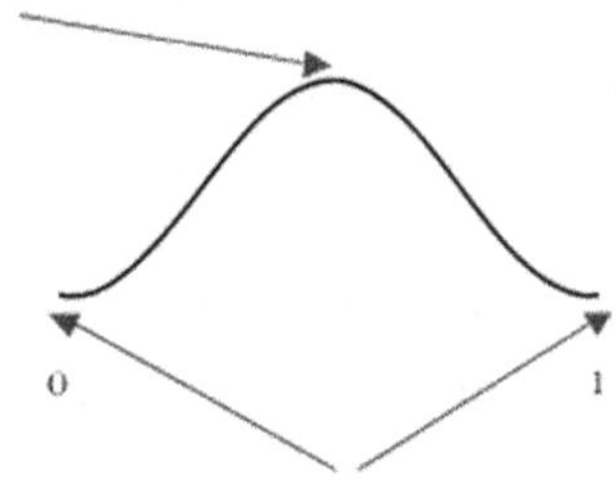

Figure 8.10. Perceived Entropy Is High in the middle (0.5) and Perceived Entropy Is Low As It Reaches Either Extreme

At 0, the structure of a joke, or a PPT, or any message would exhibit no surprise; while at or near 1, surprises would be so frequent as to become ordinary. One might say at the middle of the curve, there is sufficient familiarity for a change of structure to be surprising. Thus, the calculated distraction factors are high at either end of the curve because neither stasis nor constant change presents surprise. The structural presentation of the message does not change even when the viewer changes, but may be perceived by different viewers as having different meaning. Some viewers may possess more of the code for understanding the message. One person's template of probabilities may be another person's noise.

As is the case of clownpants and the PPT presentation: that which falls outside the parameters of regular or normal or common to that presenter is what creates the entropic burst. When the engineer attempts to fill the PPT presentation with entropic bursts, he or she is merely changing the baseline scale of normal or regular for that PPT presentation and consequently altering the pretence under which the entropic burst can occur, thusly, like in joke telling, eliciting from the audience a willing suspension of disbelief of what may be normal through audible and temporal signals. Even as far back as the first time this joke was told, people were aware of the importance of structure in the construction of humor, at least the temporal dimension (Idle, 1999). "Ask me the secret of comedy." "What is the secret of—""Timing."

Distraction is a measurable characteristic of the structure of PowerPoint documents. We present the concept of entropy measures of document structures and the corollary distraction factors as precise quantitative ways to speak about documents. This does not mean that there is one or some small set of "perfect" structures for PowerPoint, nor is there a formula to ensure distraction-free presentations, especially since the meaning is also dependent on the viewer. Comedians are funny not because they use a formula, but because they understand the set of structures of what entertains.

EXPERT VERBAL BEHAVIOR AND DOCUMENT STRUCTURE: MODELING A BINARY SYSTEM OF STRUCTURE AND MEANING

In 1981, film theorist Bertrand Augst asked, "Why can't we use a computer to measure and speak of filmic structure in the same way we can for verbal text?" Augst's comments arose after an exchange of comments on the difficulties for film studies that arise from the "literary metaphor." This is not to say there is no discourse mechanism at work in films, only that attempts at one to one correspondence between the frame and the word or the shot and the sentence or similar impositions of the verbal form onto the image form failed. Films, or moving image documents, are not textual documents. Films do not have a rigidly defined grammatical structure. Images are not words. Shots are not sentences (Pryluck, 1976, p. 224) Films are generally viewed at a set rate of presentation and linearity. Augst and O'Connor (1999) state:

> Representation of film texts for scholars and students has been fraught with difficulties imposed by the very nature of the text. The time-varying image track presented hurdles to close significant challenges to formulation of units of meaning and analysis. The digital environment offers opportunities for addressing these problems (p. 345).

The technology used in the production and viewing of moving image documents has changed considerably since Augst posed his original question; however, there has been little change or advancement in film theory as a result of better and more efficient technology for interacting with the medium.

The Structure of Moving Image Documents

It has been common in both film description and film analysis to use the "shot" as the base or minimum unit. However, the difficulties of such use have proved to be numerous. There is no definition of shot that specifies any specific set of parameters for any particular attribute—no specific number of frames or type of content. Bonitzer (1977) refers to definitions of "shot" as "endlessly bifurcated." Similarly, the terms Close Up (CU), Medium Shot (MS), and Long Shot (LS) are used in film production textbooks, film analyses, and even in the Anglo American Cataloguing Rules (2002)—see especially, Rule 7.7B18—for use by librarians to describe the relationship of the camera to the subject. Again, however, there is no specification of how much frame real estate is occupied by some object or portion of object in the frame constitutes a CU rather than MS, for example. For our purposes, we use the frame and measurable attributes of the frame in order to speak specifically and to avoid the difficulties presented by "endless bifurcation."

The signal or the information of a film is presented in small units—frames—that are in themselves self-contained signals. In many instances they are even used as messages—for example, an individual frame may become a movie poster. However, the film and other time-varying signal sets such as music and dance are signal sets of their given sort precisely because of their temporality. We see or hear the signal set (document) as a set of changes over time. The basic model of the time-varying signal document is shown in the vector space model in Figure 8.11.

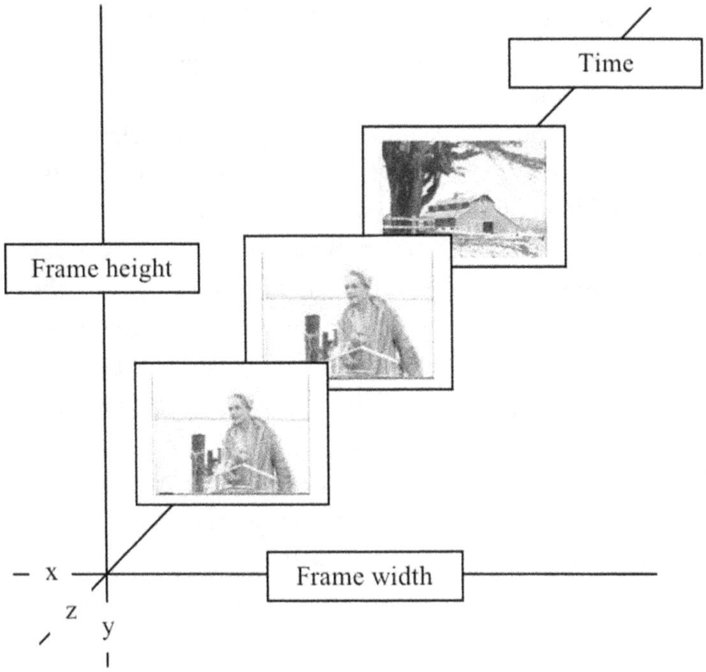

Figure 8.11. Three-Dimensional Vector Space Model of Filmic Structure Using Frame Height, Frame Width, and Time as the Three Dimensions.

It could be said that one can stare at a painting or sculpture for a few seconds or an hour from differing viewpoints, thus making the viewing a time-varying experience of the signal set. It could probably be argued that artists of various sorts construct signal sets that demand attention for a long time in order to see all the intended variations in the signal set. It can even be argued (and we have so argued) that the digital environment gives viewers reader-like control over temporality and depth of penetration into films. However, it remains the case that the majority of filmic documents produced for commercial consumption assume playback of the signal set at a standard rate and linearity.

Much of what is taught in film schools and much of what has transpired in film analysis relates to variation in the temporal aspect of the film. Eisenstein & Leyda (1949) and Vertov (1984) and some others spoke eloquently of time and its relation to structure. Structural commentary from reviewers tends to be less precise. For example, LaSalle (2005) describes *The Legend of Zorro* (LaSalle 2005) as "130-minute adventure movie that overstays its welcome by about 80 minutes," and Addiego (2005) describes *Domino* (Addiego, 2005) as "[a] psychedelic action picture that hammers away at the audience with a barrage of editing tics and tricks."

We are seeking a way to speak to of the structure of a moving image document precisely in order to enable a more productive examination of the meanings of the message for various viewers under various circumstances. In looking to previous work on the examination of the filmic message or signal set, we noted Augst's (1980) comment on Bellour's analysis of Hitchcock's *The Birds*: "It remains exemplary in the rigor and precision of the analysis performed and, to date, it is still the best example of what a genuine structural analysis of a filmic text could attempt to do. One must turn to Jakobson or Ruwet to find anything comparable in literary studies."

A comment by Augst (1980) on Bellour's response to criticism of his work as pseudoscientific and not sufficiently in touch with aesthetic aspects of film analysis addressed our particular concerns with devising an accurate and transferable means of describing the signal set: "[criticisms] continue to be leveled at any procedure that in any way exposes the gratuitousness and arbitrariness of impressionistic criticism."

Bellour's work elaborated on Metz's semiotic notions of film, particularly the concept of syntagmas, by introducing levels of segmentation greater and lesser than Metz's. This enabled structural analysis of filmic signal sets of any length and, eventually, of any sort, not simply the set, say, of classic American Hollywood features.

Difficulties for Bellour

We identified two difficulties with Bellour's signal set analysis. The first was the time-consuming nature of its practice, as demonstrated by sample output in Figure 8.12. Simply locating the proper portions of film, timing them,

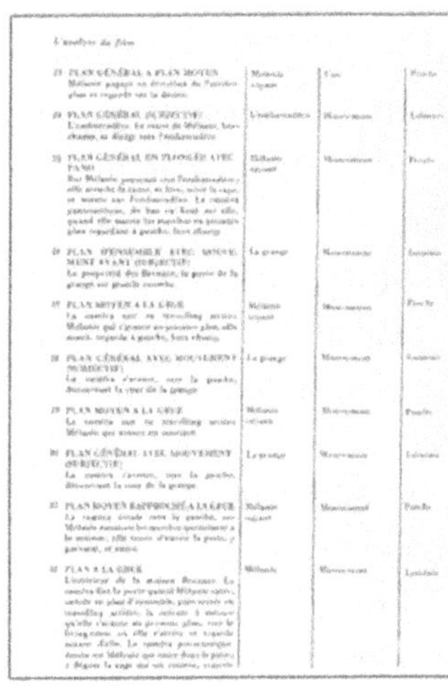

A1	23	MELANIE paddling, towards the camera, looks to the right.	2.25	MS	S	Mel ->	D	69
A1	24	THE PLATFORM seen from Melanie's POV. Forward movement.	2.37	LS	S	(Mit)	D	71
A2	25	MELANIE paddling She steps out of the boat, picks up the cage.	18.29	CS	M	Mel ->	C	548
A2	26	THE BRENNERS' HOUSE. The barn door wide open. Water noises, birds.	1.95	LS	M	(Mit)	C	59
A2	27	MELANIE smiling. The camera tracks backward.	2.54	MS	M	Mel ->	C	76
A2	28	THE BARN, Large tree in foreground and retaining wall	1.91	MS	M	(Mit)	D	57
A2	29	MELANIE smiling.	1.95	MS	M	Mel ->	C	59
A2	30	THE BARN behind the trees. Camera tracks.	2.00	MS	M	(Mit)	D	60
A2	31	MELANIE climbing the steps.	4.95	MS	M	Mel ->	C	150
A3	32	THE BRENNERS' HOUSE.	19.40	MLS/MS	M	Mel	D	581

Figure 8.12. Predigital Results—Intense Resource Requirements.

rephotographing frames for analysis and publication, to say nothing of commentary or analysis, took days and weeks.

The second is that Bellour conducted his work too early—for the remarkable precision of Bellour's analysis, without digital technology he did not have a precise system of description at the frame level. He could write of contents of the frame and of relationships holding among frames, but not with deep precision—for example, the shades of various colors and their changes from frame to frame.

The digital environment enables us to address both issues. Grabbing all the individual frames from a digital version of a film requires only seconds, not days. Also, pixels provide addressable analysis of the red, green, blue, and luminance components of any point in the frame, as well as comparisons of values at the same point or set of points across time. The mechanics of the practice of film analysis, which once would have required enormous resources of time, funding, and technology are today essentially trivial.

However, the technical ability to address and measure points within and across frames does not address Augst's earlier question; nor does it, in itself, provide a "genuine structural analysis of filmic texts." We have the technology—but what should we do with it? Techniques for analyzing the structure of moving image documents are well known and mature. Dailianas, Allen, and England (1995) reviewed a number of techniques for the segmentation of video including techniques for measuring the absolute difference between successive frames, several histogram based methods, as well as the measurement of objects within frames. These techniques proved to be robust when compared against human observers; however, all techniques were prone to false positives. Dailianas, Allen, and England (1995) note that

> . . . [b]ecause all the methods studied here have high false-identification rates, they should be thought of as providing suggestions to human observers and not as an ultimate standard of performance (p. 12).

Structure and function have a complementary, but independent relationship. In order to advance the state of both structural and theoretical analysis, the relationship between structure and function must be taken into account. In other words, an analysis that takes both structure and function into account is greater than the sum of its parts. Kearns and O'Connor (2004) provide a strong example of this approach in their demonstration of the relationship between the entropic structure of television programs and the preferences of a group of viewers.

The approach taken here combines an algorithmic structural analysis of the Bodega Bay sequence of Hitchcock's (2000) *The Birds* with the expert analysis of Bellour. Our hope is that a heuristic will emerge that will lead toward a solution to the problems identified both by film theorists and those who wish to analyze moving image documents for the purposes of indexing and retrieval. We take document description, identification of units of meaning, and identification of indexable units as fundamental foci within information science, but areas that have received only slight attention with regard to moving image documents.

Binary Systems of Structure and Function

Figure 8.13. Frames from "The Birds."

We are examining film documents here because it is so different from the word-based documents that have been at the heart of library practice. Note that the fragments of a film document presented in Figure 8.13 function without printed words. Despite their significant differences, both filmic documents and word documents are message systems, and thus information systems. The concept of information is so fundamental to our discussions of documents, their retrieval, and their use that we here reiterate a primary element of our model. We are using the technical definition posited by Claude Shannon and we state strongly our support of Warren Weaver's (Shannon & Weaver, 1949) comment in his introduction to Shannon's Mathematical Theory of Communication:

> The word information, in this theory, is used in a special sense that must not be confused with its ordinary usage. In particular information must not be confused with meaning. The concept of information developed in this theory at first seems disappointing and bizarre—disappointing because it has nothing to do with meaning, and bizarre because it deals not with a single message but rather with the statistical character of a whole ensemble of messages, bizarre also because in these statistical terms the two words information and uncertainty find themselves to be partners.

However, it is the very distinction between information and meaning that provides a theory base and descriptive tool kit for the description and analysis of film. For Shannon, information is the amount of freedom of choice in the construction of a message. This was ordinarily expressed as a logarithmic function of the number of choices, though that is not significant for our discussion. What is important is Shannon's assertion that the semantic aspects of communication have no relevance to the engineering aspects; however, the engineering aspects are not necessarily irrelevant to the semantic aspects.

Shannon's notion of information is a binary system. Message and meaning are separate, but complementary notions. This system bears a strong resemblance to the distinction between signifier and signified in semiotic theory, as well as, the separation of topography and function in the Behavior Analytic theory of verbal behavior (see Skinner, 1957 and Catania, 1998), and Wittgenstein's notion of a language game (Wittgenstein, 1953; Day, 1992).

Our model for examining this problem is a binary approach such as those discussed above. The structural analysis was conducted by measuring the changes in color palette across frames in the Bodega Bay sequence of Hitchcock's (2000), *The Birds*. The functional analysis comes from Bellour's analysis of the same sequence of the film.

FUNCTIONAL ANALYSIS OF BELLOUR'S "SYSTEM OF A FRAGMENT"

Behavior Analysis is an empirical and functional way to examine questions involving human behavior. Skinner (1953) describes the logic of a functional analysis:

> The external variables of which behavior is a function provide for what may be called a causal or functional analysis. We undertake to predict and control the behavior of an individual organism. This is our "dependent variable"—the effect for which we are to find the cause. Our 'independent variables'—the causes of behavior—are the external conditions of which behavior is a function. Relations between the two—the 'cause-and-effect relationships' in behavior are the laws of a science. A synthesis of these laws expressed in quantitative terms yields a comprehensive picture of the organism as a behaving system (p. 35).

Why is this important to our seeking a conceptual framework and set of tools for structural analysis of film? Our question concerns the relationship between the physical structure of the Bodega Bay sequence of *The Birds* and Bellour's description of the structure of the sequence. In other words, what physical attributes of the sequence prompted Bellour to make the statements he made about the film?

The notion of a binary system is so fundamental, we remake an earlier statement: a behavior analytic account of verbal behavior is a binary system. The structure or topography of a particular instance of verbal behavior has a complementary, but separate relationship, with the function or meaning of that particular instance. The behavior analytic account is similar in many respects to the separation of message and meaning in Shannon's work as well as semiotic theories of meaning. Behavior analysis provides an analytical language and framework that is appropriate for the problem at hand.

Catania (1998) defines "a tact as a verbal response occasioned by a discriminative stimulus." A discriminative stimulus is a stimulus that occasions a particular response and is correlated with reinforcement. In this particular case, the tacts or verbal responses of interest are the statements about the Bodega Bay sequence made by Bellour (2000) in *The Analysis of Film*. The discriminative stimuli are the physical dimensions of the film that prompted Bellour to make the statements he did in *The Analysis of Film*. The reinforcement in this case is assumed on the grounds that *The Analysis of Film* is considered to be a seminal work in the film theory community and Bellour and others applied the same types of analysis to other films.

Functional Analysis of Bellour's Verbal Behavior

We sought a means of structural analysis in turning to the expertise of Raymond Bellour. We selected a piece of his rigorous analysis—"System of a Fragment—On *The Birds*" (originally "les Oiseaux: Analyse d'une séquence" Bellour, 1969) using it as a record of his engagement with the signal set of a portion of the Hitchcock film (Bellour and Penley, 2000). We captured the frames from the sequence—generally termed the "Bodega Bay sequence"—for a data set of 12,803 frames. We then decided to determine how much of Bellour's response could be accounted for by one element of the data—the distribution of color across each and every frame. That is, we did not account for sound, for edge detection, or for previous knowledge.

The sequence is, on the face of it, rather simple. A young woman, Melanie Daniels, sets out in a small motorboat with a pair of lovebirds in a cage. She crosses Bodega Bay to leave the birds as a gift to catch the attention of a young man, Mitch Brenner. She enters the Brenner's house, leaves the birds, and returns to the boat. She returns across the bay. Mitch spots Melanie crossing the bay. Mitch drives around the bay to the pier where Melanie will be arriving. A sea gull strikes Melanie and cuts her head before she reaches the pier. Mitch helps Melanie out of the boat and they walk toward a shot to tend to the wound.

When Melanie is on the bay, Bellour points out, we are presented with a classic Hollywood form of alternation—we see on the screen Melanie looking, then that at which she looks, then Melanie again. This form continues until she arrives at the house. While she is in the house we simply observe her behavior, except for a brief look out the window at the barn. Bellour sees this scene in the house as a "hinge" in the design of the film. It disrupts the pattern of alternation, while it also takes Melanie off the water and brings her indoors.

As Melanie returns to the boat, we see what looks rather like the beginning of her trip—she is getting into the boat and heading off. However, Mitch sees her; then, she and Mitch acknowledge one another. Bellour refers to the scene in the house (the hinge) and the double act of seeing as the "two centers" of the Bodega Bay sequence.

As an integral portion of his analytic writing, Bellour includes photographic frames from the Bodega Bay sequence—key frames. Ordinarily, these are the first frames of each of the shots in the sequence. However, this is not always the case. The difficulties of defining "shots" seem to be manifested here. We will discuss this point at greater length; for now, "shot" is ordinarily understood to be a mechanical unit—all the frames from camera original film (or a working copy) left in by an editor. Thus, all the beginning frames, where the camera comes up to speed, the director shouts: "Action," and the miscues before useable footage is available are cut out. Then a set of frames—each a still image representing approximately one-thirtieth of a second—shows the portion of the action desired by the director. Then a cut—in film, an actual mechanical cut; in video, still a cessation of a particular stream of data—is made and another shot appended. The process is repeated until the end of the film.

Ordinarily, especially in older films, there is a close correlation between the mechanical cuts and the data within the shot. However, there is a problem here for the definition of shot—data may change even in one run of the camera or one stream of frames between cuts. The camera may remain still while various objects come and go in front of it; the camera may move and present different views of the same objects or even different objects; the camera may remain still, but have the length of its lens changed during a shot; or various combinations of these may take place. For the viewer, whether several objects or views are shown in different shots or one shot may be of little overt consequence. However, in attempting do critical analysis, one is faced with finding a unit of meaning or, at least, a unit of address and measure that provides precision of description.

Bellour essentially acknowledges this problem in the final shot of the sequence. In order to follow his numbering scheme he must call the shot #84; however, there are at least five separate portions of the shot that require separate attention and there is no mechanical demarcation. So, he presents the reader with: 84a, 84b, 84c, 84d, 84e, and 84f. In our analysis, we operate at the level of the individual frame (29.97 frames per second in the system of digital video with which we worked.) We refer to Bellour's shot numbers and to his two primary divisions: "A" for Melanie's trip across the bay, her time in the house, and her return to the boat; "B" for her return trip in the boat.

According to Bellour's analysis and textual description of the Bodega Bay sequence, the following elements should be present in the physical document, the film sequence: key frames and key frame sets, alternation, two centers—the

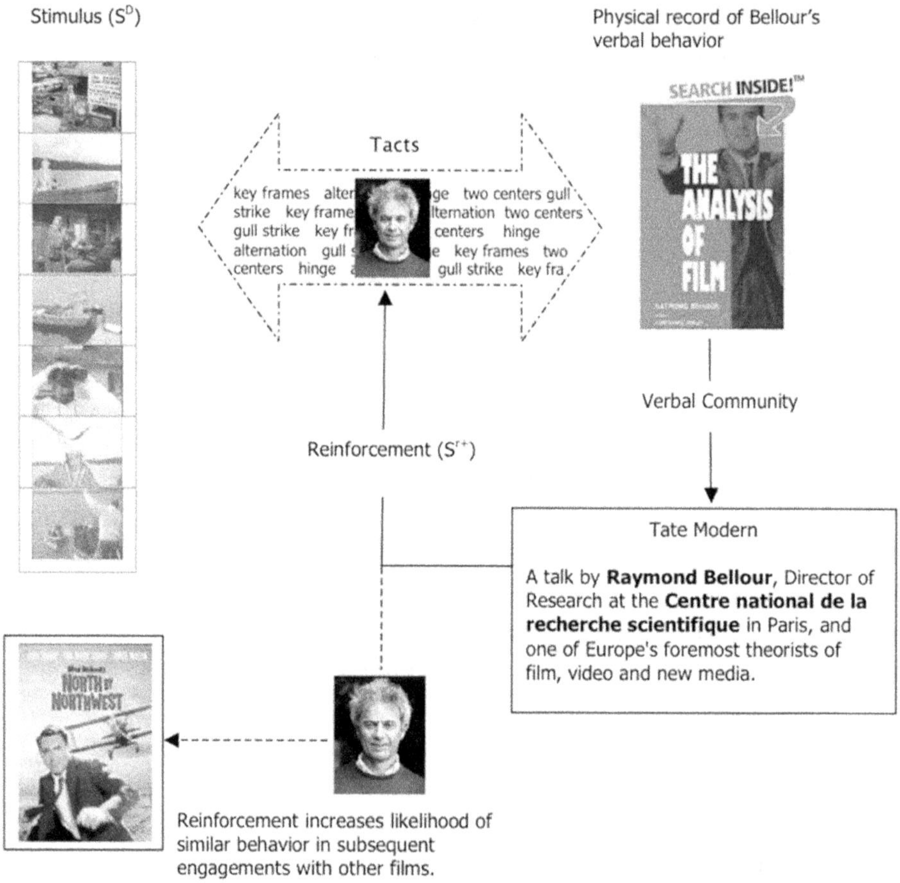

Figure 8.14. Physical Document, Bellour's verbal behavior, instantiation, and consequences.

"hinge" sequence and a second center. Figure 8.14 presents the relationship between the physical document (*The Birds*), Bellour, the physical instantiation of Bellour's verbal behavior controlled by the document environment, the verbal communities (reinforcing and punishing) that engage with Bellour's record of behavior (*The Analysis of Film*), and subsequent behavior by Bellour with respect to other physical documents of similar sort (e.g., *North by Northwest*). *The Los Angeles Times Magazine* cover story represents those opposed to the stance of Bellour and other French theorists seen as espousing "elitist psychobabble." The Tate Modern blurb represents those who regard Bellour as one of the "major figures" working in or on film and video.

STRUCTURAL ANALYSIS OF THE BODEGA BAY SEQUENCE

There are several approaches that could be applied to the structural analysis of a moving image document. Salt (2003) advocates an approach based on the notion of the "shot" and the statistical character and distribution of "shots" within a moving image document. O'Connor (1991) and Kearns and O'Connor (2004) employed an Information Theoretic approach to the analysis of moving image documents. O'Connor (1991) used a technique that measured the change of the size and position of objects, or more accurately, pixel clusters within a moving image document. Dalianas, Allen and England (1995) reviewed a number of automated techniques for the automatic segmentation of moving image documents that included the analysis of raw image differences between frames, a number of histogram-based techniques, and an edge detection-based approach.

In choosing a technique for structural analysis of a moving image document, the nature of the question one hopes to answer must be taken into account. An Information Theoretic approach such as that taken by Kearns and O'Connor (2004) measures the structure of an entire film or message in Shannon's (Shannon & Weaver, 1949) terms. Bellour described the Bodega Bay sequence in fairly microscopic detail. An Information Theoretic approach would not be granular enough to adequately match Bellour's description of the sequence. It should be noted that Kearns' (2005) concept of "entropic bursts" might provide a finer grained Information Theoretic appropriate for the task at hand. Salt's (2003) statistical approach based on the analysis of shots is limited in a number of respects. The previously discussed conceptual problems with the "shot" as a unit of analysis makes Salt's approach untenable. In addition, Salt's analysis examines the statistical character and description of shots over the course of a complete film or collection of moving image documents. Like the Information Theoretic approach, Salt's approach is macroscopic. Finally, the phenomena addressed by Salt's methods are not congruent with elements of the moving image document that Bellour addresses in his analysis. The segmentation techniques reviewed by Dalianas, Allen, and England (1995) provide the level of detail necessary for the detection of key frames and frame sets in Bellour's analysis, however, would not be appropriate for detecting alternation or detecting the centers within the sequence as identified by Bellour.

Our ultimate goal in analyzing the structure of the Bodega Bay sequence was to find the elements of the physical structure of the moving image document that prompted Bellour to make the statements (tacts) he did about the film. To accomplish this task, it was necessary to look at the structure of the segment on at least two levels. First, Bellour breaks the sequence into "shots" or frame sets and selects key frames. This requires an examination of individual frames. Second, Bellour describes alternation between the frame sets, the unique character of the "hinge," the two centers, and the gull strike. These tacts are descriptions of the relationship between frame sets.

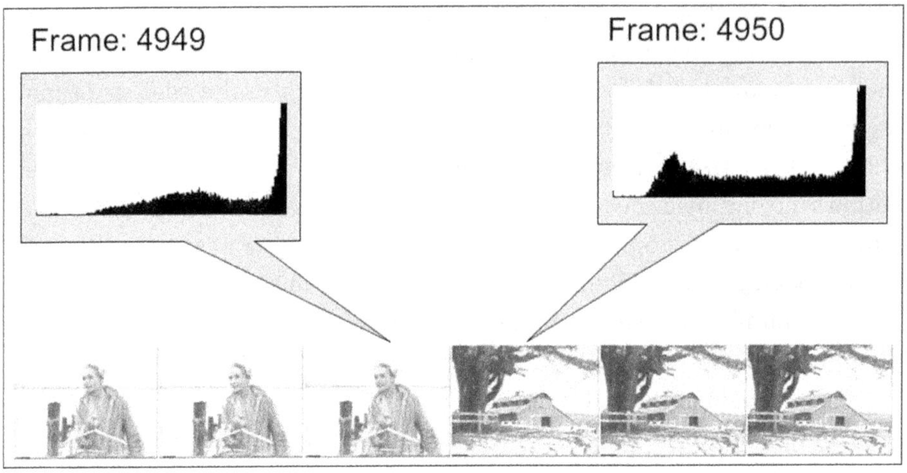

Figure 8.15. RGB Histograms for Two Frames.

We sought precise, repeatable, numeric, and graphical representations of the signal that would enable discussion of filmic structure—the message, in the terms of Shannon and Weaver. We sought the means by which we might discuss message structure, so that discussions of meaning would have a significant touchstone. It might be said that we sought a method of fingerprinting the frames.

In standard digital images each and every color is composed of a certain amount of red, a certain amount of green, and a certain amount of blue—with black being the absence of any R, G, or B and with white being maximum of each. In the frame images we captured there is a possibility of 256 shades of red, 256 shades of green, and 256 shades of blue, for a possible palette of over sixteen million colors. Deriving a histogram of each of the RGB components, as illustrated in Figure 8.15, or the aggregated values distributed across an X-axis of 255 points (the 0 origin being the 256th) yields a fingerprint—a color distribution map—of each frame.

It would seem obvious that within the large number of frames in a film (~30/sec) there is likely to be a little bit of variation in color distribution from frame to frame; however, this variation will be small in sequential frames depicting the same objects with the same composition and lighting, and the variation will be larger as the objects change or the composition changes or the lighting changes. For example, nearly all the frames of Melanie in the boat heading toward the house (Bellour's shot #15 comprised of 140 frames or approximately 4.7 seconds of screen time) will have essentially the same color distribution. When the film data stream switches to what is seen by Melanie (Brenner house for ~3.9 seconds) the color distribution is markedly different.

Perhaps one of the most appealing aspects of mapping color distribution is that it is an entirely software-based process. There is no necessity for human intervention to determine and mark what is to be considered the "subject" or how many pixels (what percentage of the frame area) make up some viewer-selected object. Not that these are not useful for some sorts of analysis, but using just the color palette enables an essentially "judgment-free" analytic process.

In behavior analytic terms, we were seeking what segments of the filmic signal set could account for Bellour's behavior of selecting certain frames as key frames, as well as the behaviors of relating certain groups of frames to other groups of frames. Reducing our analysis to a simple, unambiguous portion of the signal stream—the RGB component of the visual stream, without the input of the audio track—simplified analysis and provided the opportunity to tease apart the contributions of the entire signal bundle.

METHOD

Structural Analysis

The Bodega Bay sequence from *The Birds* was extracted and converted to AVI format from the 1986 Video Disc version of *The Birds* using Adobe Premiere on an IBM compatible personal computer running Microsoft Windows 2000. The resulting AVI file was broken into a series of 12,803 JPG image files using Apple QuickTime Pro 7.03 at a rate of 29.97 frames per second. RGB histograms were generated for each of the 12,803 frames using the Python Imaging Library.

A Lorenz transformation was then performed on each histogram. The Gini coefficient was calculated to generate a scalar value representing the color distribution of each frame, as illustrated in Figure 8.16. Differences in Gini coefficients between successive frames were calculated as a measure of change across frames, as illustrated in Figurre 8.17.

Codifying Bellour's Analysis

Bellour's analysis does not include precise times or frame numbers to either select key frames or delineate frame sets; however, he includes photographs of the key frames. The frame numbers for Bellour's key frames and frame set boundaries were selected using visual comparison between the photographs from Bellour's article and the extracted frames. Frame sets were composed of all the frames between successively identified key frames and tagged using Bellour's numbering convention. Bellour grouped framesets into higher-level groups. The frame sets were arranged into higher-level groups using Bellour's description.

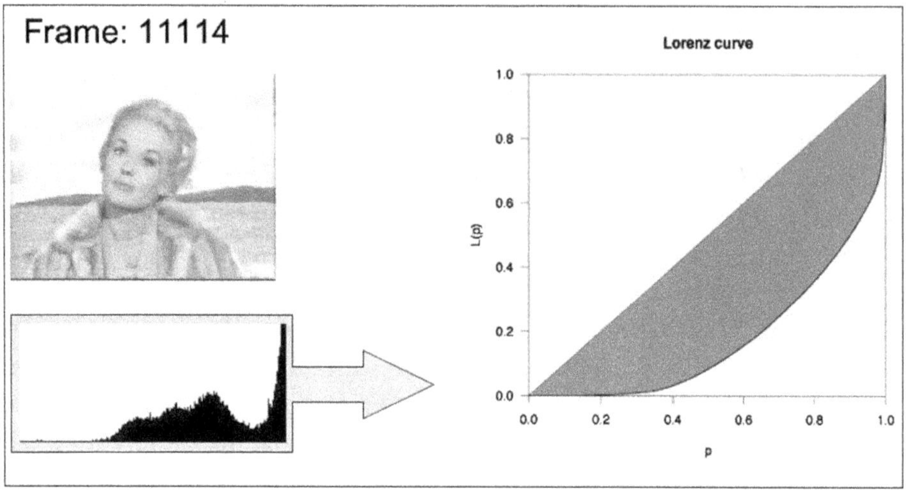

Figure 8.16. Lorenz Curve Representing RGB Values in Single Frame.

Results

Bellour's analysis began with shot number 3 of the segment and continued to shot 84. Bellour includes two groups of shots that have little bearing on his analysis of the sequence, Melanie's acquisition and boarding of the boat (3–12) and Melanie's arrival at the dock following her trip and the gull strike (84a–84f). These sets do not play into Bellour's analysis and appear to function only to demarcate the segment within the larger document—the entire film of *The Birds*.

Detection of Keyframes and Frame Sets

Figure 8.18 shows the absolute value of the difference between the Gini value of a particular frame of the Bodega Bay sequence of *The Birds* and the previous

3102	0.75823	0.730229	0.767636	0.756904		14
3103	0.752879	0.725771	0.763248	0.75239		14
3104	0.755997	0.727444	0.766893	0.75531		14
3105	0.508524	0.470775	0.48623	0.496835		15
3106	0.525335	0.491549	0.50848	0.517705		15
3107	0.516397	0.489725	0.502979	0.511506		15
3108	0.507792	0.481584	0.497303	0.504193		15
3109	0.516215	0.482181	0.509815	0.509638		15
3110	0.513575	0.490304	0.506167	0.512725		15

Figure 8.17. Sample Data: Frame Number, Red Coefficient, Green Coefficient, Blue Coefficient, Aggregated Coefficient, Frame Image, Bellour's Frame Number.

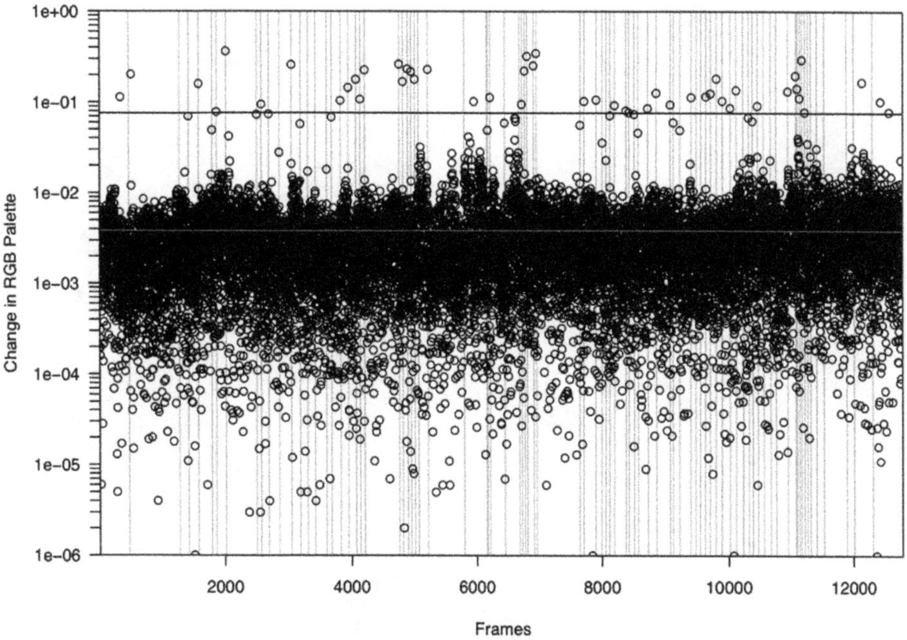

Figure 8.18. Semi-Log Graph of Absolute Frame-to-Frame Differences with Green Line Showing Mean Value for All Differences and Blue Line Showing Mean Value for Bellour's Key Frames.

frame. The mean difference between frames for all frames in the sequence is 0.003826, which is represented on the graph by the green (upper) horizontal line. The mean difference between frames identified as key frames by Bellour was 0.075678. The difference values fall into a bimodal distribution. The difference values of key frames and the proceeding frame were an order of magnitude higher than the difference values between frames that were not identified as key frames.

Figure 8.19 shows the Gini coefficients for each frame broken down into individual frame sets as identified by Bellour. Within shots, the Gini coefficients remain stable for most shots and trend in a linear manner. Notable exceptions to this pattern include the group of frame sets that make up Bellour's "hinge" sequence (25–43); the gull strike (p. 77); and Melanie's arrival to the dock following the gull strike (84a–84f).

Analysis of Frame Sets

Figure 8.20 shows the Gini coefficients of each frame of the segment broken down by shot number, presenting the "flow" of the color distributions across the time of the film sequence. We might construct a "tact map" by over-layering indicators for some of the key elements mapped by the data in Figure 8.20, as in Figure 8.21 Once Melanie is actually underway on her

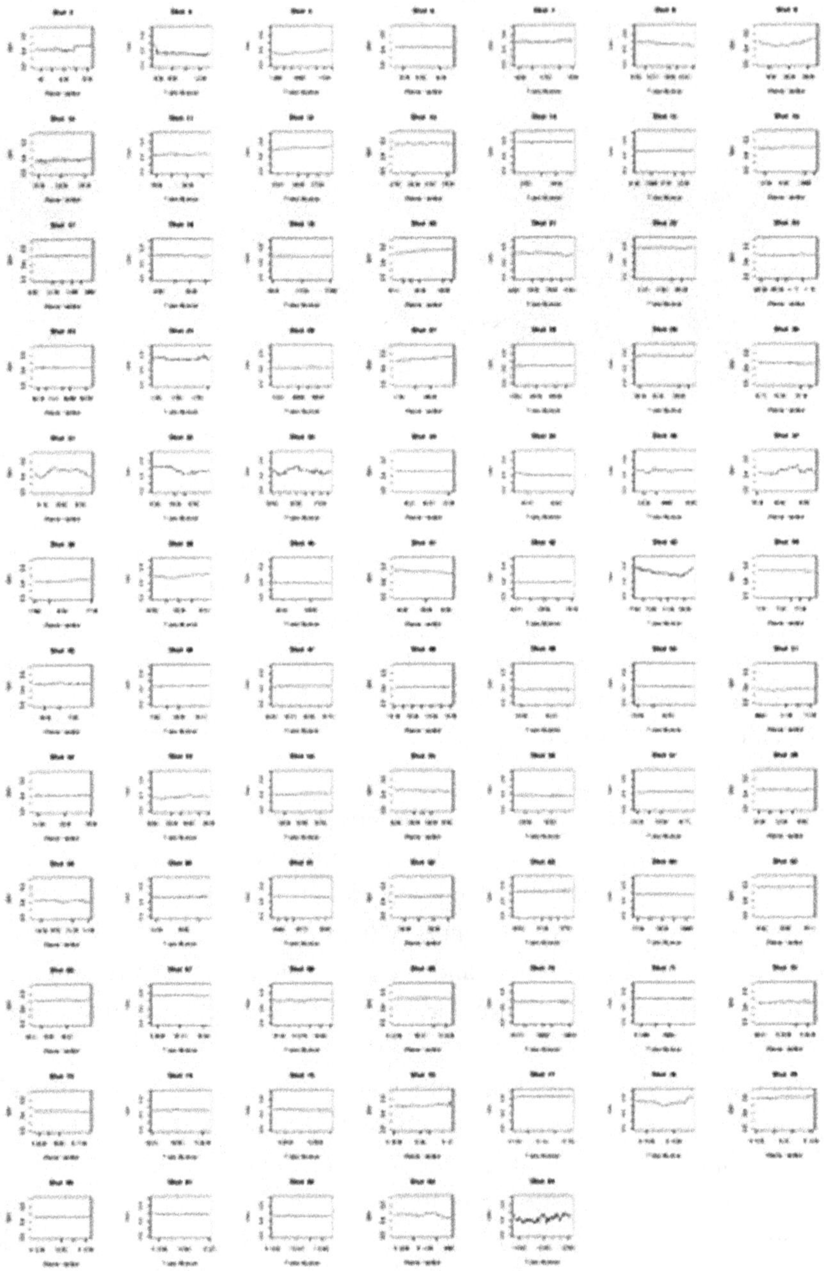

Figure 8.19. Matrix of Gini Values Grouped According to Bellour's Shot Numbers.

trip to the Brenner house, we have almost uninterrupted alternation. We are presented with Melanie in the boat, then the Brenner house as she sees it—Bellour's shots 15 through 22. Then we are presented with Melanie paddling the boat and seeing the dock—23–24; then walking on the dock and

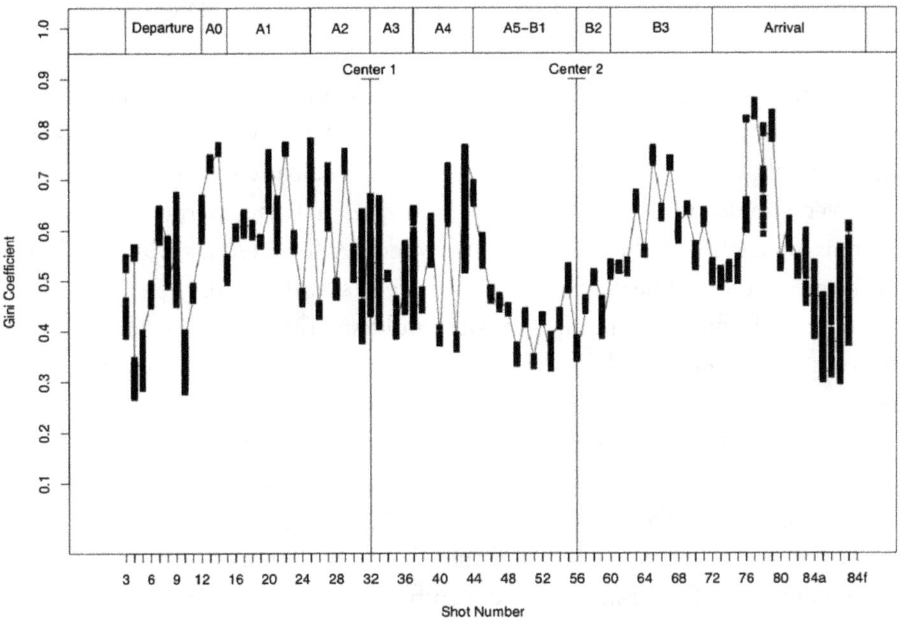

Figure 8.20. Gini Coefficients for Frames within Bellour's Shot Numbers.

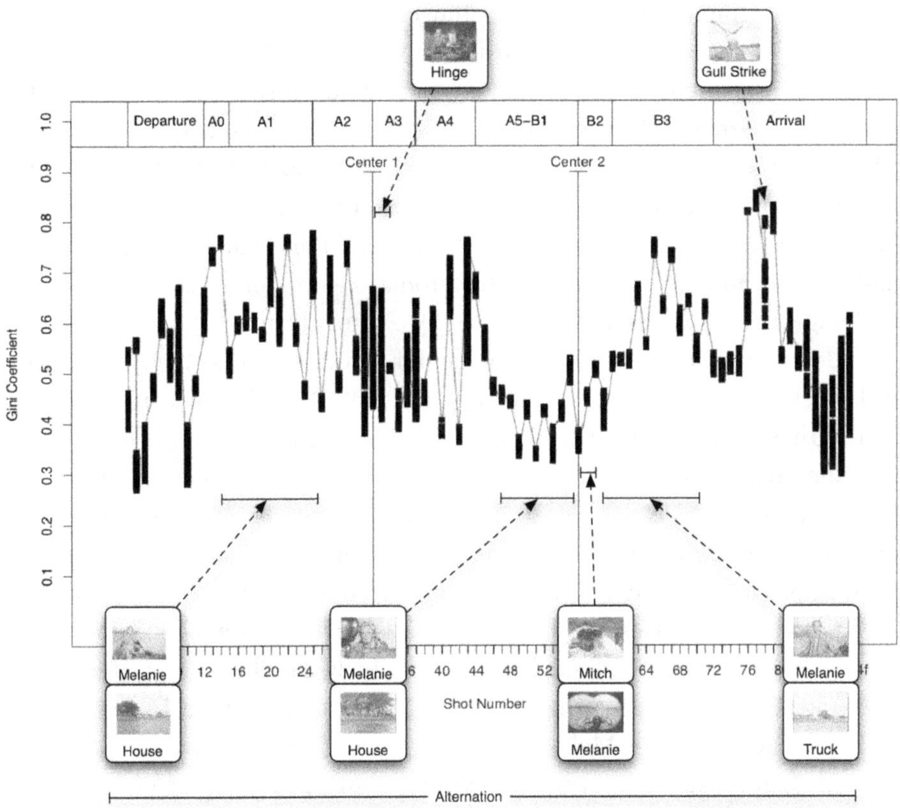

Figure 8.21. Tact Map Overlaying Alternation, Hinge, and Gull Strike Markers on Gini Plot.

seeing the barn—25–31. That is, shots 15 through 31 present Melanie, what she sees, Melanie, what she sees, and so on. The latter portion is more distinct in the graph, though the entire sequence of shots clearly shows alternation.

We should note that the RGB graph does not necessarily indicate that there is alternation in the sense of Melanie/dock/Melanie/dock/Melanie. However, one would still be able to say that there is alternation of the RGB pallets, regardless of whether a human viewer would say that the same objects were in front of the lens. Such an RGB alternation might have its own discursive power.

Bellour's "hinge" sequence runs from frame number 5219 to frame number 6447—Bellour's shot numbers 32—36 (A3). Bellour also refers to this sequence as the first of the "two centers." It would make some sense, then, that it would be in the vicinity of the center and the final frame number 6447 is very near the center of 12,803 frames. More significant is the distribution of the Gini values—they are clustered more closely to the 0.5 line and they display much less variation than we see in most of the rest of the graph. Given the different form of the distributions on either side of the "first center" it is not untenable to assert the graphic appearance of a hinge.

What is not so immediately evident graphically is the second center—that point in the sequence when Mitch sees Melanie—a second center in that it breaks up the rhyme of the trip out and the trip back for a second time. That is, Melanie has exited the house and heads back to the dock and the boat. It seems that after having been in the house—the first center—Melanie will simply head back; however, Mitch's discovery of Melanie and the eventual uniting of "hero and heroine for the first time in the ironic and ravishing complicity of an exchange" (p. 53) interrupts the simplicity of the return.

Bellour suggests that the second center "stands out less starkly"; however, it does stand out. Shot 43, whose large number of Gini values suggests both its length and the varying dataset, is where Melanie moves along the dock and into the boat. Shots 44 and 45 begin the pattern of displacement along the Gini value that was typical in the earlier alternation, This alternation pattern develops strongly between 48 and 54—alternating Gini values remain almost fixed in place along the Gini axis and they occupy a narrow band of the axis. At 55, the shot crosses the 0.5 boundary and the subsequent Gini values suggest alternation again, though of a more widely distributed sort. It is during this fragment that Melanie has watched Mitch, and then, at 54 Mitch runs to the house and at 55 Melanie stands up and tries to start the motor. The second center displays a form of alternation, but this takes place in a manner that presents almost a mirror image of the alternation in the trip out—the alternation here "hanging below" the 0.5 line. As the second center closes, the alternation repeats the pattern of the trip out—all the Gini values arcing above the 0.5 line.

CLOSING THOUGHTS

The order of magnitude differences between the mean differences for key frames and non-key frames presents a numerical representation of the key frame tact. We have a precise, numerical way of speaking of the key frames identified by Bellour, as well as an automated way of detecting those frames. The clustering of Gini coefficients in the "on water" sequences with distinctly different and separated patterns presents a numerical representation of the alternation tact. Melanie's Brenner house sequence presents a distinctly different numerical and graphical representation, giving us the hinge tact. The numerical and graphical "bunching up" in the representation of Mitch's discovery of Melanie and their double-seeing alternation, presents us with the second center and a means for speaking precisely of the two-centers tact.

Bellour does not speak to any significant degree about the gull strike on Melanie, though the strike is often mentioned in other discussions of the Bodega Bay sequence. The entire strike is approximately one second of running time and may have been too microscopic for Bellour to address in his analysis. However, the numerical analysis and graphical presentation present a striking dataset. Almost every frame presents a Gini value significantly different from its predecessor. This is a very high entropy portion of the sequence—several rapid changes in the data stream in less than a second of running time is a very different pattern from that of any other portion of the film. We might suggest that digital frame-by-frame precision might have enabled Bellour to speak of this brief fragment. In every other case the frame to frame differences that were significant were between shots; in the gull strike there are significant frame to frame differences within the shot.

One portion of Bellour's analysis on which we have not touched is his classification of shots as "Close Shot," "Medium Shot," or "Long Shot." These terms are frequently used in production and have often been used for subsequent description by theorists and catalogers. Unfortunately, these terms suffer from the same lack of precision that limits the utility of the term "shot." There is no agreed upon definition of "close," "medium," or "long" in the context of film documents. In production, the terms refer to the distance (real or apparent) of the camera from the object(s) in front of the camera; however, there is no standard stating that a close shot must have the camera no more than x centimeters or contain no more than x percent of some object. The determination of close, medium, or long is dependent on external knowledge—that is input from some source other than the physically present film document, perhaps a film course or conversation with a director.

In some sense, the hardest thing about what we are doing is seeing what is actually computable only from the physically present data. That is, film criticism and analysis have so long depended on human engagement with the physical document that the distinction between the data stream of the document and the contribution of the viewer's prior knowledge of what is represented remain difficult to tease apart, at times. So we can easily cluster shots with roughly similar RGB patterns. However, going from an MS of Melanie in the boat to an LS of Brenner's house, while it shows us an RGB change does not show us anything that would definitively indicate a change from a Medium Shot (MS) to a Long Shot (LS). Also, one could imagine a change from MS to LS (say a cityscape of one or two building fronts, to a LS of several buildings), in which the RGB would remain fairly constant. Within any one film or one director's body of work, we might be able to make some calculations that would describe/predict CS, MS, LS changes, but there is just nothing inherent only in the data that makes that a widespread property. This does not diminish either Bellour's analysis or the digital analysis—it simply speaks to the complexity of understanding filmic documents and even simply describing them accurately. Indeed, this demonstrates one of our initial assertions: that the engineering of the message structure and the semantic meaning are separate, complementary notions.

That said, the close correlation between the frame-to-frame analysis and Bellour's writing suggests that our use of an expert analyst's response to *The Birds* indeed demonstrates the validity of this approach to numerical and graphical representation of filmic structure. Perhaps one of the most significant consequences of the close correlation is the availability of a "vocabulary" for description and analysis. A fundamental problem with previous systems of analysis has been the reliance on words to describe visual, time-varying documents. Setting about describing, analyzing, and indexing word-based documents with words is simple, though not necessarily easy or trivial. One can extract words from a document; use some rule for selecting certain words; and then subject the document and the representative words to scrutiny. If the supposed representative words do not occur frequently or at all in the document, no synonyms occur, and no words of some higher or lower lever of specificity occur, then we can easily say the words are not significantly representative. Since there is no one-to-one correspondence between words and images or parts of images; since there are no precise standardized terms for entropy values of production attributes of moving image documents (that is, "fast-paced" and "beautifully lighted" are not precisely defined); and since words are not native elements of the image track, there is no reliable way of speaking precisely of attributes and changes of attributes across frames. Being able to represent these attributes and time-varying states of the attributes at the pixel, frame, frame set ("shot"), sequence, and document level with the same processes and terms should enable deeper and more fruitful analysis.

At the same time, the same techniques provide means for discovering structural elements. It would be too facile to suggest that we now have a robust mechanism for automated description of filmic structure; however, we do at least have a robust automated means for mapping the structure. We could run any film through a frame by frame comparison of RGB and be able to state that certain portions remain stable for some time, then change; and at some points, rapid changes take place—the points of change, the points of discontinuity in the data stream, represent points where something different is happening. One function of such points of continuity might be as indexing points—pull out, for example, the forty frames at which there is the greatest frame-to-frame change and have a rough "index" of the film. Find the one, two, or three most frequent RGB fingerprints and use representative frames with those values to present the "look" of the film.

Perhaps even more intriguing, and a likely avenue of rewarding research would be the use of RGB fingerprints in classification. Do all of Hitchcock's films, or at least those from a particular period, share the same fingerprint patterns? If De Palma is the heir to Hitchcock, do his films actually bear a numerical similarity to Hitchcock's films? Do music videos and early Russian documentaries (e.g., *Vertov's Man with the Movie Camera*), films with very different structures from the classic Hollywood films studied by Bellour, yield useful numerical descriptions?

Of course, most moving image documents are made up of more than simply RGB data. Multiple sound tracks for voice, narration, sound effects, and music significantly increase the amount of data available for analysis; however, there is no reason that these time-varying data could not be described using a similar numerical and graphical technique.

As we have demonstrated here, the data available for analysis is not limited to the signals available in the physically present document. Bellour's analysis of *The Birds*, in essence, becomes another signal or memetic attribute of the document. Other critics who have commented on *The Birds* or viewer reactions to the piece could be analyzed in the same manner that we have applied to Bellour's work. Every person who interacts with a document and commits some permanent behavioral product of that interaction contributes to the document's signal set for subsequent uses.

In some sense, this becomes a fundamental aspect of the setting for considering the relationship between the document/message structure and the semantic meaning. The additional signal, for example a review, can have a significant impact on whether a document is accessed and on how it is evaluated for fitness to a given information need. The document is not necessarily static with the same impact on any given user; rather, it is an evolutionary process. The concept of document as evolutionary process receives more discussion in Anderson (2006), and Wilson (1968).

Bellour (2000) sought means to explore and represent moving image documents with the precision already applied to verbal documents at the micro and macro levels. He sought means to go beyond what Augst (1980) termed the "gratuitousness and arbitrariness of impressionistic criticism." The digital environment offers the opportunity to do so; to enable speaking directly of the native elements (e.g., the RGB components and their changes across time); and, to paraphrase Godard, to confront vague ideas with precise images.

A FRUITFUL REVIVAL

Additional studies continue to express the interdisciplinary relevance of measuring structures of all documents in order to say something about document representation, document functions, and about intentional document restructuring for improved communication. Simon (2005), for example, measured entropy within jazz improvisations to be able to quantify amounts of unpredictability and riskiness in jazz improvisation by graduate students, in order to define numerically the essence of jazz improvisation. Also, Kearns, O'Connor, and Moore (2007) show that scholarly writing often lacks perspicuous balance between content and structure. This paper urges academic writers to restructure their scholarly writing to reflect the depth of their intellectual message rather than conforming to the structurally simplistic hegemony of the mundane. The authors of this study rely on modern interpretations of Shannon's information theory for understanding scholarly document structures and interdisciplinary academic audiences.

The Shannon revival is naught without the underlying principles that all information is measurable and that all the world's a document (O'Connor, Anderson, & Kearns, DOCAM conference proceedings, 2006).

CHAPTER NINE

FUNCTIONAL ONTOLOGY CONSTRUCTION

A TURN TO THE FUNCTIONAL

HERE WE PRESENT a coherent approach for modeling the relationship between the user, the document, and the environment in which they exist. The model is interdisciplinary at heart. This approach, Functional Ontology Construction (FOC), examines the relationships between the individual, the aspects of the physical environment that have function to the individual, the functional ontology, and the consequences of those relationships. The philosophical roots are a synthesis of selectionist thought as embodied in Skinner's (1953) *Radical Behaviorism* and Dawkins' (1976) theory of memetics; empirical knowledge, research methodology, and a philosophy of science from *Behavior Analysis*; and the pragmatic oriented work of Wilson (Wilson, 1968, 1977, 1983), Blair (1990) and O'Connor (O'Connor, 1996; O'Connor et al., 2003) in Information Science.

Functional Ontology Construction

There is a strong interest in the study of behavior at the present in the field of Information Science (see Wilson, 1996; Spink & Cole, 2006; Fisher, Erdelez & McKechnie, 2005). Spink and Cole (2006), in the call for papers for a special issue of the *Journal of Documentation* states:

> Human information behavior (HIB) is a basic element of human existence. Humans have sought, organized, and used information for millennia as they evolved and learned patterns of HIB to help resolve their human problems and continue to survive. The field of library and information science (LIS) has historically been a leading discipline in conducting research that seeks to understand human information-related behaviors.

Functional ontology construction (FOC) is an approach to addressing problems in Information Science that concern the relationship between human behavior and information. The underlying philosophy of science used here comes from a Radical Behaviorist perspective grounded in the work of B. F. Skinner. The techniques come from the rich empirical history and base of behavior analysis. The general principles emerge through the replication across many individuals and settings and are synthesized in an inductive manner. The model is simply the tried and tested concepts of Behavior Analysis applied to problems within the domain of Information Science. The justification for this technique lies in a shared tradition of pragmatism between Information Science and Behavior Analysis. It is in the shared tradition of pragmatism that we find both the philosophical foundation for doing things with information and the scientific foundation for implementing means of bringing together people with problems or issues to resolve and information that is functional for them.

Pragmatism as a Shared Tradition

Pragmatism emerged as a philosophical school of thought in the late nineteenth century in the United States. The *Cambridge Dictionary of Philosophy* (Audi, 1999) defines pragmatism as,

> a philosophy that stresses the relation of theory to praxis and takes the continuity of experience and nature as the outcome of directed action as the starting point for reflection. Experience is the ongoing transaction of organism and environment, i.e., both subject and object are constituted in the process. When intelligently ordered, initial conditions are deliberately transformed according to ends-in-view, i.e., intentionally, into a subsequent state of affairs thought to be more desirable.

Knowledge is therefore guided by interests or values. Since the reality of objects cannot be known prior to experience, truth claims can be justified only as the fulfillment of conditions that are experimentally determined, that is, the outcome of inquiry (p. 730).

Pragmatism and American semiotics have entwined roots in the nineteenth century. The experience of Oliver Wendell Holmes, Jr., in the Civil War led to a philosophical rejection of the idealistic and romantic notions of his mentor, transcendental philosopher and poet, Ralph Waldo Emerson. While not to the degree of Holmes, William James and Charles Sanders Pierce were also profoundly affected by the Civil War. Their collaboration in the years following the antebellum period of the nineteenth century culminated in the publication of Pierce's seminal paper, *How to Make our Ideas Clear* (1878), and James' public introduction of pragmatism at a lecture entitled "Philosophical Conceptions and Practical Results" delivered at the University of California at Berkeley in 1898 (James and McDermott, 1968).

Pragmatism becomes a rejection of universal truth in favor of subjective experience. We accept a definition of ontology as "study of existence" as Flew (1984) suggests; that is, ontology is taken to be the environment rather than some universal "way that everything is" or Wittgenstein's early "everything that is the case" (2001).

Hjørland (1996) considers Patrick Wilson to be what he describes as a "long term" pragmatist. The following passage from *Two Kinds of Power* (Wilson, 1968) is an example of Wilson's pragmatic viewpoint:

> Much, but happily not all, of the reading we do is purposive: we read in order to find the answer to a particular question, to learn what is known of some range of phenomena, to improve our understanding of some matter, to find out how to do a certain sort of thing, to maintain or improve our social or intellectual position, to console ourselves in our misfortunes. If asked why we want to do a certain sort of thing, we are often able to cite a further goal: we want to find out how to make a chocolate mousse because we want to serve one to our dinner guests, we want to find out how much weight a given sort of rope will support because we want to hang ourselves (p. 20).

Wilson frequently cited pragmatic philosophers in his work. *Two Kinds of Power* (Wilson, 1968) includes references to James, Pierce, and Quine in the extensive notes Wilson used to support his work. In the conclusion of *Second Hand Knowledge*, Wilson claims that the work is not an epistemological work in the sense of studying the nature of knowledge for its own sake and instead refers the reader to pragmatic philosopher, Richard Rorty's notion of behavioral epistemology as expressed in *Philosophy and the Mirror of Nature* (Rorty, 1979).

Wilson is not the only adherent to pragmatism in information science. Blair's STAIRS pieces (Blair, 1986, 1996) are primarily about the failure of information retrieval systems to take pragmatic concerns into account. *Language and Representation* (Blair, 1990) presents the later views of Wittgenstein as a potential explanation of the type of problems described in the STAIRS studies. Copeland's (Copeland, 1997; O'Connor, Copeland, & Kearns, 2003) bears a strong resemblance to the pragmatic work of John Dewey. *Hunting and Gathering on the Information Savanna* (O'Connor, Copeland, & Kearns, 2003) is not an explicitly stated work of pragmatic information science; however, the case studies on submarine chasing, bounty hunting, and engineering are examinations of the praxis of real world information searching behavior. The foundational model presented in *Hunting and Gathering on the Information Savanna* is one of the ancestor models upon which functional ontology modeling is derived.

The justification for the integration of behavior analytic thought into Information Science lies in a shared tradition of pragmatism between the fields. Moxley (Moxley, 2002, 2003, 2004), Staddon (2001), and Day (1992) have illustrated the parallels between the pragmatic tradition and Skinner's philosophy of Radical Behaviorism that provides the philosophical basis for behavior analysis. Moxley asserts that Skinner broke with the logical positivist tradition with the publication of Skinner's essay, "The Operational Analysis of Psychological Terms" (Skinner, 1945), which was an early version of the theory presented in *Verbal Behavior* (Skinner, 1957). The views expressed in Skinner's later work are more closely aligned with pragmatic. Moxley (2004) notes that the first published use of the term "radical behaviorism" occurs in "The Operational Analysis of Psychological Terms" (Skinner, 1945). Skinner made an explicit statement linking Radical Behaviorism to pragmatism. Skinner claimed kinship to Pierce and drew parallels between his theory of operant behavior and Pierce's concept of "habits" (Moxley, 2004). Staddon (2001) summarizes the link between radical behaviorism and pragmatism as follows,

> The philosophy of radical behaviorism is a descendant of the pragmatism of C. S. Pierce. Truth is "successful working" in the words of one modern behaviorist (Morris, 1988). Skinner extended the "successful working" of pragmatism from the life of the individual to the evolution of the race: those actions not traceable to personal reinforcement must be "instincts" traceable to natural selection. The epistemology of radical behaviorism is thus a variant of evolutionary epistemology (pp. 96–97).

Staddon's quote mirrors the development of the approach taken here. The Functional Ontology Construction approach draws from the pragmatic tradition in Information Science and applies behavior analytic principles to the problems defined from that pragmatic orientation. The consequence of taking this approach is a selectionist view of both information-related behavior as well as an evolutionary epistemology.

FUNCTIONAL ONTOLOGY CONSTRUCTION: COMPONENTS AND ANCESTORS

Functional Ontology Construction (FOC) is the application of behavior analytic theory to problems in Information Science that include human behavior as a component. The FOC approach is a synthesis of a number of critical components. The first component of the system is a binary document model inspired by the *Information Theory* of Shannon and Weaver (1949), semiotic theory (Chambers, 2003; Eco, 1976), Wittgenstein's (1953) language games, Skinner's (1953) theory of verbal behavior and Dawkins' theory of memes (Dawkins, 1976, 1982).

The second component of the system is a model of a functional ontological space where the engagements between users and documents takes place. The functional ontological space provides a common ontological context for behaviors such as information seeking or browsing and the documents that would satisfy the user's needs.

The third component of the system focuses on the implications of the functional ontology model. As Staddon (2001) would suggest, one implication of adopting a behavior analytic or radical behaviorist approach to engagements between users and documents is an evolutionary selection process. Interacting with documents has a selective function on the behavior of the users in the engagement and the behavior of the user has a selective function of the document.

Ancestors and Permutations

Before proceeding with the discussion of the components of the FOC approach, we would like to discuss a number of models and ideas that had direct influence on the approach. Functional Ontology Construction is a direct application of the behavior analytic technique of functional analysis. Again, Skinner (1953) discusses the general approach taken here in *Science and Human Behavior*.

> The external variables of which behavior is a function provide for what may be called a causal or functional analysis. We undertake to predict and control the behavior of an individual organism. This is our "dependent variable"—the effect for which we are to find the cause. Our "independent variables"—the causes of behavior—are the external conditions of which behavior is a function. Relations between the two—the "cause-and-effect relationships" in behavior are the laws of a science. A synthesis of these laws expressed in quantitative terms yields a comprehensive picture of the organism as a behaving system (p. 35).

Early permutations of the Functional Ontology Construction approach were attempts to formalize a number of ancestor models including O'Connor's Knowledge State model, Wilson's (1973) concept of situational relevance, and O'Connor, Copeland and Kearns (2003) foundational model in *Hunting and Gathering on the Information Savanna*.

O'Connor's Knowledge State model (Figure 9.1) was originally designed to find a common ontological status for the person seeking information (Question) and things that might help address that need (Documents). The basic reasoning was that a question represented some significant portion of the worldview of the person seeking information—primarily the gap in the worldview, together with the surrounding territory; and that documents—which are not the only possible aids to understanding but are the primary focus of information retrieval—represent some significant portion of the worldview of an author.

Elementary category theory would suggest that if a class could be found or described that would hold both the Question Representation and one or more Document Representation(s), since all members of a class share some

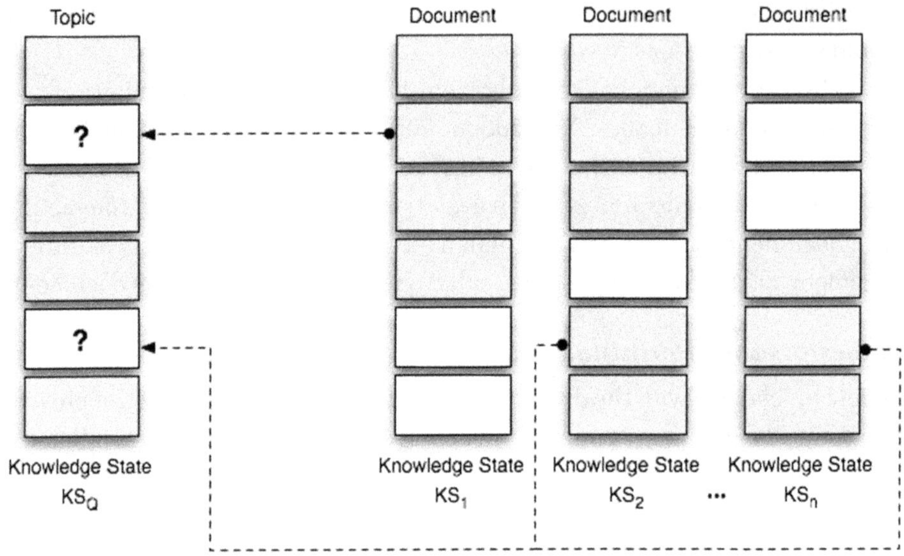

Figure 9.1. Knowledge State Model.

(probabilistic) or all (Aristotelian) defining attributes, then the empty cells in the Question Array could likely be filled with the contents of corresponding cell in one or more of the Document Arrays. It should be noted that Question Array representing the person seeking to do something is not static over time, but is sensitive to the changing environment in which the person exists. This changing environment might be seen as long-term, such learning from and looking back upon previous experience; or short-term, such as seeing one element in one document and modifying the query within a few moments. Indeed, the Question Array exists within evolving worldview of the person as it changes from moment to moment throughout his/her life.

O'Connor's knowledge state model succeeded in establishing a common ontological context between questions and the set of documents that would satisfy the questions; however, one could recast this as an attempt to find an ontological context for the behavior of questioning rather than the physical product of the behavior (e.g., the formal expression of the question). This potentially expands the model to include behaviors that are not easily expressed in terms of the question, such as browsing or watching a movie; however, the knowledge state model still does not address either the motivation for engaging in the information seeking behavior or the consequences of engaging in the behavior.

Both Wilson's (1973) notion of situational relevance and O'Connor, Copeland and Kearns' (2003) foundational model from *Hunting & Gathering on the Information Savanna* focus on the factors that would occasion the behavior of information seeking rather than focusing on the specific behavior of questioning. The FOC approach extends these models of the ontological space by applying the behavior analytic technique of functional analysis to the behavior in question.

Schamber (1994) suggests that "relevance is the field's [Information Science] central concept insofar as it serves as the fundamental criterion in evaluating the effectiveness of information retrieval (IR) and use (p. 3)." Schamber notes that there is not a clear consensus within Information Science on the topic of relevance, however she presents the following statement as general consensus within the field:

> The generally accepted theoretical conceptualization of relevance involves the relationship between a user's information problem or need and the information that could solve the problem. The generally accepted operational conceptualization involves a user's decision to accept or reject information retrieved from an information system (p. 3).

Schamber also notes that notions of relevance have a great impact on the engineering aspects of Information Science as well as "the theoretical and empirical understandings of human behavior in seeking and using information (p. 3)." One model of relevance that is of particular interest is Wilson's (1973) notion of situational relevance.

Situational relevance is both a criticism and an expansion of Cooper's (1971) concept of logical relevance. Wilson notes that the relevance of a particular document or piece of it is a function of the situation in which the need arises and the consequences of having or not having the information in question. Wilson presents a salient example of this phenomenon. One's insurance policy becomes considerably more relevant than it otherwise would be when one sees smoke from a house fire near one's home. In this example, the smoke sets the occasion for the behavior of seeking information about the insurance policy. The consequence in this particular example would be the peace of mind associated with knowing that one's house is insured.

Wilson's notion of relevance as expressed in *Situational Relevance* (1973) and *Two Kinds of Power* (1968) is similar in concept to the idea of a three-term contingency (Skinner, 1969) in behavior analytic terms. The three-term contingency, a central concept in behavior analysis is a relation that includes three parts: antecedent conditions that set the occasion for a behavior's occurrence, the behavior of interest, and the events that follow the behavior and have behavioral function. The assumption of relevance is an assumption that the document that is returned as a result of information seeking behavior fits the needs of the information seeker.

O'Connor, Copeland, and Kearns (2003) presented a model of information seeking in *Hunting and Gathering on the Information Savanna* (Figure 9.2)

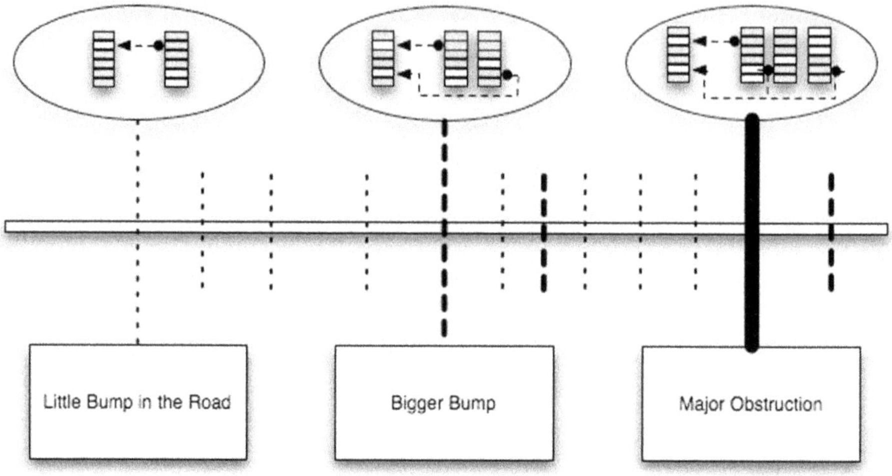

Figure 9.2. Doing Things Model.

that blends O'Connor's (1996) earlier knowledge state model with a notion of relevance similar to Wilson's notion of situational relevance, and a model with some resonance with Dervin and Nilan (1986). A small "bump in the road" may represent a scenario such as finding a mechanic to work on a 1968 VW Bus, finding directions to a night club, or remembering how to calculate the hypotenuse of a right triangle. These are not necessarily trivial needs, though, in terms of search strategies and resources expended, it is not difficult for the questioner to determine an information seeking strategy or to determine the fitness of the results.

A "bigger bump" would involve issues like deciding whether or not to buy a hybrid car (is the technology advanced enough, etc.), writing an article for a peer-reviewed journal, building a skin-on-frame kayak, or formulating a new university policy. A "major obstruction" would constitute scenarios like making the decision to buy a new home, deciding whether or not to have a surgical procedure performed, making a career change, or writing a dissertation. The distinction between the different sorts of information seeking events lies in the resources expended in developing a search strategy, the resources expended, and the fitness requirements of the results. The distinction does not necessarily have anything to do with the importance of the information need as the examples may imply; however there is a likely a correlation between the amount of effort expended in an information search and the importance of the information need.

The Functional Ontology Construction (FOC) approach formalizes the O'Connor, Copeland, and Kearns (2003) model in behavior analytic terms.

Figure 9.3 shows an early version of the version of the FOC approach. This early permutation is little more than the behavior analytic three-term

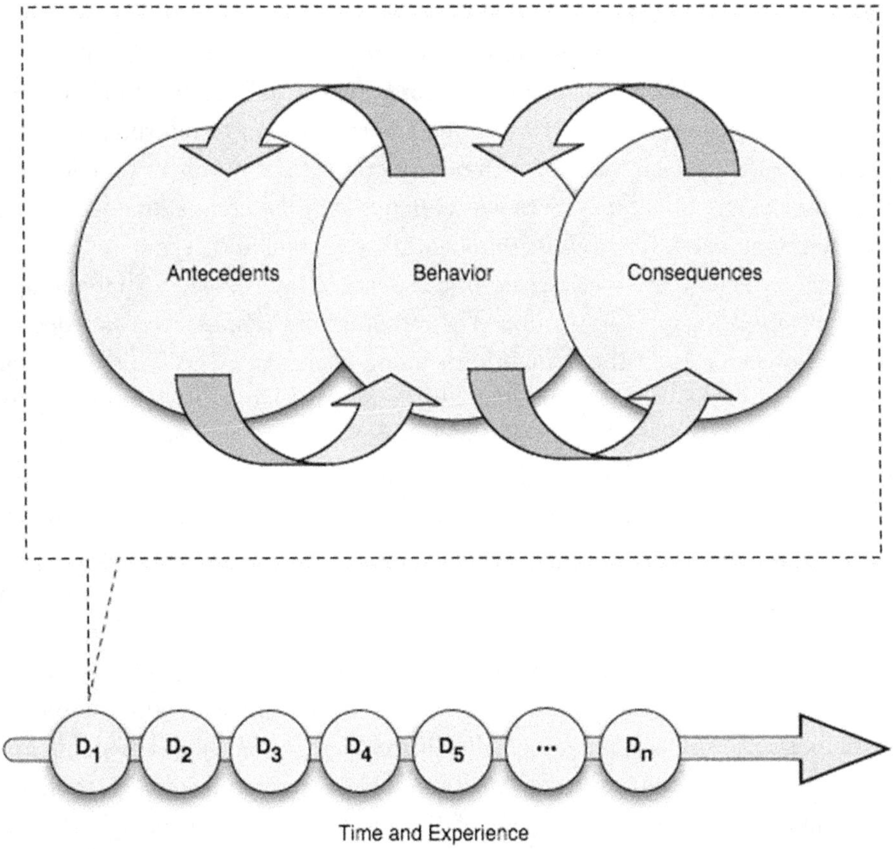

Figure 9.3. Early Instance of Functional Ontology Model.

contingency mapped onto O'Connor, Copeland, and Kearns "road of life." The early conception of the model did not make any distinction between antecedent conditions as conceptualized in behavior analytic theory and the richer concept of information (or those things of an informing nature) found in Information Science. Although one can find a common, shared tradition between radical behaviorism and information science, the assertion that the behavior of a pigeon pecking a key in an operant chamber is equivalent to a person seeking information is, perhaps, too large of a conceptual leap and offers little practical utility to a discipline focused, as Buckland and Liu (1995) suggest, on "documents and messages that are created for use by humans" (p. 385). A model of the document was necessary in order to make the FOC approach a useful and relevant tool for the discipline of Information Science.

The Document as a Binary System of Structure and Function

That model of the document is founded in Shannon and Weaver, along with insights from other fields. While there are a number of ways the term "information" is used in Information Science (see Belkin, 1978; Hayes, 1993; and Buckland, 1991 for reviews of the different meanings of the term information), the term will be used in a manner consistent with Shannon and Weaver's (1949) technical definition of the term. Their definition of information is expressed mathematically as a logarithmic function of the number of choices for a given message. Shannon's work was conducted in the context of engineering telecommunication systems. In this context, the semantic aspects of a given message are secondary to the structural aspects of the message. Shannon and Weaver's model is a binary system. The structure of the message has a degree of independence from the semantic meaning of the message. This is similar in concept to other ways of conceptualizing meaning such as semiotic theory (Eco, 1976; Chandler, 2004); Wittgenstein's "language games"; and the behavior analytic account of verbal behavior (Skinner, 1957). Eco (1976) states that semiotics is "concerned with everything that can be taken as a sign" (p. 7). Semiotics breaks meaningful phenomena into a dyadic or binary system between signifier, the structure of the sign, and signified, the concept associated with the sign (Chandler, 2002).

For clarity, we repeat an earlier passage here. Like Information Theory and Semiotics, Wittgenstein's (1953) concept of "language games" is a binary system of structure and meaning. Meaning emerges from the relationship between the participants in the conversation. Wittgenstein puts greater emphasis on meaning than on the structure of the message. In a sense, it is the inverse of Shannon and Weaver's (1949) focus on the message independently of the message's intended meaning. Wittgenstein's concept of language games is similar to Skinner's (1957) system of verbal behavior (Day, 1992). The main difference between the two systems is the analytic nature of Skinner's system. Wittgenstein asserts that there are as many types of language games as there are conversations or instances of language games. In a somewhat different but compatible vein, Dawkins' (1982) notion of memes and memetic phenotypes is also a binary system of function and structure where memes are a unit of meaning and the memetic phenotype or vehicle is the physical expression or container for the meme. Dawkins (1982) describes the relationship between memes and memetic phenotypes in the following way:

> The phenotypic effects of a meme may be in the form of words, music, visual images, styles of clothes, facial or hand gestures, skills such as opening milk bottles in tits, or panning wheat in Japanese macaques. They are outward and visible (audible, etc.) manifestations of the memes within the brain. They may be perceived by the sense organs of other individuals, and they may so imprint themselves on the brains of receiving individuals that a copy (not necessarily exact)

> of the original meme is then in a position to broadcast its phenotypic effects, with the result that further copies of itself may be made in yet other brains (p. 109).

The model of the document used in the FOC approach is similar in principle to Dawkins' concept of the meme. The document is a bundle of signals that have behavioral function. Schjeldahl, writing of the paintings of Gustave Courbet gives expression to this binary relationship:

> Looking gets you only so far with his work. Then decoding—an onerous task at this distance in time, like explaining moldy jokes—must take over. (Painting by Numbers, in *The New Yorker*, July 30, 2007, p. 83)

Drucker offers another expression of the complex relationship between the signal set of the document and how it might function:

> Stretching the definition of a document along a material axis offers its own challenges to the structures of belief. But the conceptual axes that shoot through any point introduce another set of warps in our understanding. I don't see a simple, positive material fact when I look at a document, I see fields of shifting relations momentarily stabilized in an artifact that exists in a continuum of temporal and spatial and quantum dimensions, only constituted through the framing acts of intervention. (*Excerpts and Entanglements, in a Document (Re)turn*, Skare, Lund, Vårheim, eds. Frankfurt: Peter Lang, 2007).

ONTOLOGY AS ENVIRONMENT

The functional ontology is similar to the behavior analytic notion of behavioral environment. The functional ontology is the set of environmental stimuli and historical factors that have function for an individual at a particular point in time—those things that select behavior. This usage of the term ontology is closer to the philosophical usage (Flew, 1984) than the technical use of the term in Information Science.

In Information Science, ontology describes a categorization system such as the Library of Congress system or a hierarchy of categories such as Yahoo's Web directory. This use of the term is more akin to the notion of a foundational or upper ontology (Smith, 2004); an ontology that contains "everything that is the case" as Wittgenstein (1922) pursued in the *Tractatus Logico-Philosophicus*. Wittgenstein's (1953) later work on language games suggests that the relative nature of language games makes a universal ontology untenable. This position marked Wittgenstein's break with the logical positivists. Smith (2003) suggests that "the project of building one single ontology, even one single top-level ontology, which would be at the same time nontrivial and also readily adopted by a broad population of different information systems communities, has largely been abandoned" (p. 115). Shirky (2005), commenting on the rise of tagging as an emerging organizing principle for the World Wide Web, states:

> Today I want to talk about categorization, and I want to convince you that a lot of what we think we know about categorization is wrong. In particular, I want to convince you that many of the ways we're attempting to apply categorization to the electronic world are actually a bad fit, because we've adopted habits of mind that are left over from earlier strategies.
>
> I also want to convince you that what we're seeing when we see the Web is actually a radical break with previous categorization strategies, rather than an extension of them. What I think is coming instead are much more organic ways of organizing information than our current categorization schemes allow, based on two units—the link, which can point to anything, and the tag, which is a way of attaching labels to links. The strategy of tagging—free-form labeling, without regard to categorical constraints—seems like a recipe for disaster, but as the Web has shown us, you can extract a surprising amount of value from big messy data sets.

Ontology within the context of this work is simply that which exists within the environment of an individual. The functional ontology is comprised of those elements of the individual's environment that have behavioral function. Ontology as traditionally used in Information Science emerges as a consequence of the collective instances of individual behavior.

The Functional Ontology Construction Approach

A document can be conceptualized as a bundle of attributes or signals. The term signal is preferred for two reasons. First, the term signal has a dynamic connotation. The FOC approach has an underlying assumption that relationship between users and documents is a system of selection, which requires the examination of change over time. Second, if one were to use the FOC strategy in a research or engineering setting, then a signal detection approach would be a likely tactical approach to the problem at hand. Three types of signals were discussed with regard to the playing cards: diachronic, synchronic, and memetic. These types of signals can be conceptualized as being independent spaces into which signals fall (see Figure 9.4, panel 1).

In order to speak to the relationship between the document and the user, the behavioral space must be added to the model. Behavior occurs in time. We can conceptualize in terms of an antecedent space and a consequent space (see Figure 9.4, panel 2). The boundary between the antecedent and consequent

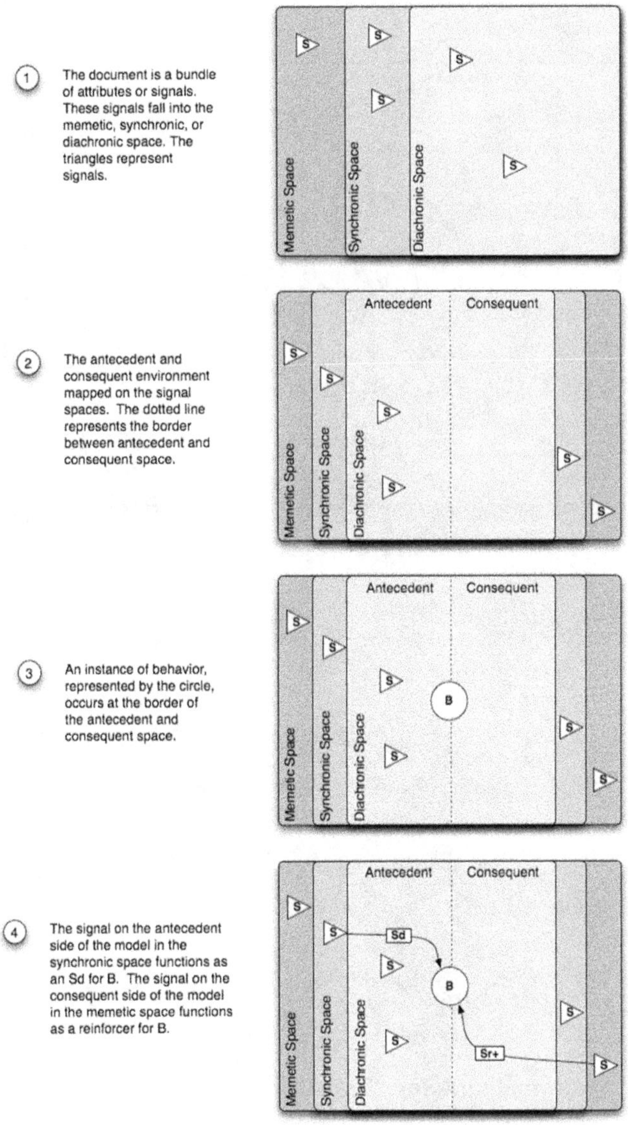

Figure 9.4. Functional Ontology Model.

spaces is the point where an instance of behavior occurs (see Figure 9.4, panel 3). The signals present in a given document may have or acquire behavioral function for a particular person (see Figure 9.4, panel 4). For example, a synchronic signal may function as a discriminative stimulus (SD) for a given instance of behavior and a signal in the memetic space may function as a reinforcer for the behavior (Sr+). It should be noted that the nature of a given signal is not relevant when discussing how the signal functions in relation to the individual's behavior. Figure 9.5 represents a model for a single instance of behavior.

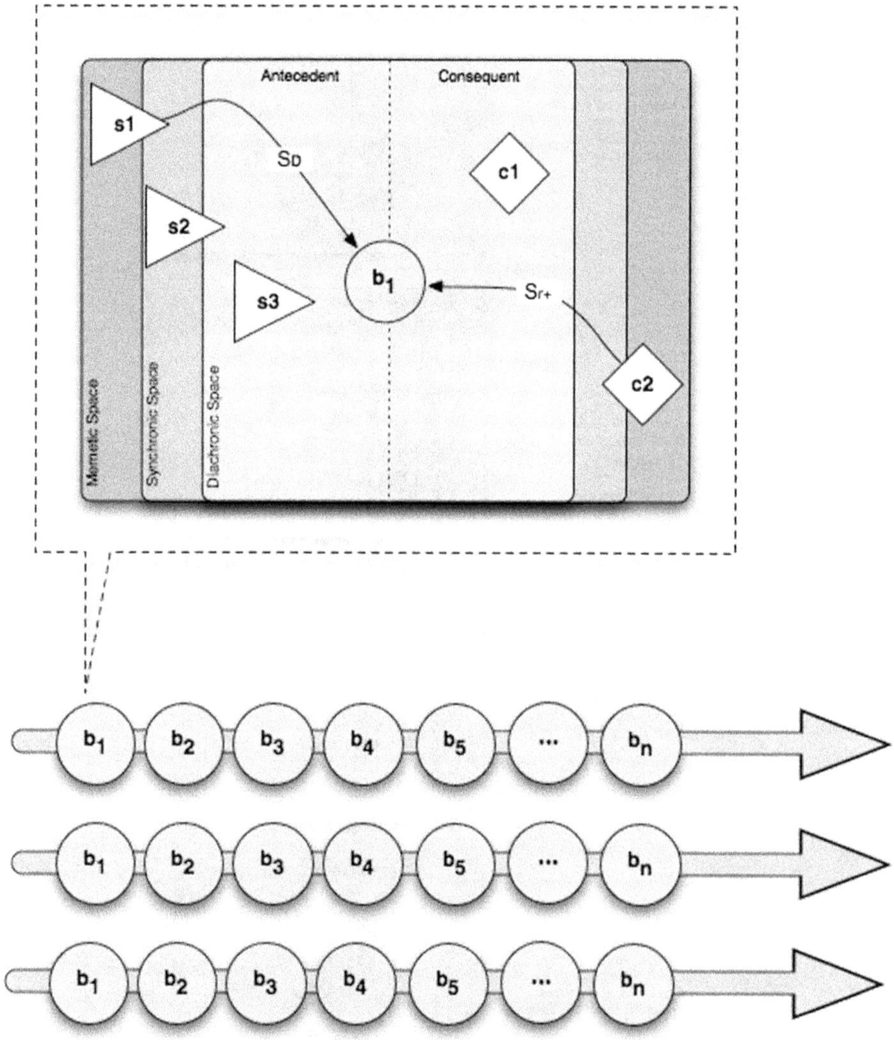

Figure 9.5. Functional Ontology Construction.

A single instance of behavior occurs within a continuous stream of behavior that makes up the life span of an individual. Operant behavior is selected or extinguished by the consequences of individual instances of behavior. Figure 9.5 shows an individual instance with in the context of a behavior stream.

CHAPTER TEN

CREEK PEBBLES: A SUMMARY METAPHOR AND TOUCHSTONE FOR EXPLORATION

CREEK PEBBLES in a bag are one metaphor proposed by William Least Heat-Moon for organizing thoughts about a journey one has just made. Standing on a hill in rural Kansas, he asks if one should just take one's impressions, insights, and facts and let them fall as they will, like pebbles scooped up from a creek and tossed into a bag, taking on their own order. The random order may not be entirely satisfactory, but it can be instructive. We want to come to know the pebbles and their environment and their workings individually and collectively. The subtitle of the book resulting from Heat-Moon's travels and contemplations, *A Deep Map*, offers a provocative concept for our considerations of reducing search space.

Our explorations of doing things with information have had us venture over a large and varied terrain. Some regions have been crisscrossed several times; others have been sighted only in the distance. We strongly suggest the study of works on travel and exploration because traditional indexing, abstracting, and classifying, as well as newer means of doing things with information bear more than a metaphorical relationship to the mapping of geographical territory. The concepts of how one comes to know things about an area hold whether we speak of an intellectual or geographical area. Indeed, it may be only a matter of convenience to make the distinction at all. We might also say that it is critical that we come to know the knowledge territories of those for whom we construct information systems, or at least how to account for their ways of knowing. The Functional Ontology Construct might be said to be a deep mapping system.

Explorations seldom simply end. They yield interesting insights, with luck, and perhaps material of immediate utility. They also stimulate reflection upon where we have been, where we would now like to go, whither we would like to return, and how we are to make sense of it all.

REFLECTIONS

It is time to look back briefly on where we have been and then to scoop up some more pebbles to help us think of where we might next travel. We set out with a few pathways chosen and some explicitly ignored. This was not to be a survey of indexing and abstracting practices, nor was it to be a manual for any particular sort of indexing and abstracting practice. The maps for those areas have been well constructed and are sufficiently numerous.

We followed some paths through ideas on representation and how one thing stands for another. The problems that can arise when representation of questions and documents is not thought out were examined through exercises and thought experiments. Possible responses to the problems of such representation were considered.

The seeming contradiction of increasing access by reducing a priori conceptual tagging was explored in some depth. This would be accomplished by representing only the physically present text, pointing out major discontinuities (hills and valleys) on the document's landscape, and enabling the patron to make concept and value judgments. The ability of a digital environment to process large amounts of physical data was the foundation of such an approach to mapping documents to reduce search time.

The seemingly opposite approach of using the machine to gather conceptual judgments and make them useable was also examined. Here the user group would help to train the system and thus craft it to the idiosyncrasies of the user group.

In most of our considerations and exercises, we examined different means of changing the locus of representation, so as to include the user to some greater degree. This suggested possible changes in the nature of the relationship of some users to some systems. In many ways, those changes mirror the relation one might expect to have with the neighborhood bookstore owner or video dealer or the good reference librarian. That is, one develops a relationship through which the idiosyncrasies of interests and seeking habits become known and can be incorporated into the system. The possible search space is increasing by leaps and bounds; search time is not. The challenge is to design systems for reducing search time in a useful manner. The variety in question types and searching styles adds to the challenge.

DOCUMENTS IN THE WORLD/REALITY

Here we would like to specifically align our work with the group that exists as the Document Academy. This group has revivified the area termed "documentation." Several annual gatherings fostered by Buckland and Lund have brought together scholars who investigate "relationships between documentary practices and a rich array of social, political, scientific, and cultural phenomena" (Frohmann in *A Document (Re)turn*, p. 27). The group has not established a fixed model of documents and their uses, preferring to continue to explore. Drucker summarizes the complexity of the notion of a document:

> It is a particular, distinct, illusion, the image of an area created at the intersection of overlapping frames—of historical and social references, the projections of the reader, provocations of the text, constrained conditions, and potential responses—all within the poetical field. The term embedded, is not meant to suggest that a document is embedded in these many works, like a nugget in earth, capable of extraction, but that it is constituted, the way a knot appears in a skein (*A Document (Re)turn*, p. 51).

Perhaps we should say instead that Drucker notes the simplicity of the notion of document, but its distance from the concepts of daily practice makes it seem complex.

We do not intend to make a complete elaboration of the work of the members of the Document Academy. Rather, we offer a few summary comments from Buckland as a few more pebbles in our creek of understanding how to do things with information. Buckland enumerates the primary elements of the group's approach in his description of the Documentation Studies program at the University of Tromso. The Document Academy has its origins in this program. Buckland speaks of four facets he terms: three dimensions, specific empirical, and methodological traditions, specific conceptual framework, and period of constitution. Under "three dimensions" Buckland elaborates upon meaning (at the heart of documentation), technology/technique (all documents have physical manifestations), and socioeconomic aspects (modern society is nothing if not document-pervaded). Discussing "specific empirical and methodological traditions," Buckland addresses four thrusts: who?—human agency; what?—materials and technologies; how?—techniques adopted; and why?—purpose and outcomes. The "specific conceptual framework" is set within a "document-centric perspective" and a "pan-documentary field of vision" and encompasses: document analysis, human agencies, and traditions and genres. The core problems addressed are neither novel nor left untouched by other fields. The "period of constitution" gives rise to the "new insights and practical solutions" are that are brought to bear on questions of documents. These include: structural themes—document forms, document biography, docemes; themes of value and policy—what good is a document? Crosscutting insights; and a wider agenda (Buckland, *A Document (Re)turn*, pp. 328–333).

Drucker again: What is the document? And the text? They are never the same as each other. We read and the work is called forth, provoked. Each embodiment is an interpretation. The creation of a "document" however, much as it depends upon the materiality of that textual substrate, is a more complicated matter yet (Drucker, *A Document (Re)turn*, p. 48)

INFORMATION ENVIRONMENT

There is probably some danger in speaking too closely of details of today's information environment. Surely much of this will be archaic within weeks. Yet, we should not lose sight of the fact that the quantitative changes in data availability are leading qualitative changes in the sorts of questions that can be asked and the arrangements within which they can be asked. It may be of use to look to the past. Classicist Arrowsmith suggests that changes in media will not, in and of themselves, generate better conditions; we must continue to grapple with what it means to be fully human. This may mean, among other things, careful consideration of what sorts of questions can be asked. Information exists within societal constructs. Destruction of the Alexandrian Library, the persecution of women as witches, and censorship disputes in schools are but a few of the most obvious examples of the dangers inherent in the social construction of knowledge.

Bounty hunters traverse search space and have devised methods of reducing, synthesizing, and analyzing data. They spend most of their time initiating simultaneous search subroutines and monitoring the value of each routine. They also come to understand the environment and thought patterns of those for whom they are searching. They make substantial use of small but significant pieces of information. How do they know where to look for these small bits of information and what to make of them? What might we learn from bounty hunters to enhance the abilities of search intermediaries?

Artists must constantly struggle with the manner in which to present their views of the object/event space. What is the proper mix of novelty and familiarity? What can we learn from artists about repackaging information to make it most useful to individual clients? What are the means artists use to make new connections and new combinations? How might we incorporate this sort of knowledge into the design of access systems?

Who are the other people whose professional insights into humanity and use of information could contribute to our understanding of information and its use? What must we know, so that when a patron walks in the door or logs onto a computer system, or uses whatever mediating systems may become available, we can provide the most powerful, the most highly crafted, the most precise tools available to help that person meet with success?

THERE ARE STILL TOO MANY DOCUMENTS

There are still too many documents. At the time of the writing of *Explorations in Indexing and Abstracting* there was no YouTube.com for posting videos, now as we write this 250,000 hits have been recorded on the campaign videos of the leading Democrat and Republican and 19,979 hits have been recorded for "boxer [dog] drinks milk." There weren't photo-sharing websites, now there are so many images on photo social network sites that on flickr.com there are at the time of this writing 23,879,162 photos labeled with the tag "me." The Massachusetts Institute of Technology makes course materials for 1800 courses available free on the web. When we were writing *Explorations in Indexing and Abstracting* amazon.com was run out of a garage in Seattle; today it has available 80,000 titles for its new digital reading platform. Web sites have multiplied, books and magazines have not disappeared, and new hybrid media have been developed. People are now receiving RSS feeds and downloading podcasts and creating blogs. Telephones play music, connect to the Internet, and take photographs and video clips that can be sent to family and friends or to YouTube.com or any major news network. Our creek seems to be in the middle of spring runoff, with a torrent of water carrying pebbles and logs and an occasional old tire along. There are still too many documents for any one person to be able to be familiar with them all. There are so many documents and means for their production and use that more gems may well exist for anyone seeking to do something with information.

Humans long ago invented means for storing information outside individual brains. This invention of recorded information offers data and insights no longer bound to a single time and place. Schmandt-Besserat even argues that recordings of numbers and words enabled "cognitive evolution." We need no longer depend on personal experience or the recollections of those with whom we have physical contact. Yet, the search space presented by the mass of recorded documents present us with a significant dilemma—how are we to choose and use the "right documents"?

We have offered examples of new ways to think about messages in all sorts of media and how they might be discovered, analyzed, synthesized, and generated. We brought together philosophical, scientific, and engineering notions into a fundamental model for just how we might understand doing things with information. We have tried to generate questions that will challenge us and enlighten our efforts to improve the ways we do things with information. We have scooped up a few more pebbles to expand our thoughts. We have, perhaps, gotten a feel for the territory and for the various paths within it. Certainly there will be some frustrations that we did not discover a simple mechanism, a single prescription, and a main highway across the territory. Yet this can also be the source of wonder and encouragement.

REFERENCES

AAUP Book, Jacket, and Journal Show, 1996. *Show Catalog by the Book, Jacket, and Journal Show Committee of the American Association of University Presses.*

Addiego, Walter. "Domino Quit Modeling for the Glamour of Guns." *San Francisco Chronicle* October 14, 2005.

Anderson, Richard L. *Functional Ontology Construction: A Pragmatic Approach to Addressing Problems Concerning the Individual and the Information Environment.* Doctoral dissertation. Denton, TX: University of North Texas, 2006.

Anderson, Richard L., Brian C. O'Connor, and Jodi L. Kearns. "The Functional Ontology of Filmic Documents." *A Document (Re)turn: Contributions from a Research Field in Transition.* Ed. Roswitha Skare, Niels Windfeld Lund, and Andreas Vårheim. Frankfurt am Main, Germany: Peter Lang GmbH, 2007, 345–363.

Arrowsmith, William. "Film As Educator." *Journal of Aesthetic Education* 3(3) (1969): 75–83.

Audi, Robert. *The Cambridge Dictionary of Philosophy.* Cambridge, MA: Cambridge University Press, 1999.

Augst, Bertrand. Course notes on Bellour's "les Oiseaux: Analyse d'une sequence." University of California, Berkeley, 1980.

———. Personal communication on the possibilities of computational structural analysis of motion pictures. University of California, Berkeley, 1981.

Augst, Bertrand, and Brian C. O'Connor. "No Longer a Shot in the Dark: Engineering a Robust Environment for Film Study." *Computers and the Humanities* 33 (1999): 345–363.

Bartsch, Robert A., and Kristi M. Cobern. "Effectiveness of PowerPoint Presentations in Lectures." *Computers and Education* 41(1) (2003): 77–86.

Bates, Marcia J. "The Biological and Social Consequences of Information Seeking." *Lazerow Lecture,* University of Kentucky (2000).

Bateson, Gregory. *Mind and Nature: A Necessary Unity.* New York: E. P. Dutton, 1979.

Belkin, Nicholas J. "Anomalous States of Knowledge As a Basis for Information Retrieval." *Canadian Journal of Information Science* 5 (1980).

———. "Information Concepts for Information Science" *Journal of Information Science* 34 (1978): 55–85.

———. "The Cognitive Viewpoint in Information Science" *Journal of Information Science* 16 (1990): 11–15.

Belkin, Nicholas J., Robert N. Oddy, and Helen M. Brooks. Part I: Background and Theory; Part II: Results of a Design Study," *Journal of Documentation* 3(2&3) (1982): 61–71, 145–164.

Bellour, Raymond. "*Les Oiseaux:* Analyse d'une sequence," *Cahiers du Cinéma* 216 (October 1969): 24–38.

Bellour, Raymond, and Constance Penley. *The Analysis of Film.* Bloomington, IN: Indiana University Press, 2000.

Bingham, Roger. *The Nature of Human Nature.* Princeton, NJ: Films for the Humanities & Sciences, 1995.

Bird, Linda. "Avoid the Mistakes of PowerPoint Rookies." *Office Computing* 12(1) (2001): 62–65.

Blair, David C. "Indeterminacy in the Subject Access to Documents." *Information Processing and Management* 22(3) (1986): 229–241.

———. "STAIRS Redux: Thoughts on the STAIRS Evaluation Ten Years After." *Journal of the American Society for Information Science* 47 (1996): 4–22.

———. *Language and Representation in Information Retrieval*. Dordrecht, The Netherlands: Elsevier Science Publishers, 1990.

Bonitzer, Pascal. "Here: The Notion of the Shot and the Subject of Cinema." *Cahiers Du Cinema* (1977): 273.

Brookes, Bertram C. "Information Science." *Information Science (excluding IR)*. Ed. H A Whatley. The Library Association, 1972, 137–149.

———. "The Foundations of Information Science: Part I: Philosophical Aspects" *Journal of Information Science* 2 (1980): 125–133.

Brown, David G. "PowerPoint-Induced Sleep." *Syllabus* (2001).

Buckland, Michael K. "Northern Light: Fresh Insights into Enduring Concerns." *A Document (Re)turn: Contributions from a Research Field in Transition*. Ed. Roswitha Skare, Niels Windfeld Lund, and Andreas Vårheim. Frankfurt am Main, Germany: Peter Lang GmbH, 2007.

———. "Information As a Thing." *Journal of the American Society for Information Science* 42 (1991): 351–360.

———. *Redesigning Library Services*. Chicago, IL: American Library Association, 1992.

Buckland, Michael K., and Ziming Liu. "History of Information Science." Ed. Martha E Williams. *Information Today* 30 (1995): 385–416.

Byrne, David. "Learning to Love PowerPoint." *Wired* 11(9) (2003).

Campbell, Jeremy. *Grammatical Man: Information, Entropy, Language, and Life*. New York: Simon and Schuster, 1982.

Catania, A. Charles. *Learning*. 4th ed. Englewood Cliffs, NJ: Prentice Hall, 1998.

Chandler, Daniel. *Semiotics: The Basics*. London: Routledge, 2004.

Churchland, Paul M. *The Engine of Reason, The Seat of the Soul: A Philosophical Journey into the Brain*. Cambridge, MA: MIT Press, 1995.

Cooper, William S., "Is Inter-Indexer Consistency a Deep Hobgoblin?" *American Documentation* 20(3) (July 1969): 100–110.

Cooper, William. "A Definition of Relevance for Information Retrieval." *Information Storage and Retrieval* 7(1) (1971): 19–37.

Copeland, Jud H. *Engineering Design as a Foundational Metaphor for Information Science: A Resistive Postmodern Alternative to the "Scientific Model."* Doctoral dissertation. Emporia, KS: Emporia State University, 1997.

Dailianas, Apostolos, Robert B. Allen, and Paul England. "Comparison of Automatic Video Segmentation Algorithms." *Integration Issues in Large Commercial Media Delivery Systems* (1995): 2–16.

Dawkins, Richard. *The Extended Phenotype*. Oxford: Oxford University Press, 1982.

———. *The Selfish Gene*. 1989 ed. Oxford: Oxford University Press, 1989.

Day, Willard F., and Sam Leigland. *Radical Behaviorism: Willard Day on Psychology and Philosophy*. Reno, NV: Context Press, 1992.

Dervin, Brenda, and Michael Nilan. "Information Needs and Uses." Ed. Martha E Williams. *Annual Review of Information Science and Technology* 21 (1986): 3–33.

Dijkstra, Bram. *Idols of Perversity*. New York: Oxford University Press, 1986.

Donahoe, John W., David C. Palmer, and Vivian Packard Dorsel. *Learning and Complex Behavior*. Boston, MA: Allyn and Bacon, 1994.
Dreyfus, Hubert. *What Computers Still Can't Do*. Cambridge, MA: MIT Press, 1992.
Drucker, Johanna. "Excerpts and Entanglements." *A Document (Re)turn: Contributions from a Research Field in Transition*. Ed. Roswitha Skare, Niels Windfeld Lund, and Andreas Vårheim. Frankfurt am Main, Germany: Peter Lang GmbH, 2007.
———. *Alphabetic Labyrinth: The Letters in History and Imagination*. New York: Thames & Hudson, 1995.
DuFrene, Debbie D., and Carol M. Lehman. "Concept, Content, Construction, and Contingencies: Getting the Horse Before the PowerPoint Cart." *Business Communication Quarterly* 67(1) (2004): 84–88.
Dwyer, James. "You Can't Judge a Book without a Cover." *Technicalities* 13(12) (1993): 3–4.
Eco, Umberto. *A Theory of Semiotics*. Bloomington, IN: Indiana University Press, 1976.
———. *The Name of the Rose*. San Diego, CA: Harcourt Brace Jovanovich, 1983.
Eisenstein, Sergei, and Jay Leyda. *Film Form; Essays in Film Theory*. 1st ed. New York: Harcourt, Brace, 1949.
Ellis, David. "A Behavioral Approach to Information Retrieval System Design." *Journal of Documentation* 45(3) (1989): 171–212.
Ellwod, John. "Presence Or Powerpoint: Why PowerPoint Has Become a Cliché." *Development and Learning in Organizations* 19(3) (2005): 12–14.
Farrow, John F. "A Cognitive Process Model of Document Indexing." *Journal of Documentation* 47(2) (1991).
Fischler, Martin, and Oscar Firschein. *Intelligence: The Eye, the Brain, and the Computer*. Reading, MA: Addison-Wesley, 1987.
Fisher, Karen E., Sanda Erdelez, and Lynne McKechnie. *Theories of Information Behavior* (ASIST Monograph). Medford, NJ: Information Today, 2005.
Flew, Antony. *A Dictionary of Philosophy*. New York: St. Martin's Press, 1984.
Frohmann, Bernd. *A Document (Re)turn: Contributions from a Research Field in Transition*. Ed. Niels Windfeld Lund, Andreas Vårheim, and Roswitha Skare. Frankfurt am Main, Germany: Peter Lang GmbH, 2007.
Gardner, Howard. *The Mind's New Science*. New York: Basic Books, 1995.
Gibson, William, and Bruce Sterling. *The Difference Engine*. New York: Bantam Books, 1991.
Glenn, Sigrid, Janet Ellis, and J. Greenspoon. "On the Revolutionary Nature of the Operant As a Unit of Behavioral Selection." *American Psychologist* 47 (1992): 1329–1336.
Greisdorf, Howard F. *Relevance Thresholds: A Conjunctive/Disjunctive Model of End-User Cognition as an Evaluative Process*. Doctoral dissertation. Denton, TX: University of North Texas, 2000.
Greisdorf, Howard F., and Brian C. O'Connor. "Modeling What Users See When They Look at Images." *Journal of Documentation* 58(1) (2002a): 1–24.
———. "What Do Users See?" *Proceedings of the 65th ASIST Annual Meeting* 39 (2002b): 383–390.
Guilford, Joy P. "Varieties of Divergent Thinking." *Journal of Creative Behavior* 18(1) (1985): 1–10.
Harris, Michael H. "The Dialectic of Defeat: Antimonies in Research in Library and Information Science." *Library Trends* 34(3) (1986): 515–531.
Hayes, Robert M. "Measurement of Information." *Information Processing and Management* 29(1) (1993): 1–11.

Heat Moon, William Least. *PrairyErth: (A Deep Map)*. Boston, MA: Houghton Mifflin, 1991.

Hitchcock, Alfred. *The Birds*. Universal Studios Home Video, 2000.

Hjørland, Birger. "Overload, Quality and Changing Conceptual Frameworks." *Information Science: From the Development of the Discipline to Social Interaction*. Ed. Johan Olaisen, Erland Munch-Petersen, and Patrick Wilson. Oslo, Norway: Scandinavian University Press, 1996, 35–68.

Hull, David L., Rodney E. Langman, and Sigrid Glenn. "A General Account of Selection: Biology Immunology, and Behavior." *Behavioral and Brain Sciences* 24(3) (2001): 511–573.

Idle, Eric. *The Road to Mars: A Post-Modem Novel*. New York: Pantheon Books, 1999.

Ingwersen, Peter. "Information and Information Science in Context." *Information and Information Science in Context*. Ed. Johan Olaisen, Erland Munch-Petersen, and Patrick Wilson. Oslo, Norway: Scandinavian University Press, 1996, 69–112.

James, William, and John J. McDermott. *The Writings of William James; A Comprehensive Edition*. New York: Modern Library, 1968.

Kearns, Jodi. *A Mechanism for Richer Representation of Videos for Children: Calibrating Calculated Entropy to Perceived Entropy*. Doctoral dissertation. Denton, TX: University of North Texas, 2001.

———. "Clownpants in the Classroom? Entropy, Humor, and Distraction in Multimedia Instructional Materials." *Document Academy* (2005).

Kearns, Jodi, and Brian C. O'Connor. "Dancing with Entropy: Form Attributes, Children, and Representation." *Journal of Documentation* 60(2) (2004): 144–163.

Kuhlthau, Carol Collier. *Seeking Meaning: A Process Approach to Library and Information Services*. Information Management, Policy, and Services. Norwood, NJ: Ablex Pub. Co., 1993.

LaSalle, Mick. "This Guy Just Can't Hang Up His Mask." *San Francisco Chronicle*, October 28, 2005.

Livraghi, Giancarlo. "PowerPointitis: Glitz Over Content." Visionarymarketing.com (2005). http://visionarymarketing.com/articles/powerpointdisease.html.

Mahin, Linda. "PowerPoint Pedagogy." *Business Communication Quarterly* 67(2) (2004): 219–222.

Maron, M. E. "On Indexing, Retrieval, and the Meaning of About." *Journal of the American Society for Information Science* 28(1) (1977).

———. Ed. "Theory and Foundations of Information Retrieval." *Drexel Library Quarterly* 14 (1978).

Maron, M. E. Notes for Course on Information Retrieval. Berkeley, CA: University of California, 1982.

Maron, M. E. William S. Cooper, and Stephen E. Robertson. "Probability of Relevance: A Unification of Two Competing Models for Document Retrieval." *Information Technology: Research and Development* 1(1) (1982): 1–21.

Marr, David. *Vision: A Computational Investigation into the Human Representation and Processing of Visual Information*. San Francisco, CA: W. H. Freeman, 1982.

Meadow, Charles T. *Text Information Retrieval Systems*. San Diego, CA: Academic Press, 1988.

Menand, Louis. *Pragmatism: A Reader*. New York: Vintage, 1997.

———. *The Metaphysical Club: A Story of Ideas in America*. New York: Farrar, Straus and Giroux, 2002.

Minsky, Marvin. *The Society of Mind*. New York: Simon & Schuster, 1986.

Moles, Abraham A. *Information Theory and Esthetic Perception*. Urbana, IL: University of Illinois Press, 1966.

Morse, Philip M. "Browsing and Search Theory." *Toward a Theory of Librarianship: Papers in Honor of Jesse Hauk Shera*. Ed. Rawsi. Metuchen, NJ: Scarecrow Press, 1973.

Moxley, Roy A. "The Selectionist Meaning of C. S. Pierce and B. F. Skinner." *The Analysis of Verbal Behavior* 18 (2002): 71–91.

———. "Pragmatic Selectionism: The Philosophy of Behavior Analysis." *The Behavior Analyst Today* 4 (2003): 289–305.

———. "B. F. Skinner's Adoption of Pierce's Pragmatic Meaning for Habits." *Transactions of the Charles S. Pierce Society* XL (2004): 743–769.

Neill, Samuel D. *Dilemmas in the Study of Information: Exploring the Boundaries of Information Science*. Contributions in Librarianship and Information Science; no. 70. Westport, CT: Greenwood Press, 1992.

Norvig, Peter. "PowerPoint Shot with Its Own Bullets." *The Lancet* 362(9381) (2003): 343–344.

Norvig, Peter. "The Making of the Gettysburg PowerPoint Presentation." http://www.norvig.com. Accessed June 25, 2008.

Novitz, David. *Pictures and Their Use in Communication: A Philosophical Essay*. The Hague, The Netherlands: Martinus Nijhoff, 1977.

O'Connor, Brian C. "Access to Moving Image Documents: Background Concepts and Proposals for Surrogates for Film and Video Works." *Journal of Documentation* 41 (1985): 209–220.

———. "Browsing: Frameworks for Seeking Functional Information." *Knowledge: Creation, Diffusion, Utilization* 15 (1993).

———. *Explorations in Indexing and Abstracting: Pointing, Virtue, and Power*. Englewood, CO: Libraries Unlimited, 1996.

———. "Fostering Creativity: Enhancing the Browsing Environment." *International Journal of Information Management* 8(19) (1988): 203–210.

———. "Pheromones of Meaning: Surrogates and Keyframes for Video." *Symposium on Understanding Video* (2002).

———. "Preservation and Repackaging of Lantern Slides in a Desktop Digital Environment." *Microcomputers in Information Management* 9 (1992).

O'Connor, Brian C., and Mary K. O'Connor. "Book Jacket as Access Mechanism: An Attribute Rich Resource for Functional Access to Academic Books." *First Monday* 3(9) 1998. http://www.firstmonday.org/Issues/issue3_9/oconnor/index.html. Accessed June 24, 2008.

O'Connor, Brian C., Jud H. Copeland, and Jodi L. Kearns. *Hunting and Gathering on the Information Savanna: Conversations on Modeling Human Search Abilities*. Lanham, MD: Scarecrow Press, 2003.

O'Connor, Brian C., Mary K. O'Connor, and June Abbas. "User Reactions As Access Mechanism: An Exploration Based on Captions for Images." *Journal of the American Society for Information Science* 50(8) (1999): 681–697.

Overhage, Carl F. J., and R. Joyce Harman. Eds. Planning Conference on Information Transfer Experiments (INTREX). Cambridge, MA: MIT Press, 1965.

Pai, Edward. Personal communication on Modeling the Relationship between Users and Documents, 1995.

Petroski, Henry. *The Evolution of Useful Things*. 1st Vintage Books ed. New York: Vintage Books, 1994.

Pierce, C. S. "How to Make Our Ideas Clear." *Pragmatism: A Reader*. Ed. L. Menand. New York: Vintage, 1997, 26–48.

Pius XII, Pope. "Divino Afflante Spiritu." Encyclical. Rome, Italy: Holy See, 1943.

Plotkin, Henry C. *Darwin Machines and the Nature of Knowledge*. Cambridge, MA: Harvard University Press, 1994.

Pratt, Allan D. *The Information of the Image*. Norwood, NJ: Ablex Pub. Co., 1982.

Pryluck, Calvin. *Sources of Meaning in Motion Pictures and Television*. Manchester, NH: Arno Press, 1976.

Rezendes, Paul. *Tracking & the Art of Seeing: How to Read Animal Tracks & Signs*. Charlotte, VT: Camden House, 1992.

Rice, Ronald E., Maureen McCreadie, and Shan-Ju L. Chang. *Accessing and Browsing Information and Communication*. Cambridge, MA: MIT Press, 2001.

Robertson, Stephen E. "Between Aboutness and Meaning" in *The Analysis of Meaning: Informatics* 5, eds. Maxine MacCafferty and Kathleen Gray. London: Aslib, 1979.

Rorty, Richard. *Philosophy and the Mirror of Nature*. Princeton, NJ: Princeton University Press, 1979.

Sagan, Carl. *Cosmos*. New York: Ballantine Books, 1985.

Salt, Barry. *Film Style and Technology: History, and Analysis*. London: Starword, 2003.

Savolainen, Reijo. "The Sense-Making Theory—An Alternative to Intermediary-Centered Approaches in Library and Information Science?" *Conceptions of Library and Information Science. Historical, Empirical and Theoretical Perspectives*. Ed. Pertti Vakkari and Blaise Cronin. Taylor Graham, 1992, 149–164.

Schamber, Linda. "Relevance and Information Behavior." Ed. Martha E. Williams, *ARIST 29* (1994): 3–48.

Schjeldahl, Peter. "Painting by Numbers: Gustave Courbet and the Making of a Master." *New Yorker*, July 2007.

Schmandt-Besserat, Denise. *How Writing Came About*. Austin, TX: University of Texas Press, 1997.

Schott, Susan. Personal conversation with Brian O'Connor about her role as Sales and Marketing Director for the University Press of Kansas. 1997.

Shannon, Claude Elwood, and Warren Weaver. *The Mathematical Theory of Communication*. Urbana, IL: University of Illinois Press, 1949.

Shirky, Clay. "Ontology Is Overrated: Categories, Links, and Tags." Clay Shirky's Writings about the Internet, 2005. http://www.shirky.com/writings/ontology_overrated.html.

Simon, Scott. A Multi-Dimensional Entropy Model of Jazz Improvisation for Music Information Retrieval. Doctoral Dissertation. Denton, TX: University of North Texas, 2005.

Simpson, John A., and Edmund Weiner. *Oxford English Dictionary*. Oxford: Libri, 1989.

Skinner, Burrhus F. *Contingencies of Reinforcement: a Theoretical Analysis*. New York: Appleton-Century-Crofts, 1969.

———. "The Evolution of Behavior." *Journal of the Experimental Analysis of Behavior* 41 (1984): 217–221.

———. "The Operational Analysis of Psychological Terms." *Psychological Review* 52 (1945): 270–277, 291–294.

———. *Science and Human Behavior*. New York: Macmillan, 1953.

———. "Selection by Consequences." *Science* 213 (1981): 477–481, 502–510.
———. *Verbal Behavior*. New York: Appleton-Century-Crofts, 1957.
Smith, Barry. "Ontology." *The Blackwell Guide to the Philosophy of Computing and Information*. Ed. L. Floridi. Oxford: Blackwell Publishing, 2004, 155–167.
Smith, Edward, and Douglas Medin. *Categories and Concepts*. Cambridge, MA: Harvard University Press, 1981.
Sober, Elliott. *Conceptual Issues in Evolutionary Biology*. 2nd ed. Cambridge, MA: MIT Press, 1994.
Spink, Amanda, and Charles Cole. *New Directions in Human Information Behavior* (Information Science and Knowledge Management). Dordrecht, The Netherlands: Springer, 2006.
Staddon, John E. R. *The New Behaviorism: Mind, Mechanism, and Society*. Philadelphia, PA: Psychology Press, 2001.
Stigler, Stephen M. *Statistics on the Table: The History of Statistical Concepts and Methods*. Cambridge, MA: Harvard University Press, 1999.
Swanson, Donald R. "Undiscovered Public Knowledge." *Library Quarterly* 56(2) (1986): 103–118.
Thorson, John E. *River of Promise, River of Peril: The Politics of Managing the Missouri River*. Kansas: University Press of Kansas, 1994.
Tufte, Edward. *The Cognitive Style of Power Point: Pitching Out Corrupts Within.* Cheshire, CT: Graphics Press, 2003.
Twain, Mark. "On Girls" in "English as She is Taught" in *The Complete Essays of Mark Twain.* Edited and with an Introduction by Charles Neider. New York: De Capo Press, 2000.
van Rijsbergen, Cornelis. J. *Information Retrieval*. London: Butterworth-Heinemann, 1979.
Vik, Gretchen N. "Breaking Bad Habits: Teaching Effective PowerPoint Use to Working Graduate Students." *Business Communication Quarterly* 67(2) (2004): 225–228.
Vertov, Dziga, and Annette Michelson. *Kino-Eye: The Writings of Dziga Vertov*. Berkeley, CA: University of California Press, 1984.
Watt, James H. "Television Form, Content Attributes, and Viewer Behavior." *Progress in Communication*. Ed. Voight. Norwood, NJ: Ablex Pub. Co., 1979.
Watt, James H., and Krull. "An Information Theory Measure for Television Programming." *Communication Research* 1(1) (1974): 44–68.
Weisburd, Stefi. "The Spark: Personal Testimonies of Creativity" *Science News* 132(19) (1987): 299.
Wheeler, John A., "Information, Physics, Quantum: The Search for Links" in *Complexity, Entropy, and the Physics of Information*, ed. Wojciech H. Zurek. Redwood City, CA: Addison-Wesley, 1990, 3–18.
White, Howard D., Marcia J. Bates, and Patrick Wilson. *For Information Specialists: Interpretations of Reference and Bibliographic Work*. Norwood, NJ: Ablex Pub. Co., 1992.
Wilson, Patrick G. "Catalog as Access Mechanism: Background and Concepts." *Foundations of Cataloguing: A Sourcebook*. Ed. Michael Carpenter and Elaine Svenonius. Littleton, CO: Libraries Unlimited, 1985.
———. *Doctoral Dissertation*. Berkeley, CA: University of California, Berkeley, 1960.
———. Personal communication with Brian C. O'Connor, April 18, 1980.

———. *Public Knowledge, Private Ignorance: Toward a Library and Information Policy.* Contributions in Librarianship and Information Science, no. 10. Westport, CT: Greenwood Press, 1977.

———. *Second-Hand Knowledge: An Inquiry into Cognitive Authority.* Contributions in Librarianship and Information Science, no. 44. Westport, CT: Greenwood Press, 1983.

———. "Situational Relevance." *Information Storage and Retrieval* 9 (1973): 457–471.

———. "Some Consequences of Information Overload and Rapid Conceptual Change." *Information Science: From the Development of the Discipline to Social Interaction*. Ed. Johan Olaisen, Erland Munch-Petersen, and Patrick Wilson. Oslo, Norway: Scandinavian University Press, 1996. 21–34.

———. *Two Kinds of Power: An Essay on Bibliographical Control.* California Library Reprint Series. Berkeley, CA: University of California Press, 1968.

———. "The Value of Currency." *Library Trends* 41 (1993): 632–644.

Wilson, T. D. "Information Behaviour: An Interdisciplinary Perspective." *Information Processing and Management* 33(4) (1997): 551–572.

Wittgenstein, Ludwig. *Philosophical Investigations*. New York: Macmillan, 1953.

———. *Tractatus Logico-Philosophicus*. London: Routledge, 2001.

Wooden, Wayne S., and Gavin Ehringer. *Rodeo in America: Wranglers, Roughstock, and Paydirt.* Lawrence, KS: University Press of Kansas, 1996.

Worley, and Dyrud. "Presentations and the Powerpoint Problem." *Business Communication Quarterly* 67(1) (2004): 78–80.

Yoon, JungWon. *Improving Recall of Browsing Sets in Image Retrieval from a Semiotics Perspective*. Doctoral dissertation. Denton, TX: University of North Texas, 2006.

INDEX

Aboutness, 5, 16, 91, 94, 97, 99, 106, 125
Abstract, 10, 25, 36, 37, 69, 121, 139, 141, 145
Abstracting, 2–7, 9–11, 25, 32, 33, 48, 56, 58, 75, 76, 81, 110, 133, 134, 138–40, 148, 221, 222, 225
Access, 1, 18, 42, 52, 60, 63–65, 70, 71, 73, 74, 88, 93, 99, 101, 103, 107, 110, 112, 122, 123, 125, 129, 130, 131, 134, 148, 151, 222, 224
Adaptation, 9, 36, 37, 100
Adjectival, component of aboutness, 99, descriptors, 100, forms, 152, representations, 171
Adjective, 104, 140, 145, 153, 154, 157
Alphabet, 35, 36
Alternation, 192, 193, 195, 200–3
Ambiguity, 65, 112
Analysis, 8, 64, 65, 85, 98, 104, 112, 119, 120, 123, 127–29, 133, 151, 158, 160, 186–92, 194, 198, 203, 207, 208, 210, 211, 213, 223
Anomalous State of Knowledge, 19–20, 112, 113, 117, 151
Antecedent, conditions, 213, 215, space, 218
Antonyms, 104, 105
Apparatus, 12, 75, 80, 81, 109, 110, 112–14, 116, 119, 121–23
Attribute, 10, 22–25, 28, 33, 41–44, 50, 56, 70, 76, 77, 88, 91, 100, 103, 105, 106, 108–19, 121, 123, 125, 126, 129, 139, 145, 147, 150, 156, 169, 170–72, 175–84, 186, 191, 204, 205, 211, 218, diachronic, 33, 41–44, 76, 77, 130, 139, 218, form, 170–72, 176, 178, 179, 181, 182, palette, 108, 109, synchronic, 33, 41, 42, 44, 130, 141, 218, 219
Author, 6, 17, 41, 42, 48, 49, 53–55, 71, 73, 76, 107, 112, 116, 122–24, 127, 130, 141, 152, 158, 169, 211
Awareness, 50, 51, 113, 114, 118

Behavior, 37, 39, 43, 44, 61, 91, 103, 133, 172, 185, 191, 192, 194, 197, 207–20, analysis, 191, 192, 207, 208, 210, 213, verbal, 39, 61, 191, 192, 194, 210, 216
Behavioral, environment, 217, function, 39, 213, 217–19, phenomenon, 43, product, 205, reaction, 99, space, 218
Behaviorism, 37, 207, 209, 210, 215
Behaviorist, 210, approach, 211, perspective, 207
Bellour, Raymond, 188, 189, 191–206
Bibliographic(al), agency, 75, 87, 110, 112, 154, apparatus, 75, 80, 81, 110, 112–14, 119, 121, 123, essays, 6, instruction, 79, 151
Bibliography, 36, 37
Binary, 38, 39, 55, 57, 58, 64, 85, 137, 141, 170, 175, 185, 190, 191, 210, 215, 216, 217
Boolean, operators, 134, search, 14, 136, terms, 135
Brain, 38, 39, 94, 216, 217, 225
Breadth, 15, 86–88, 116, 151, 158
Browser, 81, 82, 111
Browsing, 50, 52, 67, 81, 107, 108, 110–19, 121–23, 134, 148, 149, 151, 153, 154, 156, 211, 212
Buckland, Michael, 38, 64, 215, 216, 223, 224

Card, 3, 14, 69, 107, 218
Catalog, 3, 5, 14, 69, 71, 107, 123, 129, 130, 137
Cataloger, 110, 138, 203
Cataloging, 112, 124
Cataloging in Publication, 135
Category, 28, 41, 43, 49, 60, 103, 104, 106, 127–30, 211, 217

Characteristic, 11, 12, 14, 22, 24, 60, 65, 94, 104, 116, 119, 125, 127, 130, 150, 170, 185
Class, 24, 30, 35, 41, 60, 65, 74, 77, 114, 116, 119, 211
Classification, 5, 7, 9–11, 13, 14, 40, 52, 76, 205
Closeness, 5, 113
Clown pants, 174–78, 181, 182, 185
Clownpantsiness, 176
Clusters, 2, 94, 106, 109, 138, 140, 142, 145, 154, 160, 195
Code, 17, 22, 31, 33, 35, 40, 57, 59, 60, 75, 140–42, 145, 170, 185
Cognitive, authority, 122, 124, 130, evaluation, 36, 225, maps, 51, state, 181, structure, 181, style, 113
Collection, 1, 2, 4, 9, 10, 12, 14, 25, 36, 37, 40, 42, 44, 49, 52, 54, 58, 65, 67–69, 71, 75, 79, 81–86, 88, 100, 102, 103, 107, 108, 109–18, 121, 124, 131, 133, 134, 136, 137, 148, 154, 158, 165, 195
Color, 16, 23, 25, 34, 70, 113, 118, 128, 165, 168, 169, 177–79, 191, 192, 196, 197, 199
Comedy, 8, 41, 184, 185
Communication, 8, 15, 38, 64, 68, 72, 94, 169, 170, 175, 176, 178, 181, 182, 190, 191, 206
Community, 8, 29, 75, 101–3, 106, 128, 146, 192, 194, constructs, 29, memory, 5, 99, 100, 102, 106, tags, 101
Complexity, 14, 35, 175, 204, 223
Concordance, 25, 27, 145
Congruence, 49, 116
Consistency, 76, 150, 160
Constraints, 12, 36, 37, 50, 53, 60, 68, 73, 77, 111, 113, 134, 138, 155, 172, 181
Content, 2, 15–17, 37, 40, 43, 59, 70, 75, 104, 106, 109, 113, 118, 124, 127, 128, 131, 138, 153, 170, 171, 175–77, 181, 182, 184, 186, 189, 206, 212
Context, 4, 8, 10, 37, 43, 45, 54, 58, 74, 145, 146, 210, 212, 216, 218, 220
Contingency, 43, 61, 213, 215
Control, 63, 88, 110, 115, 118, 134, 148, 187, 191, 211
Convenience, 69, 174, 222
Convention, 36, 48, 52–56, 107–9, 134, 141, 197
Credentials, 122, 127, 130, 131
Credibility, 125, 130, 131
Criteria, 2, 113, 129, 213
Critic, 99, 205
Criticism, 188, 203–4, 206, 213
Critique, 48, 88, 128
Curve, 182, 184, 185, 198

Data, 7, 8, 12, 24, 30, 37, 42, 47, 49, 50, 56, 59, 64, 69, 94, 100, 101, 114, 118, 119, 122, 138, 139, 141, 146, 147, 158, 165–67, 169, 192, 193, 196, 200, 203–5, 218, 222, 224, 225
Depth, 13, 15, 19, 63, 75, 77, 81–83, 88, 110, 118, 127, 134, 141, 148, 151, 154–58, 160, 169, 187
Descendant, 36, 210
Describing, 64, 86, 91, 99, 103, 110, 135, 151, 165, 188, 204
Description, 12, 41, 78, 86, 87, 91, 93, 94, 99, 103–6, 112, 119, 123, 124, 127, 130, 134, 136, 137, 151, 165, 178, 179, 186, 189, 190, 191, 193, 195, 197, 203–5, 223
Descriptors, 82, 83, 88, 91–93, 97, 99, 100, 101, 103–6, 112, 115, 116, 119, 135, 151, 154
Difference, 48, 50, 77, 79, 80, 91, 117, 138–40, 142, 152, 170, 177, 189, 197, 199, 203
Discontinuity, 19, 138, 139, 147, 165, 184, 205
Discovering, 110, 117, 205
Distraction, 174–77, 181–85
Distribution, 53, 54, 60, 86, 178, 179, 182, 192, 195, 196, 197, 199, 202
Document, 1–6, 10–12, 14–18, 20, 21, 25, 33, 36–45, 49, 50, 51, 53–56, 58–60, 63–65, 69, 70, 73–78, 80–89, 91, 93, 94, 97, 99–103, 107–19, 121–25, 129–31, 133–42, 145–51, 153–58, 161, 163, 165, 169–71, 174, 175, 178, 185–87, 189, 190, 193–95, 203–7, 210–13, 215, 217–19, 222–25

Effect, 39, 174, 178, 179, 181, 182, 191, 205, 211, 216, 217

Entropic burst 181, 182, 185, 195, elements, 174, structure, 189
Entropy, 8, 15, 16, 20, 170–72, 174–76, 178–82, 184, 185, 203, 204, 206, calculated, 171, 172, 174, 182, perceived, 171, 174, 185
Environment, 5, 9, 12, 14, 21, 40, 48, 51, 52, 54, 57, 59, 71, 72, 79, 100, 107, 110, 113, 115, 131, 134, 137, 146, 147, 169, 186, 187, 189, 194, 206–8, 212, 217, 218, 221, 222, 224
Evaluation, 4–6, 8, 49, 51, 55, 103, 109, 111, 113, 119–21, 131, 148, 150, 176
Evaluative, abilities, 119, comments, 123, 127, component, 37, conversation, 120, judgment, 55, power, 125, representations, 42, 129, 131, statements, 130
Evolution, 36, 44, 210, 225
Evolutionary, construct, 36, epistemology, 8, 48, 68, 69, 210, nature of representation, 36, process, 205, selection, 211
Experience, 21, 23, 31, 45, 48, 55, 99, 115, 187, 208, 212, 225
Expert, 185, 189, 204
Expertise, 1, 118, 120, 146, 192
Extraction, 5, 14, 23, 24, 40, 73, 94, 133, 140, 141–43, 147–52, 160, 165, 223

Factor, 125, 181–85, 212, 217
Failure, 40, 58, 63, 79, 80, 97, 107, 108, 119, 123, 134, 209
Familiarity, 15, 48, 182, 185, 224
Frequency, 16, 25, 40, 140, 141, 143–49, 153–55, 157, 158, 160
Function, 15–18, 20, 37–39, 43–45, 47, 49, 51, 53, 55, 91, 169, 189, 190, 191, 207, 211, 213, 215–19
Functional, access, 110, analysis, 191, 192, 211, 213, application, 170, attributes, 112, boundary between topical and, 114, concepts, 100, connections, 43, description, 103, 104, descriptors, 100, information, 81, 208, model, 38, need, 108, ontology, 38, 39, 207, 209–11, 214, 215, 217–20, 222, representation, 46, 99, 112, 131, 170, 174, requirements, 49, 51, 113, search, 108, 114, sense, 106, tips, 174, uses, 170
Functionality, 16, 18, 37, 105, 130

Game, 39, 191, 210, 216, 217
Generality, 14, 35, 59, 74, 77, 106, 107, 151, 154, 155
Generalization, 40, 73, 94
Gini coefficient, 197, 199–203
Grazing, 111, 113, 114
Gullibility, 118, 120, 154

Heading, 2, 14, 36, 40, 51, 59, 64, 69, 70–72, 74, 76, 77, 79, 80, 85, 101, 103, 107, 110, 112, 114–16, 124, 125, 134–38
Highlighting, 14, 24, 40, 42, 75, 88, 105, 110, 125, 140, 141, 148, 149, 170
Human, 2, 13, 21, 38, 40, 46, 76, 94, 133, 148–50, 207, 215, 224, 225, ability, 71, agency, 223, behavior, 191, 210, 211, 213, body, 10, capability, 67, engagement, 204, existence 207, ideas, 36, indexer, 16, 76, 77, 13, 147, 149, 155, 160, information behavior, 207, information processing, 119, intervention, 197, librarian, 150, memory, 37, observer, 189, problems, 207, programmer, 76, scholars, 81, systems, 64, viewers, 202

Idea, 9, 10, 12, 18, 21, 33–36, 40, 43, 49, 52, 53, 64, 68, 70, 77, 79, 80, 100–2, 117, 119, 133, 135, 170, 206, 208, 211, 213, 222
Ideal, 55, 73, 85, percentage, 73, raw number, 73, set of indexing terms, 85, situation, 77, 78, system, 73
Identification, 5, 79, 117, 190
Idiosyncrasies, 100, 222
Idiosyncratic, browsing, 116, 121, code, 14, conventions, 52, sampling, 108, searching, 111, 119
Ignorance, 65, 75
Image, 15, 16, 18, 27–31, 33, 35, 39, 73, 91–94, 97–101, 103–6, 114, 115, 128, 130, 140, 165, 166, 175, 178, 179, 186, 187, 189, 190, 193–98, 202, 204–6, 216, 223, 225

Indeterminacy, 63, 77, 97, 107–9, 111, 113, 115, 117, 119, 121–23, 125, 127, 129, 131, 139
Index, 2, 6, 9, 16, 36, 37, 68–71, 76, 77, 86, 139, 143–45, 148, 154, 170, 181, 182, 205
Indexer, 14, 16, 18, 44, 63, 74, 76–79, 85, 93, 133–35, 138, 147–52, 155, 160
Indexical, pebbles, 27, photograph, 27, relationship, 33, representation, 25, 28, 32, 33
Indexing, 2–7, 9–11, 25, 32, 33, 40–42, 44, 45, 48, 56, 58, 63, 67, 68, 71–77, 81, 82, 85, 87, 91, 110, 133, 134, 137–40, 147–51, 190, 204, 205, 221, 222, 225
Information, 1–11, 12, 14–22, 24, 26, 28, 30, 32, 34, 36–40, 42–46, 48–52, 54–61, 63, 64, 66–72, 74, 76–78, 80–82, 84, 86–88, 94, 98, 100, 102, 104, 106–10, 112–16, 118–22, 124–26, 128–30, 132, 134, 136, 138, 140–42, 146–48, 150, 152, 154, 156, 158, 160, 162, 165–71, 173–78, 181, 182, 184–200, 202–26
Intelligence, 5, 7, 8, 22, 46, 66, 68–71
Interaction, 25, 43, 48, 55, 145, 205
Interface, 21, 58, 99–103, 106, 108
Intermediary, 65, 107–9, 122, 224, 141, 150
Intervention, 64, 107, 197, 217
Isomorphic, photograph, 25, representation, 24, 25, 28

Judgments, 51, 55, 93, 99, 123, 125, 149, 171, 173, 222

Key frame, 193, 195, 197, 199, 203
Keyword, 16, 25, 59, 79, 121, 129, 133, 136, 137, 138, 146, 148, 165, 169–71
Knowledge, 4–9, 16, 18–20, 24, 33, 40, 42, 43, 49, 51, 52, 55, 56, 58–60, 65, 71, 80, 88, 99, 106, 107, 109–13, 115–19, 121, 135, 146, 149, 150, 151, 192, 204, 207–9, 211, 212, 214, 222, 224

Language, 4, 16, 18, 37, 39, 42, 44, 48, 52, 67, 71, 75, 76, 87, 115, 191, 192, 210, 216, 217
Letters, 31, 35, 55, 57, 138, 140, 142, 152, 154, 155, 184
Librarian, 16, 42, 49, 59, 65, 68, 70, 71, 81, 100, 103, 107, 108, 111, 112, 134, 150, 154, 186, 222
Library, 4, 14–17, 38, 40, 42, 52, 53, 63, 65, 69, 72, 75, 100, 103, 107, 111, 116, 121, 123–25, 129, 137, 170, 190, 207, 222
Library of Congress, 100
Library of Congress Cataloging in Publication, 135
Library of Congress Subject Headings, 14, 33, 40, 69, 70, 72, 74, 77, 79, 100, 103, 110, 114, 125, 134, 135, 153, 217
Library of Congress MARC record, 16
Library of Congress system, 217
Lineage, 36
Location, 4, 105, 110, 114–16, 118, 121, 141, 166, 171
Locus of representation, 110, 222

Machine browsing, 67
Machine indexing, 40, 74, 140, 148, 160
Machine representation, 76, 138, 140, 141, 147, 148, 150, 151, 160
Map, 6, 8, 33, 51, 89, 147, 148, 158, 196, 199, 201, 218, 221, 222
MARC record, 16,17
Meaning, 5, 15–20, 29, 30, 37–41, 43, 44, 48, 54–56, 63, 64, 69, 73, 94, 158, 167, 169, 175, 181, 185–87, 190–93, 196, 204, 205, 216, 223
Membership, 10, 127, 156
Meme, 39, 210, 216, 217
Memetic, attribute, 205, phenotypes, 39, 216, signals, 218, space, 219
Memetics, theory, 207
Message, 15, 17, 18, 38, 39, 41, 43, 48, 49, 54, 55, 59, 60, 63, 64, 68, 88, 89, 91, 122, 138, 165, 167, 169, 174–77, 182, 185, 187, 188, 190–92, 195, 196, 204, 206, 215, 216, 225
Moving image documents, 175, 178, 186, 187, 189, 190, 194, 195, 204–6

Multimedia, design, 175, documents, 10, 140, 141, presentations, 174, 175, 178, 182, systems, 94
Music, 9, 25, 39, 41, 42, 47, 52, 53, 91, 135, 186, 205, 216, 225
Native, elements, 59, 91, 169, 204, 206, tongue, 55
Need, 1, 3, 7, 14, 21, 34, 35, 37, 44, 49, 51, 54, 55, 59, 74, 77, 99–101, 107–9, 135, 147, 150, 205, 211, 213, 214
Noise, 175, 182, 185
Noun, 88, 94, 99, 140, 152, 154
Novelty, 15, 48, 116, 174, 182, 224

Object, 14, 22, 24, 27, 28, 31, 35, 41, 44, 45, 58, 60, 93, 94, 100, 101, 106, 186, 193, 195–97, 202, 203, 208
Object/event space, 45, 48, 53, 61, 108,
Observation, 48–50, 52, 68, 80, 108, 126, 128, 158
Ontological, contexts, 54, 210, 212, space, 232, status, 211
Ontology, 38, 39, 207–11, 213–15, 217–20, 222
Operant, behavior, 210, 220 contingencies, 43
Organism, 36, 37, 169, 191, 208, 211
Organization, 5, 7, 12, 14, 36, 88
Palette, attribute, 108, 109, 130, color, 180, 191, 196, 197, 202, representation, 130–32

Patron, 3, 14, 24, 25, 33, 40, 42, 44, 49, 51, 53, 54, 56, 58, 59, 63–65, 69, 71, 73, 75–80, 83–85, 87, 88, 99–101, 106–10, 122, 138, 139, 141, 147, 148, 150–54, 157, 158, 160, 222, 225
Pattern, 71, 94, 119, 120, 169, 192, 199, 202–5, 207, 224
Penetration, 64, 75, 110, 118, 134, 141, 148, 150, 154, 156, 187
Phenotype, 39, 216
Photograph, 23–25, 27, 28, 30, 31, 68, 72, 85, 91, 93–97, 101–3, 106, 124, 128, 137, 165–69, 174, 178, 197, 225
Picture, 9, 16, 23, 27, 29, 30, 54, 60, 66, 67, 85, 93, 94, 99–101, 103–6, 165, 167, 178, 179, 182, 187, 191, 211
Pixel, 165–67, 178, 179, 189, 195, 197, 204
Pointing, 9, 81, 110, 111, 134, 148
Postcoordinate indexing, 14, 110, 134, 136, 137
PowerPoint, 15, 165, 174–76, 179–85
Pragmatic, information science, 209, 210, orientation, 210, work of John Dewey, 209, work of Patrick Wilson, 207, 209
Pragmatism, 208–10
Precision, 83, 84, 87, 88, 188, 189, 193, 203, 206
Precoordinate indexing, 110, 134, 135
Predictability, 15, 169, 174, 175
Probabilistic, indexing, 5, classification, 211–12
Probabilities, 114, 121, 185
Probability of satisfaction, 125
Purpose, 22, 33, 37, 41, 44, 49, 53, 56, 87, 125, 175, 178, 223

Query, 5, 7, 59, 81, 103, 105, 108, 112, 114–16, 119, 136, 137, 154, 212
Question, 3, 4, 6, 12, 15, 19–20, 23, 33, 37, 40, 41, 45, 49–52, 56, 60, 61, 63–65, 68, 69, 71–75, 77, 81, 85, 87, 88, 97, 100, 109, 110, 112, 117, 119, 121, 122, 130, 134, 150, 154, 171, 173, 177, 186, 189, 191, 195, 209, 211–13, 222–25

Reasoning, 7, 8, 11, 12, 13, 24
Recall, 83–85, 87, 88
Record, 16, 17, 129, 130, 145, 192, 194
Recorded behaviors, 103, documents, 45, 225, information, 225, knowledge, 4
Recording, 25, 27, 36, 103, 225
Records, 21, 118, 170
Reference, 16, 51, 78, 107, 114–16, 134, 141, desk, 3, 100, intermediary, 134, interview, 76, librarian, 42, 59, 65, 71, 100, 108, 112, 150, 222
Referent, 22, 25, 31
Relevance, 5, 115, 123, 125, 191, 206, 211–14
Representation, 2, 3, 5, 7, 12–14, 18, 21–29, 31–33, 35–37, 39–47, 49–61, 63, 65, 67–89, 93, 94, 97, 99, 100, 105–10, 112–15, 117–19, 121–26, 128–34, 138–40, 141, 145, 147–52, 156, 160, 169–71, 173–76, 182, 184,

Representation (*cont.*)
186, 196, 203, 204, 206, 209, 211, 222
Retrieval, 5, 6, 12, 21, 24, 33, 37, 40, 42, 44, 50, 51, 53, 58, 65, 76, 78, 81, 82, 103, 106, 109, 112, 113, 125, 134, 135, 137, 170, 190, 209, 211, 213
Review, 36, 37, 63, 69, 99, 130, 131, 149, 205
Reviewer, 53, 99, 124, 127, 130, 131, 187
RGB (Red, Green, Blue), 196–98, 202, 204–6
Rightness, 49, 50, 52, 116

Sampling, 85, 94, 108, 110–17, 119, 121
Satisfaction, 5, 82, 85, 112, 125
Search, 1, 3–5, 7, 10, 11, 14, 25, 27, 44, 58, 59, 65, 66, 70, 71, 78–80, 83, 87, 97, 100, 106–8, 110–21, 124, 125, 129, 134–37, 150–52, 154–58, 214, 221–25
Searcher, 2, 70, 81, 82, 102, 103, 108, 110, 112–19, 121, 122, 125, 130, 134–37, 141, 150, 151, 155, 156
Searching, 1, 4, 17, 40, 51, 55, 65, 75, 81, 85, 101, 103, 109–11, 116, 121, 122, 125, 129, 134, 135, 137, 148, 151, 209, 223, 224
Seeking, 6, 14, 37, 38, 45, 49, 51, 56, 60, 91, 99, 103, 117, 122, 139, 187, 191, 197, 211–15, 222, 225
Segmentation, 188, 189, 195
Segmenting, 113, 115, 121
Selecting, 2, 128, 197, 204
Selection, 2, 38, 44, 55, 56, 82, 86, 110, 117, 123, 131, 150, 170, 210, 211, 218
Semantics, 175, 176, 182
Semiotic, notion, 45, 188, theory, 39, 191, 192, 210, 216
Semiotics, 39, 48, 55, 208, 216
Shannon, Claude E., 8, 15, 38, 39, 54, 55, 63, 64, 169–71, 175, 176, 178, 181, 182, 190–92, 195, 196, 206, 210, 215, 216
Signal, 39, 169, 185–88, 196–97, 205, 217, set, 177, 186–88, 192, 197, 217
Significance, 109, 139, 141, 145
Signified, 31, 39, 191, 216
Signifier, 39, 191, 216
Signs, 9, 21, 22, 30, 31, 35, 36, 40, 42, 44, 60, 97
Similarity, 6, 60, 113, 118, 148, 158, 205
Situation, 6, 9, 40, 44, 48, 51, 60, 77, 78, 89, 112, 124, 133, 150, 151, 213
Situational, function, 19–20, relevance, 211–14
Skinner, B. F., 39, 55, 191, 207, 209, 210, 211, 213, 216
Space, 22, 50, 107, antecedent, 218, behavioral, 218, blank, 13, 138, 140, 142, 165, consequent, 218, memetic, 219, ontological, 210, 213, search, 4, 44, 116, 221, 222, 224, 225, vector, 5, 186, 187
Specification, 115, 116, 186
Specificity, 15, 74, 77, 82, 85–87, 94, 100, 107, 109, 118, 148, 154, 204
Squiggles, 40, 41, 60, 69, 138, 139, 145
Standard, 57, 70, 98, 110, 123, 140, 146, 187, 189, 196, 203
State, 1, 3, 15, 19, 57, 60, 65, 88, 99, 104, 106, 109, 112, 113, 117, 140, 150, 151, 181, 204, 211, 212, 214
Stimulus, 7, 192, 217, 219
Structure, 15, 17, 20, 30, 38, 39, 43, 44, 48, 63, 64, 88, 94, 99, 107, 109, 122, 123, 133, 158, 169–71, 174, 175, 181, 184–87, 189, 190, 191, 195, 196, 204–6, 215–17
Studiousness, 54–56, 61, 113, 114, 120
Style, 33, 39, 42, 113, 118, 125–28, 131, 171, 216, 223
Subject, 9, 29, 44, 63, 65, 67, 69, 70, 72, 74, 76, 77, 79, 91, 94, 97, 99, 103, 108, 110, 112–15, 118, 119, 123, 125–29, 130, 134, 135, 137, 186, 197, 204, 208
Subject heading, 2, 14, 36, 40, 51, 59, 64, 70, 71, 76, 80, 85, 101, 107, 112, 115, 116, 124, 136, 138
Surprise, 15, 102, 123, 174, 175, 177, 181, 184, 185
Surrogate, 18, 99, 125, 129, 170, 174
Symbol, 13, 29, 30, 60
Symbols, 60

Synchronic, attributes, 33, 41, 42, 44, representation, 130, changes, 141, signals, 218, 219
Synonym, 59, 69, 73, 109, 153, 154, 156, 158, 160, 204
Synonymy, 40

Tact, 192, 195, 199, 201, 203
Tag, 103, 141, 218, 225, conceptual, 74, 93, 97, 139, 147, community, 101, descriptive, 112
Tag cloud, 25, 158
Tagging, 40, 102, 103, 139, 141, 150, 151, 218, 222
Template, 16–20, 65, 185
Text, 23, 25, 36, 41, 42, 53, 54, 60, 61, 88, 93, 94, 99, 118, 138, 140, 141, 142, 145, 147, 148, 152, 158, 174, 178, 179, 181, 184, 186, 188, 189, 222–24
Time, 1, 2, 4, 5, 10, 22, 24, 32, 41, 44, 45, 49, 50, 51, 54, 58, 65, 73, 76, 78, 79, 81, 88, 100, 105, 110, 111, 115–17, 120–22, 124, 125, 130, 134, 135, 150, 151, 172, 181, 186, 187, 189, 199, 203, 206, 212, 217, 218, 222, 223, search, 2, 5, 10, 44, 116, 222, 223
Timeliness, 125, 130
Title, 4, 24, 25, 42, 55, 58, 59, 64, 69–71, 76, 79, 107, 112, 113, 115, 116, 118, 124, 129, 130, 135, 136, 138, 140, 153, 154, 169, 170, 181, 225
Topic, 2, 9, 12, 16, 42, 48, 53, 59, 69, 76, 91, 94, 99, 100, 107–9, 111–14, 119, 120, 122, 125, 137, 138, 140, 146
Topographic map, 148
Topography, 133, 191
Translation, 7, 16, 23, 40, 66, 74, 94, 108, 109, 118, 141

Uncertainty, 8, 38, 165, 167, 169, 190
Understanding, 7, 15, 17, 18, 20, 48, 82, 141, 146, 169, 185, 204, 206, 209, 217, 223, 224
Unit of meaning, 94, 186, 190, 193, 216
Unpredictability, 15, 182
Utility, 6, 10, 33, 38, 42, 45, 47, 49, 51, 53, 55, 56–59, 61, 73, 84, 85, 103, 108, 114, 116, 121, 122, 125, 147, 203, 215, 222

Vague awareness, 50, 51, 113, 114, 117, 118
Vague idea, 80, 206
Vague query, 112
Variables, 85, 170, 191, 211
Vector space model, 5, 186, 187
Verb, 73, 140, 145, 152, 153
Vocabulary, 7, 86, 99, 118, 130, 134, 204

Weighted, descriptor system, 136, lists, 137, query, 108, request system, 135, system, 137
Wilson, Patrick, 16, 18, 54, 77, 91, 93, 107, 108, 122, 123, 125, 130, 181, 205, 207, 209, 211–14
Wisdom, 7–9, 60, 81
Wittgenstein, Ludwig, 31, 33, 39, 191, 209, 210, 216, 217

ABOUT THE AUTHORS

BRIAN C. O'CONNOR, Ph.D., is a professor at the School of Library and Information Sciences, University of North Texas.

JODI KEARNS, Ph.D., is an archivist at the Archives of the History of American Psychology, University of Akron, Ohio.

RICHARD ANDERSON, Ph.D., is Information Security Coordinator in the Computing & Information Technology Center, University of North Texas.

CPSIA information can be obtained
at www.ICGtesting.com
Printed in the USA
JSHW041238120123
36171JS00004B/16

9 781591 585770